College Rules!

College Rules!

How to Study, Survive, and Succeed in College

SHERRIE NIST, PH.D., and
JODI PATRICK HOLSCHUH, PH.D.

TEN SPEED PRESS
Berkeley / Toronto

Ten Speed Press
P.O. Box 7123
Berkeley, California 94707
www.tenspeed.com

Distributed in Australia by Simon and Schuster Australia, in Canada by
Ten Speed Press Canada, in New Zealand by Southern Publishers Group, in South
Africa by Real Books, in Southeast Asia by Berkeley Books, and in the United
Kingdom and Europe by Airlift Book Company.

Cover and text design by Susan Van Horn
Cover photography by Stephen Olejnik

Library of Congress Cataloging-in-Publication Data
Nist, Sherrie L. (Sherrie Lee), 1946–
College rules! : how to study, survive, and succeed in college / Sherrie Nist,
Jodi Patrick Holschuh.
p. cm.
Includes index.
ISBN 1-58008-390-0 (pbk.)
1. College student orientation—United States. 2. Study skills—United
States. 3. College students—United States—Conduct of life.
I. Holschuh, Jodi. II. Title.
LB2343.32 .N57 2002
378.1'98—dc21   2001007711

First printing, 2002

Printed in Canada
3 4 5 6 7 8 9 10 — 06 05 04 03 02

DEDICATION

To our husbands, Steve and Doug, and to our daughters, Kama and Maia, with love.

ACKNOWLEDGMENTS

For Sherrie Nist, this book—written late in her tenure—represents a career-spanning culmination of her many interactions with mentors, colleagues, students, and teachers. For Jodi Holschuh, this book—written early in her tenure—represents a means to put into practice the research on college-student learning that she had been reading about and conducting. One full professor, one assistant professor—neither of whom would have been able to accomplish her goal of writing *College Rules!* without the help and support of many individuals.

First, our heartfelt thanks to Michael Rosenberg, our agent, who loved our idea and did a terrific job of connecting us with a publishing company willing to take on this project wholeheartedly. Michael liked our proposal so much that he added it to his Web site as an example of how to write a good proposal. We thank him for his support and encouragement. Also, thanks to Barbara Collins-Rosenberg who assumed the role as our agent when Michael returned to the field of publishing.

Second, thanks to everyone at Ten Speed Press: Lorena Jones, who decided that *College Rules!* would be a good addition to the Ten Speed catalogue; Meghan Keeffe, whose energy and effort helped make this book appealing and cool; Susan Van Horn, Kristi Hein, Clancy Drake, Barbara King, and Ken DellaPenta who in various and wonderful ways, helped spruce up *College Rules!* for its readers.

Third, there's not a "thank you" big enough for our mentors, colleagues, and teachers, both past and current, who taught us to be teachers, researchers, writers, and questioners. These individuals, although too numerous to mention, also gave us the self-confidence and skills to be successful in the sometimes treacherous world of academe.

Fourth, a special thanks to Dr. Deborah Martin and Dr. David Zehr for allowing us to share parts of their syllabi with our readers (and their potential future students).

Fifth, this book could not have existed without our students. We have learned as much from them—even more, perhaps—than they have ever learned from us. For both of us, teaching continues to breathe new life into our research and other writing. It adds meaning to what we do, and on many a day simply makes us smile.

Sixth, thanks go to our parents, Charlene and Roy Miller and Mary and Stanley Patrick, who instilled in us the love and pleasure of learning. Their curiosity and love of learning helped us recognize these characteristics in ourselves. For that, we are eternally grateful.

But most of all, we thank our spouses and children: Steve and Kama, Doug and Maia. Our husbands, Steve Olejnik and Doug Holschuh, encouraged us to write this book and believed in our idea that if students knew how to learn in college right from the start, they would ultimately have an easier and more enjoyable college experience. They were also very understanding when dinner was late (or take-out sushi or pizza) as we were wrapping up the final chapters. Our daughters, Kama and Maia, had very different roles. Kama drew on her own college experiences to offer advice and guidance. Maia, who was born while we were working on *College Rules!*, often gave us big smiles of encouragement while we were trying to finish up this project. We both thank Maia for napping at the appropriate times to let her mommy write.

CONTENTS

Contents

Contents

INTRODUCTION

We introduce you to *College Rules!* by telling you some of our deep, dark, secrets—the confessions of two professors who (in all honesty) didn't have the most stellar beginnings as college students. For the first year and a half of college, each of us held our breaths when grades came out at the end of the term; we were clueless about what it took to be successful students. We both felt guilty about our lack of attention to schoolwork—we did sort of want to learn something—but not guilty enough to make any real changes. But did we have fun! If we could have earned grades in social life, both of us would have made A+s.

Sherrie began to turn things around when she received an ultimatum from her dad. She remembers his words clearly: "I'm not paying for Cs—or worse—anymore. You made good grades in high school; you either do better in college or you come home." Talk about a dose of reality. It had never occurred to Sherrie, who had always done well in school, that she might not make it in college unless she made some real changes. It had never occurred to her that she had to discipline herself and rethink the way she approached learning. The possibility of having to return home without a degree in hand was a big wake-up call.

Jodi remembers walking into her first college class, Introduction to Sociology. She filed into the large auditorium with 300 other students. The professor started class by stating that he did not care whether students came to class or not—he'd teach the same material either way. "Great," thought Jodi. "I'll get to sleep in on Tuesdays and Thursdays." She kept the mindset that class was optional until she noticed that her friends who were doing well in college were doing things differently. They were going to class every day and they were studying most evenings, and as a result of their efforts, they were much less stressed out about the workload. Once Jodi decided to adopt this strategy, things (and grades) improved greatly. Jodi wished that she had realized what to do before she entered college.

Now you might say, so what? It ended up great for you guys. You must have done all right. After all you got into graduate school, earned Ph.D.'s, and have great careers. Life is sweet. But although we ended up in academe, we seriously wish we had been better students right from the start. Honestly. In fact, we believe that we chose to study the ways students make the transition from high school to college learning because we did not do such good jobs ourselves. Which brings us to why we wrote *College Rules!*. If we had known then what we know now, well, let's just say we wouldn't have had so much catching up to do. We want you to learn from our mistakes and our successes.

We know you're smart. You know you're smart. You wouldn't have been accepted to college if you weren't. So why do you need *College Rules!?* Because *College Rules!* draws on our years of experience as both students and professors to bring you the very best advice on how to have a successful college career.

Your high school probably did a fairly decent job of teaching you information: you'll go off to college armed with lots of facts. What might give you a bit of a challenge, however, is how to turn these facts into knowledge. In other words, do you know how to think critically and learn actively? Do you know how to manage your time? Are you self-disciplined? Can you synthesize? Analyze? Critique? Do you know how to take good notes in a lecture or discussion class? Can you learn lots of new information quickly? Do you know the best ways to prepare for and take college-level exams? Yikes. Lots of questions to answer. But if you don't think about them before you start college, you might just spend the first year (or at least the first semester) trying to figure out what college is all about and how to maintain the grades you made in high school.

Take Maggie for example. We remember Maggie because she reminded us so much of ourselves. She was a good student in high school, but we could tell that she didn't think how she studied and learned would have to change in college. She pledged a sorority her first semester and had an active social life. And although she enrolled in some tough courses, Maggie stuck to what worked in high school, which translated into studying (or what she called studying—flipping through the pages in her textbook and notes to memorize key terms) about four hours a *week*. To make a long story short, by the end of her freshman year, Maggie had dug herself into an academic hole that was difficult for her to climb out of. She realized that getting into college is the easy part; staying in is more difficult.

So how can you avoid these mistakes and start out on the right track? Enter *College Rules!*. Although we have written "how to learn" textbooks that are used in college courses, we firmly believe that the message of active learning needs to be in your hands *before* you begin college. We also believe that it's important to demystify learning by letting you in on the secrets of postsecondary academic expectations. And we believe in the importance of emphasizing academics as a way for you to have a satisfying and well-rounded college experience. By this we mean that, all else aside, your college experience will suffer if you are in trouble academically. Plain and simple. Poor grades simply make you spiral downward both socially and psychologically.

College Rules! focuses on how you can do well academically, thereby opening the door for you to enrich your life in other ways. We expect (and want) you to have a full social life and we encourage you to become involved in campus groups and organizations. We want you to understand the importance of knowledge and how you must be the one responsible for gaining it. We want you to seek purpose in your knowledge quest and to have the self-discipline to make learning happen. Perhaps most important, we want you to be able to make good choices. We want you to do it all *and* make good grades. We expect lots from you, but probably no more than you expect from yourself.

We realize that there are lots of "college success" books out there, so what makes *College Rules!* different? Unlike some, this book does not tell you how to keep your underwear from turning pink (don't wash it with a red T-shirt). It does not tell you how to buy football tickets (get your order in early) or how to get a fake ID (just don't even go there). It does not tell you how to get along with weird roommates nor does it suggest how to get around the system. What it does provide are "rules" on studying and learning that will help you be both efficient and effective in achieving academic success in college. We attempt to paint a realistic picture of what you should expect academically and what your college will expect from you. Attending college can be a life-changing experience. It can also be a great adventure. We hope that *College Rules!* will introduce you to lots of ideas that will help you make the most of the experience.

HOW TO USE *COLLEGE RULES!*

Although the primary audience for *College Rules!* is students heading off to campus, we certainly wouldn't discourage sophomores, juniors, or seniors from reading it (we even know some graduate students who would benefit). We believe that there is valuable information here for students at any point in their college career. However, our major goal is helping college freshmen make the often treacherous transition from learning in high school to learning in college.

To this end, approach reading *College Rules!* in any way that suits your needs. You can read it the traditional way—start at chapter 1 and read through chapter 22 in consecutive order. If you're a high school student who will be starting college, this ordered approach might be the best. Read a chapter or two every day and then, once you get to college, go back and reread chapters that piqued your interest or that did not quite sink in.

You can also use *College Rules!* as an at-your-fingertips reference for college success. If you're a bit hesitant as you're packing up your stuff to head off to campus, read chapter 6. If you're getting ready to take your first college exams (and you haven't even opened this book yet), read chapters 20 to 22. If you can't manage your time worth a hoot, read chapter 7. In other words, read the chapters that you think will benefit you at any particular time.

With the second approach, we offer a few words of caution, however. We know for a fact that learning in college is a complex process. Being successful is not about doing this *or* that. Being successful is usually about doing this *and* that (and then doing some more). There's no one particular suggestion in *College Rules!* that's guaranteed to make you a better student. There are no "magic beans" for college success. Rather, we have provided you with a comprehensive guide to help you hit the campus running at least ten paces ahead of your fellow students. So though you can read *College Rules!* on an as-needed basis, if you want to get the most out of the book you should read all of it—not necessarily in the order in which the chapters are presented, but do give it a good, comprehensive read.

Finally, a bit about how *College Rules!* is laid out. If you thumb through the chapters (a good strategy to use with any book—see chapter 15) you will notice that there are lots of sidebars. Here's what you'll see:

- **Sad but True**—These student stories focus on some of the troubles that are common to students regardless of what college they attend. Although you might find some of these stories difficult to believe, we have actually encountered all of these students over our careers. (The names have been changed to protect the innocent.) Hopefully, you can learn from their mistakes so that you don't fall into these traps.

- **The Inside Scoop**—These sidebars provide advice for being successful based on putting research into practice.

- **Listen Up**—These sidebars give you tried-and-true study tips to help you make your learning more efficient and effective.

- **Do Your Homework**—These sidebars give advice on things you should do routinely outside of class.

- **For Adults Only**—These sidebars give advice to nontraditional students—those who are heading back to college after several years in the workforce.

- **Get Wired**—These sidebars give tips for maximizing learning through the use of computers and other technology.

- **Urban Legend**—These sidebars focus on a variety of untrue stories that have been circulating around college campuses for years. They are sort of like computer hoaxes. They sound probable, but really aren't true.

CHAPTER 1

YOU'RE IN
THE BIG TIME NOW

The university is not engaged in making ideas safe for students. It is engaged in making students safe for ideas.

—Clark Kerr

ollege. You've dreamed about what it would be like for years now. Perhaps you envisioned four (or five) years of partying, whirlwind social events, and fun. Or maybe you thought just the opposite—that college would be nothing but hard work. Classes, exams, papers. Never having your nose out of a book. Yikes.

But most of you probably don't think in such extremes. Instead, you anticipate making new friends, learning lots of new things, and of course experiencing some good old-fashioned college fun.

Success in college requires a considerable amount of hard work, determination, motivation, and some just-plain-luck. It also requires you to make some changes, because one thing we know for certain: College is different from high school. Plain and simple. You may have the idea that college is high school with a little more freedom. In some ways, that's true, but in the classroom college is very different from high school. Sure, you have more freedom, but you also have more responsibility, harder courses, more reading, and longer hours of studying. Academic responsibilities can often conflict with the P-A-R-T-Y part of the college experience. Although we think that both are important to a well-rounded college experience, you can get

Research suggests that students often enter college lacking the study strategies they need to be successful. Not much of a surprise. What is a bit surprising, however, is the reason why. It seems that in high school many students aren't challenged to any great degree. Tests in high school may not be very demanding, so students really don't have to use studying techniques that require them to think at higher levels. This could explain why students have a difficult time adjusting to the academic demands of college.

in trouble if you begin college unaware of the academic adjustments you'll have to make.

Your college years can end up being the best of your life if you begin college with the understanding that some things will change—in fact, change dramatically—and if you become a savvy student and an efficient, effective learner.

Doing College

In high school you may not have had to work very hard to make decent grades. You listened to what the teachers said, dutifully wrote down the information they put on the board, and answered all the questions they gave you on a study guide. Because that same information was on the exam, you may never have had to take your textbooks home at all and you still aced the test. Your teacher was probably deeply committed to making sure that everyone learned in her classroom. If you were having trouble, she probably took time to help you (or find you help). And if you showed real aptitude in her subject, she was very encouraging as well.

When you get to college, though, it's as if the rules you've spent 12 years mastering have changed. Gone are flipping through study guides and memorizing facts as accepted ways of learning.

If you can't use the standbys, just what *do* you need to do to be successful once you are in college? According to the thousands of students we've interacted with, you need at least some of the following.

● **Self-discipline.** You have probably thought about this already. In college you need to find ways to make yourself do the things you need to do every day. But sometimes finding the discipline you need is tough—especially when assignments pile up and you would rather be outside shooting hoops than reading yet another chapter of history. (In fact, you would rather walk on hot coals than read another word of history.) Self-discipline is a skill that you must develop. It won't happen overnight, but with a little effort you will establish the self-discipline you need.

● **Motivation.** Just as you must nurture self-discipline, you must find motivation for learning. As you will learn later, you are always motivated to do *something*. The trick is to motivate yourself to do the tasks involved in college.

● **A game plan.** Everyone needs a plan of action and this is especially true for college students, who often have lots of commitments to keep track of (like assignments, meetings, social obligations, and so on). To create a game plan, you must figure out exactly what you need to do, then set aside time to get it all done.

● **A bunch of effective learning strategies.** Many students begin college using strategies that have worked for them in the past, such as rereading a text, or relying only on information supplied by the teacher. To succeed in college you'll need to

LISTEN UP

If you do not have a system for managing your time, the first thing you should do is to run (very fast) to your campus bookstore or nearest office supply store and buy a schedule book to keep track of assignments, readings, exams, and all of the other things you need to do each day.

THE INSIDE SCOOP

Some students believe that they enter college unprepared because their high school teachers should have prepared them to handle the college workload, but failed to do so. We don't believe this is the case. The way our educational system is structured, a high school teacher's goal is not to prepare his students for college (no matter what the conventional wisdom is), but to prepare them to finish high school—mission accomplished.

change your strategies to meet the new challenges. You'll need to create a learning cycle, which means knowing lots of different ways to approach learning.

If you have already started college, think about the changes you have made. Were there any that you weren't expecting? If you are getting ready to enter college, think about the changes you are anticipating. How will you cope with these new situations?

But What If I Wasn't the World's Greatest High School Student?

Let's face it, not everyone leaves high school with a great GPA (or great entrance exam scores). You may be worried that if you goofed off in high school you will never make it through college. Although this is a legitimate concern, don't let this fear keep you from pursuing your goals of getting that college degree. If your high school record isn't stellar, you may not be able to get into Harvard, but like most students, you probably can get in somewhere.

We've found that many students blossom academically once they get to college. They may feel challenged for the first time or they may suddenly become motivated to reach their goals. Almost overnight, some students decide to take responsibility for their own actions and want to prove they can succeed academically. Whatever the case, we have seen this happen over and over again. We call it the clean slate phenomenon. Students who start out believing that their weak academic slate has been wiped clean tend to do better than those who are carrying around the baggage of their high school record.

To give yourself a clean slate, you need to believe that you are capable of college work. Picture yourself acing that first exam, or in a cap and gown marching up to get your diploma—whatever works for you. You'll also need to make some changes in how you set your priorities, manage your time, and study for classes. This book shows you how. Of course, you already know that if you messed up in high school, you *will* have to work hard to make it through college—but it probably helps to realize that so will everyone else.

Six Ways College Differs from High School

You may have already considered how college is different from high school. Perhaps you've talked to relatives or friends about their experiences. Chances are you've seen lots of college scenes in movies and on television, so you have a mental picture of what college is like and how it differs from your previous school experiences. To get you thinking a little more about this, here are six ways in which you can expect college to be different from high school. (You'll probably think of much more in your own personal experience, but these six generally apply to just about every college student.)

1. GREATER RESPONSIBILITY

In high school, most of your time is usually planned by others. Someone else tells you when to go to class, when to do homework, and maybe even when you can go out with friends. In college, you not only set your own class schedule, but you also manage your own free time. You can no longer count on your teacher or your parents to remind you when something is due or when you have to be somewhere. *You* set your own priorities and manage all your new responsibilities. It may also be the first time you have lived away from home; this means the additional responsibility of fending for yourself—eating properly, doing laundry, managing money, getting medical attention, and studying when you should.

> **FOR ADULTS ONLY** Ⓧ
>
> If you are returning to college after some years away from schooling, you may find that you are experiencing just the opposite: it may have been quite a while since anyone told you what to do and how to do it. You may find the deadlines and bureaucracy of college frustrating, especially if you are juggling a full-time job and family responsibilities as well. We suggest you meet with your professors or your advisor to speak about these concerns.

2. DIFFERENT CLASS STRUCTURE AND INSTRUCTION

Unlike high school classes, college classes generally don't meet every day. Usually college classes meet on either a Monday-Wednesday-Friday or Tuesday-Thursday schedule and you don't necessarily go from one class directly to the next. You will also spend less time in class each week—usually just 12 to 15 hours, depending on how many courses you're taking. This is quite a change from the 30-plus hours you spent in high school classes.

You will also find that class sizes are much different in college. You may be in a class with as few as five students (although this is extremely rare, it does happen occasionally) or you may find yourself in a classroom with over 300 fellow students. If you are in one of the large lecture sections, you will find that the professor probably will not even attempt to learn students' names.

You may find that the way you are taught differs. Your professors will often make assignments (such as reading the text or completing practice problems) and then not check them. They assume that you are responsible and that you are eager to do the work. On top of that, they assume that if you don't ask any questions, you must understand the information. Unlike your high school teachers, your college professors usually don't approach you if you are experiencing trouble in the course. Instead, they expect you to seek them out if you need any extra assistance (which, in most cases, they are happy to supply during their office hours). Nor will your professor approach you if you miss a class. In high school, your teachers probably gave you the information you missed (handouts, notes, assignments), but in college you will need to get notes from a classmate and ask the professor for any other assignments or important information you may have missed.

DO YOUR HOMEWORK

Actually, that's our advice: *do your homework*. If your precalculus professor tells you that it would be a good idea to do certain problems and you know for a fact that she will never in a million years collect them, do the problems anyway. It will help you in the long run as you prepare to take the exam.

We must add another word about assignments: more than likely, professors won't remind you about impending due dates. Instead, they expect you to consult your syllabus regularly and turn in assignments on the proper dates.

3. FASTER PACE

You will soon notice that instruction moves at a much faster pace in college. The amount of material you may have covered in a year in high school may take up only one semester's worth of college work. Not only that, professors lecture nonstop during class time, especially in the introductory courses that first-year students have to take. Your professors have high expectations of you: they expect you to be able to keep up with what they are saying *and* to take good, comprehensive notes. Whew. Also, many professors don't lecture straight from the text, but they expect you to be able to relate text information to the lecture topics without discussing it in class. Of course, this activity is always done on your own time. Finally, it's also reasonable to expect to cover three or more text chapters in one week. At first you may feel like one of those little hamsters in a wheel, running faster and faster and not getting anywhere, but most students eventually adjust to the pace.

4. NEW (AND IMPROVED) KINDS OF STUDYING

Many students begin college thinking that they just need to study more. This is not particularly surprising, since the average high school student studies less than two hours a week. Although it's correct to assume that you will need to study longer, it's also important to understand that you need to study *differently*. You need to be able to connect new information with what you already know and with other content. You are also responsible for learning large amounts of information with very little guidance. We will talk about this issue in greater depth throughout *College Rules!*. For now, know that you will have to spend some time each day studying for your classes and that the way you approach studying will change.

5. FEWER EXAMS

In college there are fewer exams—often only two or three per semester per course. Although this initially sounds like a good thing, it actually makes your life tougher. Because there are so few exams, each one covers a great deal of information. Do the math. If you only have three tests in a 15-week semester, each test covers 5 weeks' worth of reading and lecture notes. In a heavy reading course such as psychology or political science, that can translate into reading hundreds of pages and remembering even more information presented in lectures. In addition, many college exams are cumulative, which means that the test covers all of the information taught in the class during that term. If you make a poor grade on an exam in high school, it's not a particularly big deal because you have a lot of other opportunities for grades and your teacher is likely to drop (or just not count) a bad grade if the rest of your grades are good. In college, however, grading works a bit differently.

Professor Jones looks out over his 300 students taking their biology final exam. His eye catches a student in the upper left-hand side of the classroom who is sneakily looking at the floor beneath his desk, then quickly bubbling in an answer on his test. "Gee," thinks Professor Jones, "this student must have some kind of crib sheet."

When the student brings his test up to the front to leave it in the pile accumulating on the lectern, Professor Jones shakes his head. "You can't turn that in," he says. "You were cheating. I saw you."

The student looks the professor directly in the eye and demands, "Do you know who I am? Do you even know my name?"

Professor Jones replies, "Of course not. There are over 300 students in this class."

The student smiles, shoves his test into the middle of the pile, and runs out of the room.

This urban legend has been going around college campuses for several years. Although we don't know if this ever really happened, it does say a lot about how students can feel unknown in their classes.

6. FEWER GRADES

In high school it might have seemed as though you were being graded on every move you made. But in college you are often assigned work that is not graded. Usually, only the scores on exams, papers, computer assignments—the big things—make up what counts in your overall course grade. There are also far fewer opportunities (make that almost no opportunities) to receive extra credit in college, so you need to do well on the few graded assignments you have.

It is well to remember that the entire population of the universe, with one trifling exception, is composed of others.

—John Andrew Holmes

In addition, in high school you may have been rewarded for "effort"; in other words, as long as the teacher thought you were trying hard to learn, at a bare-bones minimum you would pass. In college, however, not only is your professor largely unaware of the effort you make, but she also actually expects you to be working

14

hard and working smart. Therefore, when computing your final course grade, most professors rely solely on your exam scores, papers, and other major projects.

Don't Mess Up

Starting off on the right foot is important for your future success in college. You really can't "blow off" a semester before you get serious about your academics, no matter what anyone tells you. Students who take too long "adjusting" to the demands of college learning and studying can find themselves in a deep academic pit that's very difficult to get out of. That's why it's important to start out strong. As with other challenges in life, you can always lighten up, but it's much more difficult to tighten up.

Getting off on the right foot isn't too difficult if you understand some fundamentals. Think of it as basic training. If you can get through the first few weeks by following the advice of our former students, you should be on your way to smooth sailing.

LISTEN UP

If you have a diagnosed learning disability (or think you may have a learning disability), getting the help you need also works differently in college. Chances are you won't have special tutors or teachers and your instructors probably won't call you at home. You are responsible for your own success. You are also responsible for working out the accommodations you're entitled to with your professors. However, be sure to check with the disabilities services office on your campus to find out what you need to do. Colleges are ready to give you the support you need, but you must seek it out and ask for help.

KEEP UP

We often ask our students at the end of a term to give advice to the next class concerning what it takes to be successful at our university. The number one answer each and every time is...keep up with your work. Most college students find themselves behind in their work at one time or another. This isn't much of an issue when it happens occasionally, but you can get into big trouble if it becomes a way of life. You can avoid this by establishing a reading and studying schedule and following it each day.

GO TO CLASS

Our students also say that it's important to attend class every day. You may have heard the rumor that professors don't care whether you are in class. However, in our experience this is simply not true. In fact, some professors—even those with more than 200 students in their class—take attendance every day because they feel so strongly about the importance of students' being in class. Even professors who don't take attendance want you to be there. So go to class. Get all of the information that you (or your parents) are paying for.

TAKE A BALANCED COURSE LOAD

Taking a balanced course load means taking a range of courses that are a combination of subjects you are interested in and subjects that don't require too much of the same type of task. In other words, don't take four (or worse yet, five) courses that all require tons of reading (such as history, biology, sociology, psychology, literature) or writing (such as English, political science, comparative literature) or problem sets (such as mathematics, statistics, chemistry) all in one semester.

BE AWARE OF YOUR STATUS

Another good piece of advice that we hear from students is the importance of monitoring your status in every course. Know where you stand and be honest with yourself. If you have made a C– on your last two chemistry tests, don't delude yourself into thinking that you can get an A in the course when you have only one test left. If you have already missed three English classes and your grade is docked points if you miss any more, be sure to roust yourself out of bed and get to class. Many of your classmates will be in denial about where they stand. Don't let it happen to you.

Use this advice from our former students to help get yourself started on the right foot. Remember, once you enter college you are, for the most part, in control of the experience you will have.

The dictionary is the only place in which success comes before work.

—Author unknown

Many students hear stories of what college is like from friends and family, but some of these tales contain misinformation that can actually hurt your college performance. For example, Andrew, one of our students, recently missed class because he was running late and heard from his brother that you shouldn't bother to even go to class if you will be more than ten minutes late. He told Andrew that professors don't let anyone in when they are so late. Although this may be true for some classes, it was not for ours and Andrew missed some very important information (and was not able to turn in an assignment due that day, so he also lost some points). The moral of this story is to find out your professors' rules for attendance and follow them—don't take for granted that the rules are the same in all cases, and don't rely on another student's "expertise." Go to the source of the information you want.

Quick and Dirty

○ Prepare to make some changes in how you think about school, learning, and studying. Doing college right means thinking about (and maybe improving) your motivation, self-discipline, and strategies for learning.

○ College requires greater personal responsibility. You must keep track of all of the many things you need to do as a college student.

○ Start out strong. Keep up with your assignments and go to class every day.

CHAPTER 2

WHERE TO FIND THE HELP YOU NEED

No student knows his subject: the most
he knows is where and how to find out
the things he does not know.
                          —Woodrow Wilson

An article by humorist Dave Barry reminded us of the importance of devoting a chapter in *College Rules!* to seeking help. Mr. Barry's teenage son was going to Europe for a few weeks of backpacking. Being an experienced father (and also having been a teenager himself eons ago), Mr. Barry "reminded" his son several times about being careful with his passport. The last thing he said to his son before he boarded the plane was, "Don't lose your passport." His son rolled his eyes, confident that everything would be fine. Unfortunately, his passport and all of his traveler's checks were stolen before he even got off the plane. So he ended up in a foreign country where he couldn't speak the language and he didn't have the foggiest idea what to do. He hadn't thought ahead because he was certain that nothing like that would happen to him.

As a college student, no matter how independent or mature you are, you're going to need help at some point in time. You may need help finding out about financial aid, lining up a tutor for an impossibly difficult chemistry course, seeing a doctor when you are too sick to die, locating the counseling center when your life is falling apart, or connecting with the registrar when you're sure a terrible mistake has been made on your transcript. Our advice: Be proactive. Know whom to contact in a variety of situations before you actually need the service, and know how to get what you need in the least stressful way.

Why is it important to be proactive? Because college students are busy, involved people. And when busy, involved people have anything more, different, or out of the ordinary added to an already hectic schedule, they tend not to handle it very well. Let's take a simple example, one that is guaranteed to happen to you sometime in your college career: illness—more specifically, the dreaded flu! On our campus it usually hits about six or eight weeks into the semester (it seems not to matter whether it's fall or spring semester). You wake up one morning. You can't breathe. Your throat feels like a piece of raw meat. You're coughing so hard that your ribs ache. And, oh my gosh, you have tests to prepare for, you're behind in your reading, you're supposed to put in three hours of service learning, you have a fraternity/sorority/team meeting, you have library books due today... the list goes on.

How would you handle this? Do you know the procedure for getting medical attention on your campus? Can you get an excused absence for today's classes? How will you get the notes you missed? Whom can you contact about not participating in the service learning? What happens if your library books aren't returned today? If you have to try to find out all the answers to these questions while you are as sick as you've ever been in your life, we guarantee that you will not be a happy camper. But you can prevent yourself from getting into this situation.

> **DO YOUR HOMEWORK**
>
> Early in the term, think about all of the services that you might need to know about. Write down phone numbers or email addresses. Find out where offices are located on campus. Ask questions. Don't wait until you need something to start tracking it down. That approach can only lead to unnecessary frustration.

I Need Help!

The first step in getting the assistance you need is admitting that you need it. We can pretty much assure you that unless your residence hall is on fire, no one is going to come knocking on your door asking if you need help with something. But for some reason, a large portion of college students would rather ignore the fact that a problem exists than get some relief from what's bogging them down. Depending on what your problem is, you may be able to do one-stop shopping, or you may have to go to several offices to get it taken care of. A glance at some of the offices available on most campuses will give you an idea of the services they traditionally offer. The extent of services varies greatly, as does the quality, but nearly all campuses offer them. Once you begin college, you may want to write down the phone numbers of each office and keep them in a handy place, bookmark their Web sites, or have their email addresses in your address book just in case you need them.

GET WIRED

Most college Web sites have links to a variety of student services on campus. Look for links to services such as the counseling center, health center, library, learning center, tutoring, financial aid office—any office that might be able to help you.

Counseling Center. Is your life in the toilet? Did your girlfriend just dump you? Is your boyfriend secretly seeing your best friend? Are you having trouble adjusting to living away from home? Are you depressed or just unhappy? On a scale of one to ten, is your motivation level a zero? These are but a handful of the problems that students bring to college counseling centers every day. Friends are good for the little things, but it's better to get professional help if you know that your academics are suffering because of emotional havoc. The counseling may be provided in a freestanding center, as part of the health center or learning center, or through a student success program.

Health Center. The campus health center may be minimal—a couple of rooms staffed by a nurse and a part-time doctor—or as large as a small hospital, capable of treating ailments way beyond colds and flu. On our campus, for example, the health center is staffed by numerous full-time doctors, nurses, and other support staff; the center even includes a dentist and a travel clinic. As soon as you reach campus, find out how to navigate the rules and regulations of the health center. For example: What are the hours? Do you need to make an appointment or can you just walk in? How much do you pay per visit? More than likely you'll have to pay a health fee when you enroll, so you should know what services are covered by your fee.

Tutorial Center or Learning Center. Like other services, those that help students academically may be limited or expansive. Most campuses offer some form of peer tutoring and assistance through a learning center. Many also offer brief academic workshops focusing on topics such as time management or study skills. Sometimes you can get one-on-one tutoring or drop-in tutoring for difficult courses. The college or university generally funds these services, so they are usually free. When you are struggling academically and trying to locate help, the trick is figuring out what these programs are called. Look for titles such as "Student Success," "Academic Assistance," "Learning Center," or "Tutoring Program."

THE INSIDE SCOOP

It has been shown time and time again that students who seek out help when they first begin to struggle academically make a comeback and do well. Those who don't seek the assistance they need tend to spiral downward, earning poor grades and low GPAs. So remember, it's good to ask for help early in the game.

Registrar. Need a transcript? Have a beef about your records? It's important to know what kinds of records are kept in the registrar's office on your campus and then how to get access to them. On our campus, for example, when students are first admitted their records are handled by the Admissions Office. Once the students have taken their placement tests during orientation, the records are transferred to the Office of the Registrar.

Financial Aid Office. If you want information on the types of financial assistance that are available to you or whether you might qualify for such aid, visit one of the financial aid officers. Most students don't know that a considerable amount of scholarship money goes unused every year, mainly because the students don't have any idea that it's available. If you already receive financial aid, you'll need to stay in close contact with this office so that you know in a timely fashion that your aid money has arrived or whom to talk with if there are problems.

FOR ADULTS ONLY

If you are a returning student, or even just thinking about taking courses toward a degree, you should seek the help of the financial aid office early. Many scholarships or grants are available to students of nontraditional age that are often not available to the more traditional 18-year-old.

Police and Fire Departments. These require little explanation. Although we hope you never need the assistance of either department, keep their phone numbers handy. If you live in an apartment, store both numbers either on speed dial or close to your bedroom phone, particularly if there is no 911 access.

Email addresses and phone numbers of your professors. Although you see

---

SAD BUT TRUE 🙁

A few years ago, the nightmare of every college community happened in our usually safe town: a series of rapes in an area near our campus where many students lived. Before the rapist was caught, one young woman was able to scare him by quickly dialing 911 and then screaming into the phone. She was lucky. Her quick thinking and immediate access to her phone enabled her to escape a physical attack.

---

your professors each class day, it's still important to know how to contact them should the need arise. Most professors provide methods of contact on the syllabus, as well as the situations in which they want you to contact them. For example, some profs want you to email them if you are going to miss class; others don't care. Almost every professor wants to be contacted if you are unable to show up for a test. Know your professors' rules and contact preferences.

Your advisor. On most campuses you must have a face-to-face conversation with your advisor once a term so that she can clear you for registration. If this is the case on your campus, you should have ready access to your advisor's phone number or email address so that you can make an appointment (they tend to have tight schedules around registration time). Try to find out if your campus has online advising, which allows you to talk with your advisor via email. Many large campuses are moving to this method; although it is somewhat impersonal, it is also very convenient for students. Find out what method is used on your campus and add the contact information to your list.

Library. At the very least, you should have the main Web page of your campus library bookmarked on your computer. From this page, you can find out all the information you need about library hours, access to online

Everyone needs help from everyone.

—Bertolt Brecht

systems, and how to search databases. Another piece of good advice concerning the library: Don't wait until two days before your first paper is due to find out how to use library resources. If you have checked out the library early, you'll be able to get right down to work, making the most of those resources.

This list of services is not necessarily comprehensive; many campuses provide other specialized services that students should be aware of. Check things out on your own campus once you arrive and at least begin to identify those offices that you might need to contact.

Getting Hassle-Free Help

We hear horror stories from students about how difficult it is to get a straight answer to their questions when they call certain offices on campus. Let's face it, a college campus—whether big or small, public or private, two- or four-year institution—is a bureaucracy. You should expect a certain amount of red tape—instances in which you get the runaround or someone can't or won't help you—but if you know which office handles which kinds of problems, you can avoid a lot of frustration. Remember, one way to find out who does what on your campus is to examine each office's Web site for those services you know you'll probably need. These days, most every campus office lists pertinent information on its Web site, perhaps to avoid getting unrelated phone calls or emails.

You can also reduce the hassle of finding information by being as clear as you possibly can about the questions you want answered or the information you need. Before you send an email, make a phone call, or physically go to an office on campus, try to put yourself in the other person's shoes. Ask yourself: If I were on the receiving end, would I understand this question? Am I explaining the problem clearly? Is it even plausible that this office handles problems such as this? If you can't communicate your problems or needs very clearly, you may feel like you're getting the runaround when in fact the person you're asking simply can't figure out what it is you want or need.

In our division (the Division of Academic Assistance), we have received requests for transcripts (handled through the registrar's office); questions about transfer credit (handled through the Admissions Office); questions about disability services (handled through Disability Services); the requirements of almost every conceivable major (handled through the respective academic departments); questions about meal plans (handled through Food Services); and perhaps the strangest, a request from a student in a foreign country for help obtaining a visa. Although we attempt to answer emails and phone calls and to point students in the right direction, we get a bit miffed sometimes (only a bit—we are really nice people). If any or all of these students had taken the time to look at our Web site, they would have known that our division does not and cannot handle any of these requests.

If you have done your homework and contact exactly the right office for the information you need, but you still get the runaround (grrrrrrrrrr), here are some tips that may help in a pinch.

Be persistent but patient. If someone says, "We don't handle that," respond with something like this: "Well, on your Web site it says that [whatever it is you need] is handled through your office. Could you look with me in the FAQ (frequently asked questions) section to see if I'm misunderstanding something?" If the person still believes you have the wrong office, ask politely to speak with a supervisor or ask if they can transfer you to the office that does handle your needs. And always, always, always politely ask for the name of the person you are talking with.

Try your best to remain pleasant. Not always the easiest thing to do, we know. (It's not easy for us either when we think we are getting the runaround.) Although we won't guarantee that keeping your temper at bay will get you a straight answer, we can tell you with a fair degree of certainty that if you are rude to individuals on the other end of the phone or computer or, heaven forbid, in person (now they know what you look like!), they will be rude to you as well. Perhaps even worse, they will simply ignore you—you know, hit the delete button on email and pretend that you don't exist. Keep in mind

> It takes a village to raise a child.
>
> —African proverb

that you stand a much better chance of getting someone to help you if you keep a positive attitude.

Enlist help. Ask your advisor, friends, or professors to help you find the answers to your questions. You're probably not the first student who has had trouble finding information; if you live in a residence hall, ask your RA or others on your hall. Perhaps they can provide insights that will help you get what you need quickly.

In the big scheme of things, using the three Ps—persistence, patience, and pleasantness—will go a long way in helping you get answers to your questions.

Quick and Dirty

○ Be proactive, not reactive. Seek out assistance when you first recognize you might need it, not when the alligators are nipping at your heels.

○ Know what services are available on your campus. Every campus staffs a variety of offices that generally provide help. Make friends with these folks.

○ Get the help you need with the least amount of hassle. Articulate what you need clearly and be persistent, patient, and pleasant.

CHAPTER 3

A FEW WORDS ABOUT PROFESSORS

The mediocre teacher tells.
The good teacher explains.
The superior teacher demonstrates.
The great teacher inspires.

—William Arthur Ward

Imagine that you are sitting in a class with 150 other students, listening to your professor discussing existential philosophy. She seamlessly interweaves Latin, Arabic, and French into her lecture. And most amazingly, she is able to lecture on this difficult material for 50 minutes *without using any notes!* Who is this person, anyway? How did she get so smart? Will all the stuff in Latin be on the exam?

Your professors may seem like brilliant, unapproachable figures (especially if you find yourself in very large classes), but most faculty enjoy interacting with students. In fact, we actually hope to convince you to get to know some of your professors very well. We believe that understanding what professors do and who they are will help you learn better in all your classes.

THE INSIDE SCOOP

You may hear from other students (and the public in general) that professors don't care about their students, especially when they are professors at large research institutions. Although this may be true for a small minority of professors, the vast majority of them care greatly about you and want to be sure that you learn in their courses.

Just What the Heck Do Professors Do?

Regardless of whether you're attending a two-year community college, a public four-year university, or a small, private liberal arts school, your professors will have obligations that go beyond teaching. Unlike your high school teachers, who may teach as many as seven classes a day (can you even imagine???), your college professors may actually be in class as few as six hours per week.

"Great!" you say. "More time for him to sit patiently in his office and wait for me to stop by." On most campuses, however, that's not the case. Sure, all professors are supposed to hold office hours—times when they are available to meet with students, either through appointments or on a drop-in basis. But professors do have other obligations—tasks that are often carried out away from the office or even off campus.

Most faculty at four-year colleges are expected to "engage in creative activities." This means that they are expected to conduct research, write for professional journals, publish books, present papers at professional meetings, create portfolios of art or music compositions, interpret historical events, write poetry, find a cure for cancer, invent amazing products—the list goes on and on. The types of creative activities that faculty need to pursue depend on their discipline—obviously a biology professor working in a lab on a cure for diabetes wouldn't be expected to write poetry—but all faculty must consistently show involvement in creative activity or they risk losing their jobs (you may have heard of the *publish or perish* rule). As you probably know, creativity takes time, so at least part of a faculty member's time is spent figuring out how much of this creativity she has to produce in order to be promoted, and then (and this is the hard part) actually producing something.

All faculty, regardless of institution type, are also required to perform "service" activities. No, they don't have to sign on for a stint in the military. Service in this setting means serving on a variety of committees, acting as

DO YOUR HOMEWORK

As a way of getting to know your professors a bit even before you go to class on the first day, check to see if they have Web pages. If so, take time to visit them. Web pages often present a less formal image of your professor than you will see in class. You can often find out their hobbies (my prof has a Harley), research interests (the life cycle of the cockroach—yuck!), or whether they are dog or cat people.

student advisors, providing services to their profession by reviewing scholarly papers, holding offices in professional organizations, and attending professional meetings. And because colleges tend to have faculty committees for everything, many professors end up spending a tremendous amount of time in service-related activities.

Which brings us back to the issue of your professor's schedule. Most professors will be glad to meet with you, but it's up to you to figure out how to arrange that meeting. Start by looking at your syllabus; it should provide your professor's office hours and procedures for seeing him. Some professors will only see you if you have an appointment; others have set office hours each week during which you can simply stop by to ask questions, get clarification, or discuss your grade.

I Have an Appointment with One of "Them"—Now What?

Before we discuss the nuts and bolts of talking with professors, we want to make the radical suggestion that you get to know some of them well—very well. In fact, make a pledge to yourself that you will get to know at least one professor a year; two, if you can. Right now, you can probably remember a teacher in your past who had a tremendous impact on you. If you make the effort to get to know some of your college teachers, we guarantee that years later you will still profit from the relationships. Having good relationships with college faculty members, especially those who teach in your major, can open many doors. They may have connections for jobs after graduation and they can write letters of recommendation for jobs or graduate school. Perhaps more important, they can stimulate your curiosity beyond the classroom and help you establish lifelong connections to your institution. Some campuses have mentoring programs that pair students (if they choose) with a faculty mentor at the beginning of their freshman year. The mentor meets with the student in a variety of settings over the course of the term. It could be a casual setting such as having lunch or a more formal setting in which students get additional one-on-one attention for writing papers or discussing books. If your campus offers such a program, sign up pronto.

You're ready to get to know your professors. But where do you start? Well, you have to begin by calling them something. It was easy in high school; you called your teachers Ms. Jones or Mr. Smith or Coach. In college it gets a bit more complicated.

Here's the quick and dirty on the pecking order for college profs, especially at larger colleges and universities. With the exception of instructors, those in the other ranks most likely will have doctorates; that is, Ph.D.'s. Translate that into lots of years of schooling.

- *Instructors* sometimes teach only part-time and (at large four-year colleges, anyway) must have at least a master's degree.

- New profs, or those with only a couple of years of experience, are *assistant professors*. They are fairly easy to spot—they're the ones with bloodshot eyes from staying up late engaging in creative activities or trying to stay one step ahead of their students in terms of class preparation. These folks are working toward getting promoted and being tenured, so they never seem to have enough time. (One of the authors falls into this category.)

- When profs get promoted (the first time) they are called *associate professors*. This means that they have met the requirements at their college or university to merit this promotion. They have probably written some articles and gotten them published, or maybe they've written books—perhaps even the books you're using for their courses. They have also generally had success in the classroom (good teaching ratings) or provided lots of service to the school and community. Usually, along with promotion to associate professor comes tenure. Simply defined, tenure means that your prof has a job at the college for life (if she wants it). Pretty good, huh? It takes an assistant professor six or seven years to get to this point.

I not only use all of the brains I have, but all I can borrow.

—Woodrow Wilson

- Finally, there are the big guns—*professors*, sometimes called *full professors*. These folks have been around the block a few times and have done lots of things right in order to achieve this goal. It's hard to get promoted to professor. They're usually easy to spot, too: wrinkled brow, old leather briefcase, offices filled with years of stuff accumulated from years of teaching. (The other author falls into this category.)

With the exception of instructors, to whom you would refer much as you did your high school teachers (Ms. or Mr. Whomever), other faculty should be referred to as Dr. or Professor Whomever, until they tell you otherwise. Either title is a safe bet, but check out your syllabus to see if there is any indication what he would like to be called. We know one professor who, on the first day of class, belts out very loudly—"I'm Professor Kelly" (not his real name). No doubt about what *he* wants to be called! Even if you have no idea in the world what your professor wants to be called, under no circumstances should you refer to him (or her) as "dude."

Now that you know how to address your profs, there are still a few things you need to know if you're going to get off on the right foot with them. Because professors are just ordinary people, no two are the same. What wows and works for one will fail miserably on the next. But here's some standard fare for dealing with profs, at least on the first meeting. We'll get you through that; the rest is up to you.

LISTEN UP

Over the years, many female professors have found that students address them as Ms. or Mrs. even though they have a Ph.D. For some reason, students are more likely to address male faculty as Dr. or Professor. In order to avoid this faux pas, it is always a safe bet to call your professor...well...Professor.

1. **Make an appointment.** Even if professors have drop-in office hours, we still think it's best to set up a time. You can either approach your professor before or after class or send her an email. Try to have several times in mind that would work for you so that you can be flexible in scheduling the appointment. And don't forget to have your daily planner with you when you make the appointment so you can write down the time *and* the place. (We sometimes have students show up in the classroom when we've arranged to meet them in our offices.)

2. **Show up on time.** Tardiness is a pet peeve of many professors (including one of the authors) and you're not going to earn any points by showing up late or not showing up at all. If you have to cancel the appointment, try to give your prof some notice in advance.

3. **Be brief and to the point.** Why have you made the appointment? Is it to get help with something you don't understand? To discuss a grade? To get some studying advice? We know this may sound strange, but it doesn't hurt to have a jot list and begin your meeting by saying something such as "I made this list of questions to be certain I asked you everything." Your professor will be impressed that you have thought the issue through before coming to his office. If you really feel lost and can't clearly verbalize your problem, tell him that as well so that he may more easily help you figure it out.

4. **Ask questions or make points appropriately.** Let's say you've made an appointment to discuss your grade on your first history test. You didn't do nearly as well as you thought; in fact, you believe you deserve a much higher grade than the C– you earned. How do you approach the professor? Trust us on this one, it's best not to talk to your professor in a hostile or disrespectful way. Try to put yourself in your professor's shoes. What if someone came into your room and was hostile with you? How would you feel?

    If you're angry about a grade or something else a professor has said or done, walk away and count to ten. Count to 100 if you have to. Think things through and take a deep breath, particularly if you tend to say things that you regret later. Even if you believe that the grading was terribly unfair, be as positive as you can and communicate that you want to understand why you earned a low C so that you can improve for the next test: "I thought I did much better than this. Can we talk for a few minutes about my strengths and weaknesses on this exam so that I can do better next time?" or "I understand why I had points taken off here, but how could this part of my essay have been stronger?"

> A poor surgeon hurts one person at a time. A poor teacher hurts 130.
>
> —Ernest Boyer

32

With just a little thought and planning, meetings with professors can be almost pleasant. In fact, you just might learn something interesting.

Hangin' with Your Profs

We're not the only ones who believe that one of the smartest things you can do is to get to know some of your professors well. Recently there has been more of a push nationwide for professors to interact with undergraduate students in informal settings. In fact, on our campus there is a fund set aside for faculty to use to entertain students in their homes. Students who participate in these informal social activities usually have positive things to say about the experience because they have been able to see their professor in a different light. So if your professor invites you over for pizza or for a five-course meal, put on a clean shirt and go. You will probably end up having a good time.

There are lots of ways to get to know your professors better. Many students get involved with student government, join clubs that have faculty sponsors, take small classes whenever possible, or get a part-time job working for a professor who shares a common interest. It's a real plus to put yourself in situations where you can meet and interact with faculty, where you can get to know them as people, and where they can get to know you.

THE INSIDE SCOOP

If you know your professors better, you won't be too embarrassed or afraid to ask for help. A Harvard researcher who conducted a ten-year study of college students found evidence that students benefit from getting to know their professors. In a sample of 40 students, 20 asked for academic help in their freshman year and 20 didn't. Those who asked improved their grades. The other students...well, let's just say things didn't go so well for them.

What Do Your Profs Think about *You?*

You'll be better able to interact more comfortably with your professors and get to know them if you understand some of their general perceptions about students, particularly freshmen. Take these tidbits for what they are: generalizations that college faculty have in mind when they look out over the sea of faces. Right or wrong, faculty make assumptions like these:

You're in college to get an education. So if you're a slacker or come to them with lame excuses about why you didn't complete your paper on time ("the computer chewed up my disk just as I was putting on the finishing touches") your words will probably fall on deaf ears. They have heard more excuses than you can dream up. They do expect you to plan for the worst, so that when it occurs you actually have some extra time to finish assignments that were given way in advance.

SAD BUT TRUE

Dr. Green is a gifted teacher, exciting and dynamic in the classroom, who genuinely cares about her students. Over her many years of working with college students, she became very concerned about all of the excuses students gave her for not coming to class or not showing up on test days. She had heard it all. But the excuse that bothered her most was the "death in family" one, particularly grandparent deaths. One semester she swore one of her students had three grandparents and an uncle die. So Dr. Green started to send sympathy cards to the families of her students, with some interesting results. Sometimes these deaths were legitimate. In those cases, Dr. Green often received thank-you notes or phone calls from the families who appreciated her thoughtfulness. On other occasions, however—in which the "deaths" were anything but legit—either she or the absent student received a different kind of phone call. We suspect that these students found other excuses for missing class in the future. The message here: Don't kill off all of your relatives in one semester.

You're interested in whatever it is they teach. And if you're not interested, you'll get interested. Falling asleep in class, reading the campus newspaper, or talking to the person next to you will not endear you to your professors. Remember, showing up is only half the battle.

You're self-motivated. No matter what obstacles professors throw in your path, they're sure you can handle it because you are highly motivated. Never mind that you're taking four other classes and have the reading load of ten graduate students. You're motivated and you can do it.

You know how to study and manage your time. Profs expect you to be a studying machine and know all sorts of effective ways to learn their material. They also expect you to be just like them—you know, get to class on time and submit your work three days before it's due. Take this assumption as a compliment.

You can do more with course material than simply memorize it. Your profs expect you to think critically. This means that when they lecture on some topic that seems almost unintelligible they expect you to magically understand everything they have said. Sure, some memorizing is necessary, but they expect you to go beyond that. They expect you to be able to think about their topic like an expert would. Unrealistic? Maybe, but it is a reality that they think you're pretty smart, so you should be able to think about ideas logically and critically.

Your professors are actually just regular folks who happen to have lots of education. When they look out over the sea of faces in a class, they see students who are bright, capable, and have a real desire to learn.

Quick and Dirty

○ Professors do lots of things in addition to teaching—like research, writing, and service activities.

○ When you need to see your professor, make an appointment and be ready to talk about your issues.

○ Profs come in three sizes: assistants, associates, and fulls.

○ Get to know some of your profs very well. They can help you out down the line.

○ Your profs think that you are bright and want to learn.

CHAPTER 4

ZEN AND THE ART OF COURSE SELECTION

It is not enough to offer a smorgas-
bord of courses. We must insure that
students are not just eating at one
end of the table.

—A. Bartlett Giamatti

Y ou've been staring at a course catalog the size of a small telephone book for days now. How do you know which courses to take? You're not even sure what you are going to major in yet. (Don't worry. The next chapter will help you sort out your interests to determine the kinds of careers that suit you best.) You've talked to your advisor and are armed with a list of four possible courses to start with. You figure out how to get into the computer registration system, but find that all of the courses you've planned to take this term are filled and it seems that the only courses left have titles like *Baroque Art for Physicists* or they begin at 7:50 *in the morning!* Before you decide to quit college and work full-time at a fast food joint, try taking a different approach to course selection.

GET WIRED

Many colleges offer a lot of additional course information on their Web pages. You may find course syllabi, assignments, class notes, and even instructor evaluations to help you make your course selections.

Racking Up the Credits:
How Many Courses Should You Take?

The first thing you need to decide is how many courses you want to take each term. In most colleges, 12 hours (or four courses) is considered full-time under a semester system. At colleges using a quarter system, nine hours (or three courses) is usually considered full-time. If you are receiving scholarship or student loan funds, you may need to register for a full load to receive the money. And if you want to complete your degree in four years, you should plan on taking *more* than full-time credit hours. You will need to take say, 15 hours (or five courses) if you are under a semester system or 12 hours (four courses) under a quarter system—and if you end up drop-

DO YOUR HOMEWORK

Be sure that you know exactly how many credit hours you will need to earn your degree. This way you can plan how many courses you will need to take each term. Remember, you may need to take more credits if you want to finish in four years.

ping a course, maybe even some summer hours (we will talk more about the reasons for dropping a course later in this chapter).

However, there are many reasons that you might choose to enroll part-time. For example, if you are working full-time, or are returning to school after a long absence, it may be more realistic to start out with a part-time load to determine how many courses you can handle. In fact, any entering student may feel this way for the first term and decide to start out slowly.

Ohmmmm: Creating a Balance

Selecting courses should be easy. You just pick any three or four that you need, stir gently, and you have an instant course schedule, right? Actually, you need to ask yourself some questions as you create your course schedule each semester—and be honest with yourself. Are you really going to wake up early to make it to an 8 A.M. class? Is the only course section offered this semester taught by the professor who made your roommate so nervous she broke out in hives? Will you have to run at breakneck speed from one end of campus to the other in the 15 minutes between classes? To create a balanced schedule, you need to consider the following issues.

BALANCING TASKS

When choosing courses, think about the tasks you will be required to do. You really don't want to take four courses that all require heavy reading, like literature, sociology, history, psychology, or biology. Likewise, you don't want to be doing only mathematics problems all term either (no matter how much you enjoy them). Instead, try to create a balance between heavy reading courses and those that require less reading, courses that involve problem-solving and those that do not.

BALANCING INTERESTS

It would be great if you could be interested in each and every course you take in college (we hope you will find *something* interesting in every course). However, most colleges require a core of courses, some of which may not be your favorites. Instead of waiting until the last possible semester to take these dreaded courses, it is a much better idea to spread them out over your college career. Try to balance your semester with some courses you find highly interesting; something in your major, or a course that focuses on topics you've always wanted to know more about. For example, one of the authors of this book took an elective course on King Arthur legends that was not part of her major but was the highlight of that semester.

SAD BUT TRUE ☹

Josh, a senior ecology major, had always hated taking literature courses. He really couldn't see where his teachers got all that stuff about theme and metaphor—yuck! So in his years as a college student he just avoided them, even though he was required to take two lit courses to graduate. (Maybe he thought if he ignored them, they'd just go away.) Now, as he registers for his final semester in school, he finds that he needs to squeeze in both lit courses on top of his very tough senior-level ecology courses. He thinks to himself, If only I'd gotten these lit courses out of the way earlier, I could've really enjoyed this last semester in school.

The moral of Josh's tale: Don't wait to take the courses you are not crazy about. Instead, distribute them over your college years—who knows, you may end up liking them more than you think. At the very least, you won't have to face them all at once.

BALANCING TIME

When creating your course schedule, you should also consider when each class meets. If you know that you have grave difficulty just finding the shower early in the morning (let alone trying to make your brain function), avoid 8 A.M. classes like the plague. In addition, don't overload your schedule. We have known students who have attempted to take all of their courses on Tuesdays and Thursdays and were in class from 9 A.M. until after 6 P.M. Unless you are extremely disciplined, you will soon find this kind of schedule grueling. Also, try to schedule the courses you are least interested in at your personal peak times. This way you are more likely to make it to class every day. (Later in the book we'll have a more in-depth discussion of time management.)

Creating a balance in your schedule can often mean the difference between a great semester and a lousy one. Take the time to consider these factors each time you make your course schedule.

Working with Your Advisor

SAD BUT TRUE

Keisha thought she would be graduating spring semester with a degree in marketing. However, when she registered for classes last week she found out that she needed one more economics course that would not be offered again until the fall. Keisha is really angry with her advisor for not making sure she had this course. Now she won't graduate in four years and she won't be able to begin interviewing until next year.

If you listen to people talking on campus, everyone knows someone in Keisha's situation. Advisors get a bum rap because it seems that they are always getting blamed for misguiding students. It may be that a course the student needs is not offered, or that a prerequisite course is needed before the student can register for a course that's required for graduation, or that the student took extra courses not needed for the major. Although we strongly believe that advisors should be up on things, we also know that it is very difficult for them to keep up with the many curriculum requirement changes that occur at many colleges—especially if advising is not the advisor's full-time job. In fact, many colleges require faculty to advise students; given all that your professors have to do, it is no wonder that many of them do not invest much time in their advising duties.

No matter who your advisor may be, it is *your responsibility* to be sure you get the guidance you need. We're not saying that you need to familiarize yourself with the entire course catalogue, but you should ask lots of questions and seek answers from more than one source as you set your course load each term, particularly if something seems fishy to you. For example, at our college there was a rumor that students could not use scholarship money to take summer courses. Students said that they heard this from their advisors, but upon checking with the Registrar's Office they found this was simply not true.

Here are some basic questions to ask your advisor:

1. **Which courses are required for graduating with a major in** [fill in the blank]?

2. **Are there prerequisite courses for any of these requirements?** (You may want to ask this question every time you meet with your advisor.)

3. **How often are these courses offered—and are there any that are only offered occasionally?** On most campuses, courses are planned almost a year in advance (or at least tentatively planned), so your advisor should be able to find out what will be offered the following semester (or even, in some cases, the next two semesters).

4. **Are there any requirements governing how I must choose to use my elective credit hours?** Some colleges require that you take some electives in the humanities, sciences, and so on. Others have no such requirements for electives and you can use them as you choose.

5. **Is there a particular order I should follow when signing up for the courses in my major?**

6. **Are there any courses that need to be taken at the same time?**

Choosing Your Professors

Many students tell us that selecting professors is even more important than selecting courses. Ask your friends, your advisor, and students in your major which professors they'd suggest. Try to get some specifics about the professor. What is his general style of teaching? What kinds of tests does he give? How large is the class? What are the grading procedures? What is the overall level of difficulty? (Remember that an easy course is not always a blessing—especially if you need to really learn the information for your future career.) You may even want to go talk to the professor through email or during his office hours to find out a little more about a course before signing up.

> Not doing more than the average is what keeps the average down.
>
> –William M. Winans

In general, seeking help from advisors, peers, and professors can help you create a course schedule you can live with (and even learn to love).

Making a Plan

Once you have decided on a major (we aren't rushing you—for many students this may not happen until the end of sophomore year), you should map out a general college course plan. Your plan should include both the courses you are required to take and some electives you want to take. It should also help you figure out how long it will take you to get your degree. Most colleges have a form to help you do this. In fact, some colleges will ask you to submit your course plan when you officially declare your major. However, let's assume that you do not have such guidance. How do you make your own college course plan?

Check out the course catalogue. Most colleges send out copies of an "undergraduate bulletin" or catalogue along with the acceptance letter. Others may give it out at orientation. If you didn't study it when you first got it, now's the time to pull it out and take a look at the many fascinating courses that await you. Examine the courses offered for your major, then take a look at any electives that seem interesting to you. If some of the courses are specialty courses (like that King Arthur legends course), you should contact the appropriate departments to find out when the classes will be offered again. Sometimes departments list courses that have not been taught in years; finding out this information will save you from building a course into your college plan only to find later on that it won't be offered until after you've graduated.

LISTEN UP

It's not always easy to find out about the best, most interesting electives to take. Students have told us that they didn't catch on to how to do this until their junior year, when it was essentially too late. Our advice? Ask around. In fact, ask every-one—a professor you found interesting, your friends, advisors, people you meet at the library. In addition, skim through the course catalogue and mark the things that look interesting. Remember to search outside your major or college—there's good stuff out there you might never have even considered.

Figure out how long it will take to get your degree. Most students assume that they will finish a bachelor's degree in four years or an associate's degree in two. But the reality is that it is becoming more and more common for it to take longer. If your goal is to finish in four years, your college plan must take this into account.

Make a timeline. Plot out the courses you will take each term. Be sure to give yourself some wiggle room in case a course you'd like to take is not offered during the term you've set out in your timeline. Double-check your plan to be sure that you have created a balanced course load for each term.

THE INSIDE SCOOP

Some students think that taking courses during the summer session is like attending summer school in high school—a penance for falling behind during the regular school year. But in college, summer session courses are just like courses given in the fall and spring terms. Don't think of them as a punishment; consider them another opportunity to help you complete your college career in a timely fashion.

For example, here is Ben's sample course timeline for his first two years toward completing a degree in botany.

TERM	COURSE	CREDITS
Fall 2002	Intro Biology I w/lab	3
	Intro Psychology	3
	Freshman seminar	1
	Racquetball	2
	Precalc	3
Spring 2003	Intro Biology II w/lab	3
	Freshman English	3
	Music Appreciation	3
	Spanish I	3
	Speech Communications	3
Fall 2003	Plant Biology	3
	History I	3
	Intro to Chemistry	3
	Calculus	3
	Spanish II	3
Spring 2004	Developmental Biology	3
	Cell Biology	3
	Sophomore English	3
	Human Geography	3
	Spanish III	3

Notice how Ben has created a balance of the types of courses he plans to take, while still taking at least one course per term that relates to his major—and often also fulfills a general curriculum requirement. He has also planned to start out his first semester with fewer credit hours so he can ramp up to the challenge of college.

Once you are enrolled in college, try to plan out at least your first two semesters. What do you envision your courses will be like? Remember, if you are not sure what your major will be, focus on fulfilling your general requirements first; these courses just might help you decide.

Withdrawal Symptoms

There's a pretty good chance that, sooner or later, you will want (or need) to withdraw from a course. The reasons vary; as a general rule, if you do not think that you can successfully complete a course, it is often best to drop it. Talk to your professor and advisor before you withdraw from a course to get their advice. You'll need their signatures, too, because withdrawing is often an exercise in filling out lots of paperwork.

Students often hang onto courses they cannot pass and end up with a GPA that can get them into trouble. These students may feel that withdrawing from a course is quitting and that quitting is a greater failure than seeing the course through to the end. The decision to withdraw is difficult, but it is often the best choice. On the other hand, if you have withdrawn from more courses than you've completed, graduation may not occur until you're old enough to retire.

Some colleges set limits on the number of courses you can withdraw from over your college career. If your college falls into this category, you will need to be careful because you don't want to use up all your withdrawals in the first two years. In addition, withdrawal deadlines can vary greatly (check your college catalogue or Web site for these policies so you don't miss the drop date).

When should you withdraw from a course? There are two good indicators:

1. You are feeling overwhelmed with the number of courses you are taking and feel that you would do better in all of your other courses if you just got rid of one.

2. You are failing a course and feel that you cannot pull up your grade by the end of the term. However, we must note that some professors will only let you withdraw if you are *passing* the course. Be sure to check your syllabus before attempting to withdraw—you may need to make your decision before the first exam.

Know Thy GPA

Most students think that they have only one GPA (grade point average), but actually your grade point average is calculated in several ways. First, you have a term GPA: your average for the courses you are taking in a particular semester or quarter. It is calculated by dividing the grade points earned that term by the total number of credit hours attempted that semester. Second, you have a cumulative GPA: your average for all of the courses you have taken so far. Your cumulative GPA is calculated by dividing your total number of grade points by the total number of credits you have earned.

Since we are discussing how to figure out your grades, it is important to note that an obsessive focus on your grades presents some pitfalls:

- You're not learning for your own sake. If you are only concerned with the grade you'll earn, you'll find that you are working to please the professor instead of learning to please yourself.

- If you do not make the grade you desire, you become less interested in the course. Students have told us that when they work for a grade and they don't do as well as they would have liked, they end up feeling frustrated and often just give up. Generally, grades alone are not enough to sustain your motivation.

- You find that you put responsibility for learning on others. Students who are worried about grades tend to blame others for any failures: "I didn't do well on the test because the professor didn't go over half the material in class." Remember, you are in charge of your own learning.

What *is* a grade point, anyway? A grade point is the number assigned to each letter grade. Most colleges use the point system shown on the opposite page (top right). (Note: If your college does

🖩 DO YOUR HOMEWORK

Find out about your college's policy on transfer credits. Transfer credits are those that you bring with you from other colleges (or from joint enrollment courses between high schools and colleges). Do those grades compute into your GPA—or do the credits just count for graduation credit without impacting your GPA?

not use plusses or minuses, use only the full letter grades when calculating your GPA. Check your college's policy on grading in the course catalogue.)

A	4.0
A–	3.7
B+	3.3
B	3.0
B–	2.7
C+	2.3
C	2.0
C–	1.7
D	1.0
F	0.0

Basically, to improve your grade point average you need to make above-average grades: As or Bs. However, when you begin college it is very important to get off to a good start. This is why you need to know both your *term* GPA and your *cumulative* GPA. The more credits you have earned each term, the harder it is to improve your cumulative GPA. In addition, for some majors there are minimum GPA requirements for admission. You'll need to keep track of your GPA to be sure you meet these standards.

GET WIRED

Many colleges offer "what if?" calculators on their Web sites. These sites help you figure out the exact grades you will need to earn to get the GPA you desire.

DO YOUR HOMEWORK

Pop Quiz: Sam is taking four introductory courses this semester—English, math, Spanish, and psychology. He wants to end the semester with at least a 3.0 cumulative GPA. If he gets a B– in English, a C in math, an A in Spanish, and an A– in psychology, will he reach this goal?

Course	Grade	Grade Points x	Number of Credits =	Total Points
Engl 101	B–	2.7	3	8.1
Math 101	C	2.0	3	6.6
Span 101	A	4.0	4	16.0
Psych 101	A–	3.7	3	11.1
	Total		13	41.2

To calculate the GPA, you divide total points by total credits. Sam's 41.2 points divided by 13 credits produces a 3.17 GPA. So Sam did reach his goal this term. Way to go, Sam!

We suggest you figure out your GPA every semester. In addition, keep track of your grades in each course so you'll know where you stand at all times. Some students keep a record in the front of their binder for each course.

> Eighty percent of success is showing up.
> —Woody Allen

Quick and Dirty

○ Take only as many courses as you can handle. When you are choosing courses, remember to balance interests, tasks, requirements, and electives.

○ Work with your advisor. Ask lots of questions about course and degree requirements (even if you haven't decided on your major yet) and about which professors to take.

○ Make a college plan. Don't just chip away at course requirements; map out what you are going to take over the next four (or more) years. This way you will avoid some unpleasant surprises.

○ Figure out your GPA. Stay on top of both your term (semester) grades and your cumulative (overall) GPA.

CHAPTER 5

MAJOR DECISIONS: SELECTING A FIELD OF STUDY

> We know what we are, but know not
> what we may be.
>
> —William Shakespeare

Y ou may enter college knowing exactly what you want to major in, or you may be one of a growing number of students who begin with no idea of what they will end up doing. Let's say you are in the second category. Some studies indicate that up to 75 percent of entering freshman are uncertain of their choice of major, so you are in good company. To make the choice, you begin by figuring out the career you want for the rest of your life, right? Not really. Selecting a major is quite different from selecting a career. College majors often lead to a variety of career choices. And while you are in college, you may learn of interesting careers that you have never thought about or even heard of.

Help! I Don't Know What I Want to Do When I Grow Up

When selecting a major, there's lots for you to think about. Some students try to look to the future and select a major that will allow them to have a variety of options careerwise. Others are very focused a select a major that will prepare them for more limited careers. Whatever your approach, there are a few basic steps to follow so that you can select the major that is right for you.

1. RELAX

This is an important decision, but don't let it stress you out. Selecting a major does not mean you are cutting off other options. You will still have a chance to change your mind—many students do. So take a deep breath and read on. And by the way, if your parents are worried because they think you have no direction in your life, have them read this chapter too.

2. ASSESS YOUR STRENGTHS AND INTERESTS

What do you like to do? Do you enjoy working with other people? Do you like to read for information? Do you like working with numbers? What hobbies currently interest you? Do you prefer to work indoors or outdoors? What activities do you know you do *not* like to do? To determine what you *do* like to do, see the exercise on figuring out your interests in this chapter.

☹ SAD BUT TRUE

James, a senior accounting major, recently came to a startling realization. He discovered that he did not like accounting. Nope, didn't like any part of it. Not solving problems using accounting models, not balancing budgets, not figuring out credits and debits—not any of the tasks he had been taught to do in college. The more he thought about it, the more he discovered that he wished he had majored in something that allowed him to be more creative, like advertising, or something that really interested him, like history. James had chosen accounting at the end of his freshman year for two reasons: it led to a clear career path with a good potential for making money, and his parents seemed to think it would be a good career choice. Looking back on that decision, James says ruefully, "I mean, what would you do with a degree in history? At least with accounting I knew—or thought I knew—what I was getting into."

🏛 DO YOUR HOMEWORK

Talk to some students who are currently enrolled in the major(s) you are considering. Ask them about the department, what they like and don't like about the program, why they selected this major. Often they can provide great insight into what you can expect.

The moral of James's story: Don't allow others to pressure you into making your decision too early (pssssst...*not even your parents*). Your strengths and interests often develop and change during your first years in college, so take your time when making this very important choice.

3. FIND OUT HOW YOUR INTERESTS RELATE TO COLLEGE MAJORS

If you enjoy working with or helping people, you may want to pursue a degree that allows you to teach or provide guidance to others. If you are mechanically inclined and would rather deal with things than with people, consider degrees such as engineering or forestry, or other majors that allow you to work at building or "doing." If you are artistic or creative, seek majors that encourage those talents, such as literature, graphic arts, or music.

GET WIRED

Many colleges offer Web site questionnaires designed to help you discover how your interests relate to college majors and future careers. Also check out your college's career planning office. Such offices usually offer a combination of support services that may include assessments, one-on-one counseling, workshops, and even courses on choosing a major and a career.

4. FIND OUT HOW POTENTIAL MAJORS RELATES TO CAREER OPTIONS

Some majors relate directly to specific careers; others are more general. Basically, there are three categories of majors:

Non-career-specific. These majors do not directly prepare you for a job. Some examples are English, history, psychology, and political science. Often students choosing these majors go on for an advanced degree or seek internships or other career-related experiences while enrolled in college.

Career-oriented. These majors lead you to a general field of employment, but not to a specific job. Some good examples are degrees in marketing, communications, biology, and sociology. These degrees prepare students for a variety of entry-level positions within these fields.

Career-specific. These majors prepare you for a specific job; for example, accounting, education, engineering, and nursing. After earning a degree in many of these fields, you must pass some kind of license or certification test before you can either practice or advance in your career.

5. TAKE ADVANTAGE OF CAMPUS RESOURCES

Most colleges offer some kind of career planning services. Whether you have entered college knowing your major and career path or not, you should familiarize yourself with this valuable campus resource early in your college career. In addition to offering personalized career counselors, career discovery inventories, and computer resources to help you determine a good career or major for you, they also can help you find an internship or even teach you how to interview for a job.

X FOR ADULTS ONLY

If you are returning to college to change careers or to start a new career, the career planning office often has special resources that can help you determine ways to combine previous experiences with your current major to lead to a variety of career opportunities. Be sure to take advantage of their services.

6. DO A REALITY CHECK

Your college major will, in essence, be your full-time job for the next four (or five) years. Think about the kinds of courses you will be expected to take in the major and the types of careers that can be pursued with your degree. If you like the kinds of tasks that you will be asked to do in your major and you look forward to the types of careers this major will lead to, you are on the right path. What if, on the other hand, you are a premed major who can't stand the sight of blood; an interior design major who can't draw a straight line, or a computer science major who hates solving math problems? Are you in love with the idea of your major, but not with the realities of what completing that major would entail? Periodically ask yourself, "Can I see myself doing these kinds of tasks in my career?" If your answer is "No!" more often than "Yes!" it's time to reevaluate your major and career goals.

For most students, choosing a major is not an easy decision. Our best advice is to arm yourself with as much information as you can before you make your choice. If you decide too early and then switch your major later on, you may end up needing to take more courses (and additional semesters) if some of the courses you've taken don't count for anything in your new major.

So Many Choices!

Most people want a major and a career that are tied into their interests. But sometimes determining what those interests are is more challenging than you'd expect. Most career counselors use six generally accepted categories created by John Holland and explained in *Making Vocational Choices: A Theory of Vocational Personalities and Work Environments* (Odessa, Fla.: Psychological Assessment Resources, 1987) to determine interests for future careers and majors. See which categories you fall into. Note: Most people fit into more than one category.

Artistic. Artistic people usually like unstructured tasks in a creative environment. They like to use their imagination and enjoy work that fosters creativity. Artistic types may enjoy majoring in interior design, music, literature, drama, or other creative fields.

Enterprising. These types like to take initiative and often assume a leadership position. They enjoy persuading or influencing others. Enterprising types may enjoy majoring in marketing, speech communication, business, or other fields that encourage leadership, communication, and persuasion.

Social. Social people like to work with others. They enjoy teaching, informing, curing, or other activities that help other people. They value social situations and interpersonal relationships. Social types may enjoy majoring in education, speech communications, psychology, nursing, social work, or other fields that encourage helping and working with others.

Realistic. These types tend to be mechanically inclined and are often athletic. They may enjoy dealing with things rather than people. They are likely to enjoy working outdoors or with machines, building or fixing things. Realistic types may enjoy majoring in engineering, agriculture, or other fields that emphasize the technical or mechanical.

Investigative. These are thinking types who like to solve problems through analyzing or using data. They see themselves as scholarly and intellectually capable.

Investigative types may enjoy majoring in science, mathematics, philosophy, or other fields that encourage their intellectual spirit.

Conventional. These types are orderly and precise. They are practical and neat; they like to work in structured situations in which they know what is expected of them and where accuracy counts. Conventional types may enjoy majoring in accounting, business, management, computer science, or other fields where precision and accuracy are valued.

How can you figure out where you fit among these types? Take this little test by placing a check mark next to each activity you enjoy (check as many as apply).

REALISTIC
- ☐ build things
- ☐ work outdoors
- ☐ be active
- ☐ work with my hands
- ☐ work on cars

INVESTIGATIVE
- ☐ investigate ideas
- ☐ use computers
- ☐ work alone
- ☐ work in a lab
- ☐ solve math problems

SOCIAL
- ☐ work in groups
- ☐ help people with problems
- ☐ participate in meetings
- ☐ lead a group discussion
- ☐ teach or train others

ARTISTIC
- ☐ attend concerts, theater performances, art exhibits
- ☐ read fiction, plays, poetry
- ☐ play a musical instrument, sing, compose
- ☐ write stories, poetry, essays
- ☐ act, dance, work behind the scenes in the performing arts
- ☐ sketch, draw, paint, sculpt

ENTERPRISING
- ☐ make decisions
- ☐ give talks or speeches
- ☐ organize activities and events
- ☐ sell things
- ☐ lead a group

CONVENTIONAL
- ☐ follow procedures
- ☐ keep records and organize paperwork
- ☐ work with numbers
- ☐ create databases of information
- ☐ be responsible for details

To figure out your interests, total the number of items you have checked in each category. Remember that most people fall into more than one category. To get the broadest view of your interests, select the top three categories that describe you. So you may be enterprising, artistic, and social—or conventional, realistic, and investigative—or any combination of these six cate-

> When you have to make a choice and don't make it, that in itself is a choice.
>
> –William James

gories. This information can help guide you not only in choosing a major and a career, but also in selecting courses that match your broader interests.

SAD BUT TRUE ☹

Stacy felt pressured to declare her major before she really knew what she wanted to do. Because she'd always done well in science in high school, she chose to major in chemistry, figuring that maybe she'd go on to become a pharmacist. As she finished her sophomore year she decided that her true passion was not working in a lab, but working with people. Stacy wanted to switch over to science education. Unfortunately, because she had taken so many chemistry requirements that were not a part of the science ed curriculum, changing her major now would mean spending at least an extra year in college. If only she had waited and taken more general course requirements instead of rushing to declare a major.

Double (or Even Triple) Majors

Most colleges offer double majors in areas that are closely tied together (such as computer science and mathematics) or even in areas that seem unrelated (like sociology and agriculture). For example, if you love to learn languages, yet you know you want a career that will earn a good living and allow you to travel, your ticket to success may be a double major in language and business.

Remember, if you choose to seek a double major, you will have to fulfill the requirements of *both* majors in order to graduate. You will probably need to take a heavier course load than your classmates most semesters, especially if you hope to finish in four years. However, for most students who choose to double major, this challenge is worth the extra effort because it brings their interests together. If you choose a double major, it's important to use your electives wisely. In fact, you may end up with very few "free" electives because an elective credit in one major may fulfill a required course in the other major.

You may be wondering who in their right mind would want to pursue a double major. Some students believe that this path will lead them to a better job or more job options after college. They may be right—but it depends on what those two majors are. There's another good reason: if you know you are going to apply for an advanced degree (say, medical school), a double major in chemistry and biology will certainly be helpful. On the other hand, sometimes a single major with very strong grades and a minor in your secondary interest can serve you just as well, without the added pressure. Check with your advisor and talk to students majoring in both areas before you make your final decision.

Major Assistance Is Out There

Choosing a major is obviously not an easy decision. In fact, most college students change majors at least once. Take advantage of the many resources available to help you make this very important decision. These resources include the following:

- **Your college's course catalogue.** This book contains a wealth of information about the courses you need to take and may introduce you to some specialized or interesting majors that you've never heard of before.

- **Your professors and your academic advisor.** Many of your professors have worked in the field in which they teach and may be able to tell you about career options. In addition, when you take a course in a field that you find interesting and worth pursuing further, talk to the professor and your advisor about it.

- **Your friends (and your friends' friends).** Even talk to your parents' friends. Ask people about their majors and how they came to make their choices. Talk to students with the majors you are considering and to folks going through the job interview process to gather as much information as you can.

- **Your college career planning and placement center.** We don't know why students don't just flock to these places. Helping students choose majors and then find jobs is *the career choice of those who work in career centers.* And yet these centers are some of the most underutilized places on campus. Don't wait until your senior year to visit; go there in your very first semester. You can often find out about internships, summer jobs, and other opportunities that will help you reach your long-term goals.

- **Specialized Web sites.** Our college hosts a Web site where students can explore all of the different majors offered. In addition, the Web site provides information about careers associated with certain majors, beginning salaries, and the prospects for employment opportunities in that field. What a great resource! Check out what's offered online at your own institution.

- **Your family.** Is there someone in your family who has a job you'd just love to do? Talk to that person about choosing a major and try to visit him at his place of employment to learn more about what it entails. Heck, he might even be able to help you find an internship or summer employment in his field.

These suggestions are just to help you begin to think about the resources available to you. But don't stop there! Every time you read about someone in a newspaper or watch something on TV and think, "Gee, that person has a great job," think about how you could get on a track that leads to a career like that.

> Anyone who stops learning is old, whether at twenty or eighty. Anyone who keeps learning stays young. The greatest thing in life is to keep your mind young.
>
> —Henry Ford

Why Choosing a Major ≠ Choosing a Career

If you have chosen to major in philosophy, everyone you meet probably asks, "What in the world are you going to do with that?" In fact, majoring in fields such as philosophy, drama, literature, history, or psychology can lead to careers in business, teaching, writing, research, or a variety of other careers. Just because there is no clearly defined end-point career doesn't mean there are no jobs available for you. In fact, in a study asking college graduates what they'd do differently if they could do college over again, many responded that they would seek a liberal arts education to build a broader background.

On the other hand, if you have decided to become a lawyer, that doesn't mean you need to major in prelaw. Depending on what kind of law you'd like to practice, a major in business, history, literature, or language can serve you just as well. For example, if you are interested in pursuing environmental law, then a bachelor's degree in ecology may be very helpful.

We don't know any better than you do what the job market will look like in the future. Jobs that are plentiful now may become obsolete as we find new ways of getting things done. For example, as we finish *College Rules!* we know quite a few business majors having a difficult time finding the job they'd hoped for. New opportunities will arise that no one can predict—could anyone in your parents' generation have predicted the number of jobs created by the Internet? So our best advice is to use your college years to build skills that will apply to a variety of possible careers—skills such as written and verbal communication, computing, organizing, and problem-solving.

THE INSIDE SCOOP

There's a common misperception that choosing a major is equivalent to choosing a career. However, recent research has indicated that only 50 percent of college graduates report a close connection between their majors and their job. This means that getting a bachelor's degree can prepare you for a variety of careers.

Quick and Dirty

○ Figure out your interests and strengths before you choose a major. Use the resources available to you on campus and on the Internet to help make your decision.

○ Choosing a major does not mean that you are stuck in only one career path. Rather than focusing on your eventual career, focus on choosing a major that requires you to do the things you enjoy (such as writing, painting, solving problems, working in a lab).

○ Talk to everyone you can about your choice of major before you decide. And don't let anyone pressure you to settle too quickly. Take your time as you make your choice.

CHAPTER 6

CLASSES, WORK, AND PLAY: ADJUSTING TO THE DEMANDS OF COLLEGE

The unfortunate thing about this world is that the good habits are much easier to give up than the bad ones.

—W. Somerset Maugham

Your professors may have different beliefs than you do about why you are in college in the first place. Most likely, your professors have the almost idealistic belief that you actually want to get an education. That you hang on their every word. That you are inspired by their infinite wisdom. (College professors tend to have rather large egos.) That your major goal is to learn as much _____ (whatever it is they are teaching—you fill in the blank) as possible, no matter how much time and effort it takes. Do these people think you have no life?

You, on the other hand, have only a slightly different view of why you are in college: to land a good job and make a gazillion bucks by the time you're 25. Sure, it's important to learn stuff in college, but in the end you believe that it's the grade that counts, and the job you'll get, and the money you'll make—not how much you've really learned. Besides, if you took things as seriously as some of your professors, you'd be like a monk—locked up in your room studying from sunrise to sunset, only leaving your room to go to class and be enlightened by one of those ego-ridden professors. Not your idea of fun, right?

Okay, okay, both of these beliefs are extreme. There is a happy medium among getting an education (actually learning something—learning a lot, even), playing and having a social life, and working if you choose or need to. But before you can think about balancing everything, it's important to put the demands of college into perspective and to think a little about the changes you may need to make in order to make a smooth adjustment to college.

Lots of Changes

We said in the first chapter that college is different from high school. College requires you to think differently, act differently, deal with things differently. Once you understand that you are probably going to have to make some changes in most aspects of managing your life, you have half the battle won. It doesn't matter whether you are an 18-year-old going away to school or an older student returning to school, it's important to understand that you will need to make adjustments.

THE ROLLER-COASTER RIDE: EMOTIONAL ADJUSTMENTS

If you have mixed emotions as you arrive on campus and try to find your way, don't think that you're alone. On one hand, you're so excited about all the freedom you'll have that you could bust a gut. On the other hand, the idea that it's time to cut the cord, take on additional responsibility, and not have Mom and Dad right there to bail you out of jams may be a bit scary. For 18-year-olds heading off to college, the first term in school can be an emotional roller coaster—trying (and expected) to be an adult (or at least act like one), but still wanting (and needing) to be a kid. If you are returning to college after some years in the workforce you may feel out of place (read: old) surrounded by all those young faces, or guilty about spending time away from your family.

Your emotions during those first few weeks on campus will range from raw fear to sheer elation. Almost all new students are nervous about meeting their roommates, finding out where their classes are, figuring out how everything is done, making good grades, fitting in—the list goes on and on. Understand that (1) thousands—no, millions—of students have done this before you and survived; and (2) you are not alone.

Starting or returning to college after several years of raising a family or being in the workplace poses special concerns and adjustments. Few older students are prepared for the amount of adjusting they'll need to make. For some, this adjustment is easier, especially if family members help out or the student doesn't have a full-time job. But even if you don't have the ideal situation, don't despair. Many campuses offer special support groups for nontraditional students that can be very beneficial.

PARTY ON...SOMETIMES: SOCIAL ADJUSTMENTS

It's important to have a good social network in college. Most of you reading *College Rules!* have probably been in the same social situation for an extended period of time. You have gone to high school with the same group of people and have friends that you hang out and interact with socially—maybe even since kindergarten. Returning students have had a stable, consistent adult social network. This changes, however, once you head to college. Students who attend school away from home and live in a residence hall with lots of other students may have the most difficult time adjusting socially. New students may feel afraid that they won't fit in or that they will have a difficult time making friends. Returning students may feel that they have little in common with students fresh out of high school. Students who feel socially isolated often lack the support system that is necessary to being successful in college. To make adjusting socially a little easier, here are some tips:

- If you're living on campus, get in touch with your roommate *before* you move in. Most schools at least try to match students that have some general things in common, and you will feel better once you have talked to your roommate and find out what some of those things are. Of course, this can backfire. If you talk with your future roommate either by phone or through email and she comes across as a real freak, you may have more anxiety than you did before.

> Experience is a hard teacher because she gives the test first, the lesson afterwards.
>
> —Vernon Saunders Law

- Think about joining a club or community service organization where other members share common interests. Some students like to join fraternities and sororities just because they stand a good chance of meeting others with similar beliefs and interests. Other students find clubs that sound interesting and join them just to find out more (for example, there is a Zen meditation club on our campus).

- Get involved in your residence hall. Dorms offer both academic and social programs. These are good places to meet new people. If you don't live on campus, become part of other student groups or check out the campus newspaper to see what kinds of events are going on.

- If your campus has a peer mentor or faculty mentor program, sign up. Such programs provide great opportunities for adjusting socially.

- Be open-minded. Be willing to try new things.

- Join a study group. Although study groups shouldn't be social groups per se, they can help you meet other students. And they actually work better for studying when they don't include your good friends.

- Don't forget about the play and fun part of college and be sure you build it into your schedule. It's *almost* as important as study time.

Whatever ways you choose to become socially connected, get to know other students. Find a group of students to hang out with. Students who have social support also tend to do better academically.

Knowing where you are going is all you need to get there.
     —Carl Frederick

Paula was having a very difficult time adjusting to being away from home. She had left a boyfriend behind, one who was several years older than she and had decided that college just wasn't for him, at least not at this time. Since home was only a short two-hour drive away, Paula would make the drive to see her boyfriend and hometown friends every Friday afternoon and then return to campus each Sunday evening. During the week, she pretty much kept to herself and failed to make friends from her dorm or her classes. She said that she just wanted to concentrate on studying during the week so that she wouldn't have to worry about getting schoolwork done over the weekend when she was with her boyfriend. But by midterm, Paula was miserable. Her feelings of not wanting to be in school in the first place only increased and it became harder and harder for her to keep her mind on her courses. She lived for the weekends, when she could go home and be with friends. She made a feeble attempt at making friends with others on her hall, but they had already formed social groups and were active in a variety of things on campus. When they invited her to join them, she turned them down because she either had to study or wasn't going to be there on the weekends. So they quit asking and she was pretty much alone all week. To Paula's credit, she did keep up her grades that first semester, but then withdrew from the university and went home to attend a community college so that she could be closer to her boyfriend and high school friends.

SHOW ME THE $: FINANCIAL ADJUSTMENTS

We include a few words about financial adjustments mainly because we've seen too many students run amok academically because they have managed to get themselves into financial binds.

The money-management challenges of college are as vast and varied as the number of students attending. Some of you will continue to be supported by your parents: they will pay for your tuition, room, and board, and provide you with spending money. You guys are really lucky. Others will have partial support and be expected to take out student loans for the remainder or to work part-time. You guys probably have to watch your pennies. Still others will have to work full-time to pay for school and other expenses and can only go to school part-time. You guys really have to watch your pennies.

Our goal here is not to give you a crash course on how to manage your finances. We simply want to warn you about a problem that is becoming more pervasive on college campuses: students are graduating with a degree, sometimes hefty student loans to repay, and thousands of dollars of credit card debt.

⚡ GET WIRED

There's all kinds of nifty free software available for you to download that will frankly discuss everything you should know about managing credit cards while in college. Get a handle on responsible credit card use before you attend your first college class. Until recently, this has been one life skill that's rarely taught in high school.

🎧 LISTEN UP

On many campuses, the current trend is to offer financial literacy courses. Designed primarily for entering freshmen, these courses discuss the principles of managing your money—with considerable emphasis on responsible credit card use. If your campus offers such a course, think about enrolling.

A word to the wise: Whatever your financial situation in college, learn early on how to manage your money wisely. You can use your college years to establish credit by getting *one* credit card with a low credit limit and paying it off monthly. Don't spend what you don't have. Live within your means, not for instant gratification. If you begin college by using a credit card judiciously, you will probably continue to do so throughout your college career and beyond. We know that this is easier said than done. And as with most things, you'll need to use self-control. Credit card companies want you to spend beyond your means (that's how they stay in business), but don't fall for it.

BUT WHO'S GOING TO WASH MY CLOTHES? LIVING ADJUSTMENTS

For some of you, life before college was pretty cushy. Someone cooked your meals and made sure you ate right, did your laundry, kicked your butt out of bed in the morning, and maybe even cleaned your room. Life was easy. Life was good. But you didn't realize it at the time. Now you're in charge of just about everything.

We realize that what we are about to say may seem like a no-brainer. I mean, how difficult can it be to do your own laundry, especially when everything you need is in the basement of your residence hall? Light colors with light, dark colors with dark. How hard can it be to eat right, when you still have someone preparing most of your meals and you have such a big selection of food to choose from? Just eat something from each of the food groups and go light on the fats. And how hard can it be to keep a very small dorm room cleaned up? A place for everything and everything in its place.

Well, at times it *can* be pretty hard. It's not that doing laundry is so difficult—insert enough quarters into machine, fill washer, add clothes and soap—easy enough. It's somehow finding the time that's the hard part. And eating. Going to the dining hall and finding something good to eat is not the

> ## THE INSIDE SCOOP
>
> Ever heard of the Buckley Amendment? According to the Buckley Amendment, once you are enrolled in college, you are considered an adult, regardless of your chronological age. What this means is that your parents cannot get information about your progress in college without your permission. Your grades are sent to you, and any other information about test scores, fees, and so forth is also sent to you. P.S. You may want to pass this tidbit on to your parents!

hard part. (Isn't pizza one of the major food groups?) What's hard is eating in a healthy way so that you don't put on the dreaded "freshman 15," which really is very common. And the hard part about keeping a very small dorm room clean is that it is, well, small. There's no place to put all that stuff you need on a daily basis.

We mention this because all of these little things add up to other ways you'll have to adjust. In that first call home from campus, most students tell their mom and dad, "I never realized before how much you do for me!" (Note: Try to wait until the second call home to ask for more money.) The good news is that most students figure out how to do all these things for themselves. They find time between all of their studying and other activities to get the laundry done. Some even turn this chore into a studying session. After putting on a few pounds, they learn that the only way not to pork up is to eat less, eat healthier, and get some regular exercise. And they find creative ways to cram all their stuff into a small space.

HITTING THE BOOKS: ACADEMIC ADJUSTMENTS

Academic adjustments may be more difficult to make than any of the others, although all the other changes influence academics. One of the first adjustments you will have to make is to realize that everyone on your campus is smart—maybe even smarter than you. Remember those geeks in high school who always did their homework, aced the tests, learned effortlessly (or so it seemed), and didn't work nearly as hard as you did? Well, guess who's sitting next to you in history, English, and precalc?

The very same. So what does this mean? It means the competition for good grades is high—and in order to be competitive, you're going to have to make some academic adjustments. This isn't high school anymore. Although we'll discuss this idea in more detail later in the book (our focus in *College Rules!* is on academics) we'll briefly list some of these academic adjustments here:

- assuming greater responsibility for your own learning

- being more open-minded and receptive to new (different) ideas

- doing lots of reading that you *will* be held accountable for

- adjusting to stiffer competition

- setting goals and working toward achieving them

- having and maintaining motivation

- developing time management skills

Some students make these adjustments quickly, but it takes a while for the average student to get it together. The best way to balance all of the things you have to do is to take it a little at a time. Make small changes first and stick with them. You'll wake up one morning and find that you can handle this college thing pretty well.

Characteristics of Well-Rounded Students

In order to get the most out of college, you need to have experiences beyond the classroom. The student who graduates with only a degree and an impressive grade point average has missed out on a lot. There's so much to experience in college these days that it's hard to imagine why any student wouldn't want to get involved. The students we know who have been most successful—both as undergraduate and graduate students and in the world of work—are those who make the most of what college has to offer, both in and out of the classroom. These students are happy with themselves in many respects and feel allegiance to their school. They believe they have gotten their money's worth out of a college education and that it has prepared them for the world in many respects. Many of the friends they make are friends for life. What do these students have in common?

- Not only do they earn good grades, but they also actually like to learn.

- They know that learning and studying require effort and they are willing to put in that effort.

- They balance academics, work, and play.

- They are involved in extracurricular activities.

- They are goal oriented.

- They have strong networks of friends and/or family to help support them emotionally.

- They have connected with several faculty members.

- They enjoy being students.

- They have a variety of interests and hobbies.

- They take time for themselves.

- They budget their time wisely.

- They take responsibility for their actions.

- They take care of their health.

- They are help-seekers.

- And sometimes, they just have to make some noise to let off steam.

Getting the most out of college and being academically successful requires you to maintain balance in your life. If the only thing you do is stay cooped up in your room and study all the time, you'll be unhappy. If all you do is socialize, you may be happy for a while, but you won't stay in school very long. So work it out. All college students need to work hard and play hard.

😞 SAD BUT TRUE

Brent had looked forward to going off to college ever since he could remember. His older brother, Sid, had just graduated and had lots of stories about how much fun it had been. Sid had also warned Brent that he would have to prioritize. There was so much to get involved in that it was easy not to study. Brent paid attention to all of the fun things his brother had told him and sort of ignored the studying part. Brent wanted to be part of a fraternity and pledged one of the most social frats on campus during his first semester. He loved it! Lots of parties. Lots of new friends to hang with. It seemed like something was going on every night. His social life was full and he was having a blast. Before he knew it, midterm was upon him and he slowed down enough to take stock of how he was doing in his classes. He had started the semester with five three-credit courses, and was doing so horribly that he withdrew from two of them. He was down to only nine hours and had a respectable grade in only one of his classes. Now Brent started getting anxious, but he wasn't going to let this interfere with his social life. He knew he'd be able to pull it out in the end.

This student story brings to light the importance of balancing your life as a college student. Majoring in partying may be fun for a while, but know that it can't go on forever. You can have it all. You just have to work at it a bit.

Quick and Dirty

○ Transitioning to college means lots of change and adjustments. You'll have to adjust emotionally, socially, financially, domestically, and academically. Tough, we know. But you can do it.

○ Well-rounded students take advantage of what their college has to offer both inside and outside of the classroom. Being a well-rounded student means more than just hitting the books.

CHAPTER 7

TIMELY TIPS: THE ABC(& D)S OF TIME MANAGEMENT

Perhaps the most valuable result of all education is the ability to make yourself do the thing you have to do, when it ought to be done, whether you like it or not.

—Aldous Huxley

The only thing that you have in common with every other college student is the same number of hours in a day to get everything done—24 big ones. That's 24 hours in a day, 168 hours in a week, 672 hours in a month (give or take a few). Sounds like lots of time to get things done, doesn't it? It should be plenty of time, as long as you are not a master at the art of procrastination— and as long as you can make a pledge to spend 40 hours a week at your job, which for the next four years or so is being a college student.

DO YOUR HOMEWORK

Try making a schedule of all of the things you have to do in a complete seven-day week. Put in your classes; work and family obligations; time to eat, sleep, get dressed, and so on; and other commitments. Count up the number of hours per week that you have already committed. How many of the 168 hours do you have left? Are you doing your job—being a student—for 40 hours a week? You'll need to know this information as we progress through this chapter.

The 40-Hour Mindset

One of the most difficult adjustment issues that students face when they enter college is learning to effectively and efficiently manage their time. Students and professors alike believe that lack of time management skills leads many students down dangerous paths. If you are entering college right out of high school, most of your time has probably been managed for you. You were in school all day, and when you came home your parents may have made sure you did your homework and fulfilled many other responsibilities. If you had a job, you probably worked a limited number of hours. It's likely that someone else also took care of your basic needs for food, shelter, and so forth. It's quite possible that you really didn't have to worry very much about finding time to get things done, and that many things were actually done for you.

In college things are different. You will be in class only a few hours each day (and perhaps not at all on some days), no one will be watching over your shoulder to make sure you get things done, and no one will clean your room or do your laundry for you.

X FOR ADULTS ONLY

If you are a returning student or one who has to work 20 or more hours a week, you may think that the 40-hour rule doesn't apply to you. How could it? Where in the world will you find 40 hours to devote to academics if you have a family and also work, even part-time? You may have some decisions to make, because if you plan on taking a full load (usually 12 or 15 hours) you will have to follow the 40-hour mindset. That may mean getting fewer hours of sleep, spending less time with your family, and eating more fast food. The alternative is to ease into college life. Take a lighter load as a way of adjusting, and see how it goes.

At first glance this may seem like the ideal situation—that you will have loads of free time. You can live in as big a mess as you want to, you can wear dirty underwear, and, best of all, there's no one to bug you about stuff. It should be easy to get everything done in a relaxed, orderly fashion. Well, think again. Fitting everything into a reasonable schedule is the number one problem many college students have.

So where do you start? We suggest that you take a pledge to get into the 40-hour mindset. Please repeat: "I pledge to put at least 40 hours a week into being a student. Cross my heart and hope to die." Why 40 hours? It's the standard number of hours in a traditional work week, and it's probably the least number of hours per week that you will be expected to spend on the job once you graduate from college. But if you talk with anyone who has a full-time job, they will tell you that sometimes you have to spend more than 40 hours a week, because some tasks require more time and effort than others and you have to work until the job gets done. That's why we call it a mindset: start with 40 hours in mind, but adjust the time so that you can get your job—being a successful student—done right. Remember, these 40 hours (or so) include your time in class, reading and study time, meeting with study groups, doing library research—anything that has to do with your academics.

With the exception of the hours that you spend in class, which are fixed, you can "be a student" at any other time during the week that suits you. You can study at 2:00 in the afternoon or 4:00 in the morning. You can go to the library on Saturday or Sunday afternoon or 10:00 Wednesday night. Once you figure out your prime time for studying and learning, your schedule can be quite flexible. The world will be your oyster. Your busy life can be quite manageable and fairly stress-free. Ah—if it were only that easy.

SAD BUT TRUE

Angela was having a tremendously difficult time fitting everything into her schedule. She just couldn't understand where all the time went and why she never seemed to complete anything on time—or, if she did, she knew it wasn't her best work. After some encouragement, she made an appointment to talk with one of us. Angela's busy schedule and courses were indeed demanding, but it seemed as though she should have ample time for everything. So to find out just what the heck she was doing with her time, she was instructed to write down how she spent her time (every waking minute) for a week and then come back for a second appointment.

When she returned (on time) for the next appointment, she had an almost embarrassed look on her face. She confessed, "You won't believe this, but I think I'm spending several hours a day eating. Well, not really eating but just sitting in the dining hall after I've finished and talking with friends. Socializing. Most days it's at least an hour for breakfast, anywhere from two to three hours for lunch, and another couple hours at dinner. I never realized I was doing this." Angela had diagnosed her own problem, but could she do something about it? It was really hard for her, but she stuck to it, making small changes at first, and eventually salvaging almost three hours daily that she could then spend getting other things done. It made a tremendous difference in so many areas of her life.

The Alphabet Approach: ABC(& D)s of Managing Your Life

Three truisms about time management should be etched in your memory as you begin your college career:

- Truism #1: Time flies.

- Truism #2: Everything takes longer than you think it will.

- Truism #3: No matter what you are doing at this minute, in most cases, you would rather be doing something else.

Now that we have that out of the way, think about how you can use the 168 hours you have each week in such a way that you can meet all of your academic requirements and still have plenty of time for sleep, play, and perhaps even work, not to mention those all-important out-of-the-classroom experiences that make your time in college so rich. (Remember, you've pledged to spend only about one-quarter of those 168 hours being a student.)

Managing your time (and yourself) is as easy as A B C and, well, D. All you need to do is:

- A = Anticipate and plan
- B = Break tasks down
- C = Cross things off
- D = Don't procrastinate

A = ANTICIPATE AND PLAN

No student (not a single, solitary one) should be without some sort of tool to keep track of her busy life. It can be as simple as a paper daily planner or calendar or as high-tech as an electronic

LISTEN UP

You may have heard through the grapevine that you should spend at least two hours out of class (studying) for every hour that you spend in class. This advice is not particularly accurate, although it's probably not a bad rule of thumb. For example, if you are taking a three-hour course that is really difficult for you, you may need to spend considerably more than six hours per week studying the material outside of class. On the other hand, if you're taking a three-hour course that is a piece of cake, it wouldn't be very efficient to spend six hours hitting the books. So use common sense. Difficult courses require more time; easy courses require less. Be flexible.

planner. Whatever the cost or complexity, it needs to be something portable enough to carry with you. And you need to be able to see at least a week at a time so that projects or tests or papers don't sneak up on you. Be sure that you have it on the first day of class, because the planning for the rest of the term will begin on day one. Trying to catch up on time management is like trying to catch up on sleep—it's almost impossible to do.

Remember what we said about everything taking longer than you think? That's why the first rule of managing your life is to anticipate and plan. If you think about things in advance and try to at least plan out the certainties, you will have enough flexibility and wiggle room in your schedule to handle unexpected happenings like illness, a family crisis, or an additional paper being thrown at you at the last minute. Would you wait until Friday to try to get a date for your fraternity formal on Saturday? Would you try to plan a surprise birthday party for your best friend two days before her birthday? Chances are if you did, things wouldn't work out very well.

The best way to attack the academic planning thing is to do the following:

- Once you have your class schedule for the term set (and you've finished adding and dropping courses), block out those class times in your planner for the whole semester.

- Carefully go through the syllabus for each course and note test dates or dates on which projects or papers are due. If the professor changes the date, be sure to change it in your planner as well. (We recommend writing in pencil in case things do change.)

- If there are other certainties in your life that you know you will have to consider in planning your 40 hours a week as a student, note those as well. For example, if you are a member of an organization that meets at the same time every week or month, block out those periods of time. If you work, block out the hours you work as soon as you know them. If you exercise every day at 2:00, block that out as well.

Now you're ready to block out reading, study, and test preparation time. If you have 15 hours of class per week, that leaves you around 25 hours to be a student in other ways. Ask yourself the questions on the following page as you plan this time.

- When are you most alert? Are you a morning or an evening person? If you try to study at 8:00 A.M. and you don't become human until noon, you'll just be wasting time.

- Are you going to be able to study where you live or will you need to go somewhere that has fewer distractions, such as the library or a study room in your dorm?

- Are you going to be able to discipline yourself to study on weekends or should you just plan on getting all your schoolwork done during the week? Are there other nights when you know you just won't hit the books? On our campus, for example, Thursday is a big party night. If you know that you will want to go out along with everyone else on Thursday, be honest about it and adjust your schedule accordingly.

- How difficult are your courses this term? If you have a couple of really hard courses, you may have to put in more than 40 hours a week being a student, unless you have an easier course to balance things out. Keep in mind that the 40-hour thing is a mindset, not a hard and fast rule.

- When do you have blocks of time that you can use for extended studying? Ten minutes here and ten minutes there is fine for reviewing. But studying for ten minutes at a clip won't turn you into a scholar. Studying every day for a good block of time may.

- Do you already know that you have a procrastination problem? If so, what small steps can you take *today* to start fixing the problem?

Once you have answered these questions, you should have an idea of which courses will require more work and which will require less, be able to set reasonable goals for getting your work done on time, and be able to block out some quality study time. By "quality," we mean that you'll be alert and geared up for learning and that you'll be in a place that is relatively distraction free. Set up study blocks of two to three hours with short breaks (five or ten minutes every hour or so) planned into them. Block out these times the first week of class and see how it goes. The good thing about anticipating and planning is that you can continue to tweak your schedule so that it works for you. Just stick to the 40-hour mindset. You made a pledge. We know it seems like we're asking a lot here, but once you get the hang of it, it gets easier.

B = BREAK TASKS DOWN

Whether you're faced with a really huge task such as completing your degree in four years or a much smaller task such as studying for a psychology exam, it's eas-ier to muster the will to stick to it if you break it down into smaller, manageable parts. Even keeping up with your reading assignments can be much less painful if you read half the pages of a chapter in one sitting and the rest in a second sitting later in the same day. Students tell us that one of the terrible consequences of procrastinating is that when you finally get around to doing a task, it seems insurmountable. And when things seem insurmountable, they are generally done less than adequately or not at all.

As you decide how you will spend your 40 hours per week, think about the things you will have to complete over the semester and, right from the start, break them down into smaller tasks. For example, suppose you have a project due for your anthropology class at midterm. You have to write a 20-page paper and then do a 15-minute PowerPoint presentation to the class on the highlights. This type of assignment is actually more difficult and will require more time than you may believe. Always remember: Everything takes longer than you think it will. You have to select a relatively narrow topic, spend time in the library and on the Web finding information, synthesize what you find, write an outline and a couple of drafts, and be sure to have your citations done correctly—and all that's before you've even started making the PowerPoint slides and practicing your class presentation. Unless you start breaking this large task down into smaller pieces and getting started way before the

LISTEN UP

In order to get the hang of budgeting your time wisely, it's really important to actually make a schedule and then check it frequently. Don't just keep it in your head. Put the days of the week across the top of your paper and time blocks of an hour each down the left-hand side (or you can do it the other way around if you like). After you have your schedule filled in, count your academic hours. Do you have at least 40? Then try following your schedule for a week and make modifications as you need to—almost everyone does.

due date, you will be burning the midnight oil trying to put together something acceptable to meet the deadline. But you want to do better than just acceptable work. You want to be exceptional. So break tasks down. Here's how.

1.   Look at the big picture first. Be sure you clearly understand what the end product is supposed to look like. Ask your prof to show you some examples from previous classes.

2.   Look at the parts. What pieces will enable you to get to the whole? Figure out step-by-step what you need to do—it's not going to happen through magic.

3.   Think about the logical order of completing the pieces: what you should do first, second, last.

4.   Put yourself on a timeline for completing the task.

5.   Have a plan to help you stay on track. Put the time you will spend on the project into your study schedule so that you can set aside the time for it. And then stick with it, stick with it, stick with it. Overkill, you say? Maybe, but a plan is only good if you see it through.

6.   Complete it early enough to have some time left for a final go-though and cleanup.

Also keep in mind that you can even break smaller, less overwhelming tasks, such as reading assignments, into manageable parts. This strategy works particularly well for courses that require heavy reading, such as history. On our campus, students enrolled in an introductory history course have an average of 100 pages to read a week in this class alone! That's more than some of you may have read in a month in high school. But if you take those 100 pages and break them down with the plan of reading some history six out of seven days in a week, you would only have to read about 16 pages per day. So what would you rather do: read 16 pages per day or be 800 pages behind by the time the first exam rolls around?

Things may come to those who wait, but only the things left by those who hustle.

—Abraham Lincoln

C = CROSS THINGS OFF

We are both "to do" list freaks. In fact, everyone we know who manages their time effectively uses some form of list where they can cross things off as they are completed. Making to do lists serves a couple of purposes. First, and most obvious, it lets you see what you need to get accomplished. It serves as sort of a memory-jogger so that you don't forget things that have to get done. Because students are busy people with a variety of commitments, to do lists can help you keep your life more manageable. Second, to do lists act as psychological boosters because as you do the things you have listed, you cross them off. This gives you a feeling of accomplishment.

You can make all kinds of to do lists. Perhaps the most common type—and maybe even the type that is the most helpful—is the immediate to do list. As the name implies, it's a listing of things that you need to get done within a brief period of time: a day, a few days, maybe even as long as a week. Often, immediate to do lists include minor sorts of tasks that don't take much time but are easily forgotten. These lists can include both classroom and nonclassroom activities. A list might look something like this:

TO DO:	BY:
Read history pp. 230-263	Today
Do laundry!!!!	Friday
Meet with study group	Wednesday 7 p.m.
Statistics problems-ch. 8	Monday

As you get things finished, cross them off. Add other things to the list as they come up. You can keep a running list for a week or so and then start fresh.

But to do lists can also be more long-term as well. You can make a list at the beginning of the term that covers major projects that you need to complete by the end of the term. Also included on this type of list are smaller things that need to be done by a later date, but not immediately. List each item, along with the date it is due, beginning with what needs to be completed first. As each is taken care of, cross it off. A long-term list might look something like this:

TO DO:	DATE DUE
History term paper	April 16
Plan Dad's surprise party	February 1
MIS project	April 17 (weekly meetings Tues. 8 p.m.)
Talk to friends about spring break plans	by February 15

One final comment about lists. Once you make a list, clip it in a convenient place in your daily planner, somewhere you are sure to look at. Each time you make a new list, put it in the same place so that you know where to look for it. Making lists and then not using them will hardly lead to good time management skills.

D = DON'T PROCRASTINATE

If for most of your life you have followed the credo "Always put off until tomorrow what you don't have to do today," you stand a good chance of taking this attitude off to college with you. Procrastination is a major problem for many, many college students. Just ask any student on any campus. Procrastinating can get you into academic hot water and affect other aspects of your life. At worst, it can cause you to be a weak student and, at best, a mediocre one. Unfortunately, it may be the most difficult problem to mend, because for some people procrastination is simply a way of life. Procrastinators not only tend to put things off, but they also tend to be late for everything—classes, meetings, dates. Although some people will tell you that they thrive on the stress that procrastination brings, we don't believe them for one minute. We all need less anxiety and stress in our lives, not more.

In a nutshell, procrastinators tend not to use their time wisely, particularly small pockets of time. The 10 to 15 minutes between classes or time spent grabbing a snack could instead be spent reviewing lecture notes or practicing vocabulary for French class. These small blocks of time add up to big blocks of time in the long run. If you review your lecture notes for economics 15 minutes each day, you add 75 minutes of extra study time to this course each week. That's significant.

> It is more than probable that the average man could, with no injury to his health, increase his efficiency fifty percent.
> —Walter Scott

Dan, a junior genetics major, was a hard-core procrastinator who followed the usual pattern. He consistently (and consciously) put off changing his behavior "until tomorrow." He even joked about the problem with his friends. While he usually managed to pull things off at the last minute, earning low Cs on exams and eking out passing grades on papers and projects, Dan found that his stress level was becoming almost unmanageable. He was taking a couple of really hard courses in his major, and he had slid by for so long that now he didn't even know where to start. He couldn't keep up at all, not even enough to get by. On top of the stress, he started feeling extremely guilty about his shoddy work habits. He knew he could do better, and he really was interested in some of his courses. The crowning blow came the morning he overslept and almost missed a major exam because he had stayed up late trying to cram. He made it to the test, but made a low D.

Now Dan decided to get some help with his procrastination problems. He went to a couple of workshops, talked with an academic counselor in the learning center, and made a real attempt to change his ways. At first it was really difficult. He continued to make some low grades, but he stuck with it. Much to his surprise, his grades improved somewhat and he began feeling better about himself. Although procrastination may always be a problem for Dan, his deciding to make even small changes influenced him positively in a number of ways.

We see students like Dan all the time. The scenario usually goes something like this: Student feels guilty (often very guilty) for getting behind in her work. She wakes up in the morning panic stricken about all the things she has to do and vows that "tonight's the night!" Tonight comes and she sits down at her desk and looks for any excuse possible not to study (usually this is unconscious behavior): Can't find the book. Need to make just one phone call. Something cold to drink might help. Then the real excuse arrives: Someone bursts into her room inviting her to go get pizza. "Yes," she says, and promises herself (again) that she'll start on her studying routine tomorrow night. Don't let procrastination be a way of life for you. Manage your time right from the start. Make it a habit to take care of business first. Then go out and party down.

The Advantages of Excelling at Time Management

We return to the idea we presented at the beginning of this chapter: the only thing every college student has in common is a day with 24 hours in it. It is your choice how you use those hours. You can be productive and stay on top of things and still have ample time for those out-of-classroom learning experiences that are also important. The alternative is that you squander your time, have little to show for it, and end up feeling bad about yourself.

You probably already know the advantages of managing your time effectively, but we list a few here as a way of further convincing you of the importance of starting college on the right foot. Even if you have been the world's worst procrastinator, you have a chance to make a fresh start in college. If you can learn to manage your time and your life, you will:

- Have less stress in your life. Less stress is always good.

- Have more time for the things you want to do. Fun is good, too. It's hard to go out and have fun if you're worried about all the things you haven't done.

- Be a more well-rounded student. Remember, well-rounded students (those who have lots of different experiences) get the most out of college.

- Be able to spend more time with friends. Social connections are important, and everyone needs to have time to laugh with friends.

- Learn more. Efficient learners get more from their classes than those who keep trying to figure out how to study and learn effectively.

- Play more. Everyone loves to play. No one has ever said on his or her deathbed, "Gee, I regret that I didn't work more."

- Feel good about yourself. When you feel good about your academic accomplishments, it spills over into other parts of your life and gives you confidence.

- Be envied by all. Absolutely.

We can't stress strongly enough the importance of managing your time. Entire books have been written on the subject and businesses spend huge sums of money to provide time management training to their employees. It's a skill you will need for life.

Quick and Dirty

○ Follow the 40-hour mindset if you want to succeed academically. Be involved in academics at least 40 hours a week and you should do well.

○ Follow the ABC(& D)s of time management: anticipate and plan, break tasks down, cross things off, and don't procrastinate.

○ The advantages of effective time management are great, including having less stress in your life and feeling good about yourself.

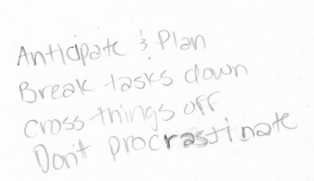

Anticipate & Plan
Break tasks down
cross things off
Don't procrastinate

CHAPTER 8

"I THINK I CAN, I THINK I CAN": GETTING AND STAYING MOTIVATED

Even if you're on the right track, you'll get run over if you just sit there.

—Arthur Godfrey

Believe it or not, you are always motivated to do something. It may be only to watch TV, talk on the phone, or sleep, but you are motivated toward something. (Right now, you are motivated to read *College Rules!*) For a college student, however, the key is to be motivated to do the right things at the right time. Although it is tempting to blame a lack of motivation on others (a really dull professor, your roommate who parties all the time), *you* are responsible for your own motivation. That's right. No one else can motivate you to do anything if you do not have your own internal motivation. Because of this and because motivation can be so fleeting—here one minute, gone the next—you need strategies for staying motivated, even in courses you don't like.

We have said it time and time again: "Show us a student who's motivated and is willing to work hard, and we'll show you a successful student." Because motivation is so important to college success, it has been called the academic glue that holds everything together. This means that even in classes that are difficult for you, even if you aren't using exactly the most effective strategies for learning the information, even if you have had the worst day in life, you'll make it through (often exceedingly well) if you are motivated.

So, how do *you* motivate *you?* The easiest place to begin is by thinking about your goals.

Q THE INSIDE SCOOP

We know that students are more motivated to do things when they are given choices and when the tasks are challenging but not overwhelming. Motivation is also higher when you can work with others and when you feel you have some control over reaching your learning goals. This explains why you may be very motivated to learn in one class and totally unmotivated in another.

GOOOOOOOOAAAAAAAAAALLLLLLLLL Setting

Students who set goals—both short-term and longer-term goals—are more motivated to complete those goals. Just think about anything you have accomplished: maybe learning to play a sport or an instrument, finishing a challenging computer game, pulling off a successful surprise party, or planning a spring break vacation. You were probably very motivated to do that activity *and* you probably even set goals to achieve whatever it was you set out to do. In fact, although you might not have even been aware that you were setting and reaching goals, there is a very strong connection between motivation and goal setting. Chances are you already set goals for personal things like losing weight and exercising, but you can and should set academic goals as well.

Having defined goals can help you become motivated even in courses you don't particularly like. But the way you set goals can also help you. Saying "I want to get an A in calculus" may not be enough. Instead, try to set smaller goals that will help you reach the ultimate goal of every college student—getting a degree.

> You are free to do whatever you like. You only need to face the consequences.
>
> —Sheldon Kopp

Often we set goals that we never achieve. It may be human nature to do so, or (more likely) it may be because of the kinds of goals we set. Saying "I want to be a better person" is great. But how will you ever know whether that goal has been achieved? Try this activity—jot down three academic goals you would like to reach within the next three months:

1. _____
2. _____
3. _____

Now check your goals to see if they meet the following criteria: are they specific, measurable, realistic, and flexible?

Specific. Are your goals clearly defined? "I want to read 20 pages of history a night" is specific; "I want to read more" is not. In fact, if you find that you are unmotivated, make your goals ultraspecific. For example, instead of saying that you want to read 20 pages a night, create a specific reading schedule by defining exactly which pages you will read each night for a week. Setting specific goals will help you keep your eyes on the prize. When goals are not specific, people tend to lose focus on achieving them.

Measurable. Your goals should also be easily measured. It is easy to know whether or not you have reached your goal of reading those 20 pages of history, but it would be difficult to measure a goal of "reading more." Setting measurable goals helps you track your progress and keeps your motivation high.

Realistic. Can your goals be reached? Often people set goals that are unrealistic. For example, a student who wants to raise his GPA from a 2.0 to a 3.0 in one semester (or even one year) may find that this goal is not mathematically possible. A better goal may be to focus on earning better grades during the current semester.

Flexible. Don't be too rigid in trying to achieve the goals you set. Sometimes when we're midway to our goals we realize that we need to make adjustments. Suppose that you had set a goal of achieving an A in chemistry. But you get very sick and miss two weeks of class, and after taking the first two exams, you realize that you will be lucky to get out of the class with a passing grade. Rather than beating yourself up about not achieving everything you've set out to do, be flexible with your goals and set your sights on catching up on what you missed and understanding the course content instead of focusing solely on the grade.

SHORT-TERM, INTERMEDIATE, AND LONG-TERM GOALS

To keep your motivation up, it is important that you set three kinds of goals: short-term, intermediate, and long-term goals. Most people are good at setting long-term goals, like getting a college degree, finding true love, and making a lot of money. But it is the short-term and intermediate goals that will help you get there. A short-term goal might be to do 15 practice problems in statistics each night. An intermediate goal might be to learn the basics of French this year.

> **🔊 LISTEN UP**
>
> Research has indicated that people who regularly set goals are more self-confident, concentrate better, and perform better. But the types of goals you set are also important in keeping your motivation up. So remember to set short-term, intermediate, and long-term goals.

SET PROCESS GOALS

Most of us do a fine job at setting outcome goals. That is, we set goals related to what we hope to achieve—getting a degree, speaking French, losing weight. But we rarely set process goals, or goals that describe what we will do to reach the desired outcome. Process goals are based on skills or knowledge you can acquire. A process goal might be to select key quotes as you read to help you write your English paper, or to make vocabulary cards to help you learn French. Process goals help you reach your short-term and intermediate goals on the way to your long-term goals.

> **🔲 DO YOUR HOMEWORK**
>
> The next time you find your motivation waning, set some process goals to help you reach your short-term goals—you just might find that they give you the boost you need.

SET YOUR GOALS AT THE RIGHT LEVEL

Your goals should be set at a level that may be a tiny bit beyond your grasp but not so far that they are completely out of reach. The ability to set goals at the right level (neither too low nor too high) is a skill that takes some practice. You need to consider such factors as tiredness, family and social commitments, and other outside influences when you set your goals. But don't set your goals too low, because there's little satisfaction in achieving goals that you knew were too easy to begin with. Give yourself a challenge. Reaching goals that are slightly challenging can do wonders for your motivation.

Take a look at the three goals you set earlier in this chapter. What changes, if any, do you need to make to these goals so you can successfully reach them? Should they be more specific, more realistic, more challenging? Goal setting is intricately linked to motivation: the better you set (and reach) your goals, the more motivated you will be.

Getting Motivated

Whenever we ask our students to give advice to incoming freshman on how to get motivated, their responses always having something to do with staying on top of things or, as they often put it, "keeping up." There is nothing more unmotivating than falling behind. But it's easier to say we'll keep up than to do it. It is amazing how quickly schoolwork can pile up. Following are some simple suggestions to help you stay motivated.

Break big assignments into smaller chunks. Sometimes thinking about writing that 20-page term paper is overwhelming. But if you break such a task into smaller, more manageable bits, it is much less intimidating. Selecting a topic early, making an outline, planning to visit the library several times, reading the papers of students who've taken the course in the past: all will help you avoid having to write the whole thing at the last minute.

Use the five-minute rule. The hardest part of schoolwork to get motivated for is just getting started. The five-minute rule can really help with this. Simply put, tell yourself you will study for five minutes (you can do anything for five minutes, right?). At the end of that time, if you still are not motivated, you can stop. Most often, once you get started you will find that you won't stop after the set time.

Kyle, a freshman, just couldn't seem to get started on his schoolwork. Every day he'd come home from classes tired from a long day of thinking. There was no way, he thought, he could get right down to studying then. He'd hang out with his dormmates in the common room watching TV, listening to music, whatever. Around 6:30 the whole group would go to dinner, and usually they'd linger there till around 8:00 talking and generally having a good time. Because the weather had been so nice, Kyle and his friends usually played some ball after dinner—football, basketball, whatever struck their mood that evening. Often Kyle wouldn't get back to his room until around 11:00, when he was far too tired to study. Kyle had gotten into this pattern during the first few weeks of classes when there wasn't much reading or studying to do. Now that the semester was in full swing he knew he needed to make some changes, but he didn't want to miss out on the fun. Kyle had formed some habits that could really hurt his chances for success in college. Our advice to Kyle was to take an hour break after classes (relaxing with his friends) and then use the five-minute rule to get started studying. Although this helped some, Kyle also needed to reassess his motivation for being a college student: was it to hang out and play ball or to get a degree?

Set goals for each study session. Goals for study sessions are even smaller than your short-term goals—in fact, consider these goals as the kind that will help you achieve your short-term goals. Instead of planning to "study," which is not very specific, set a goal—to study pages 140 to 175 in biology or to review last week's notes in accounting. Every time you sit down to study you should plan out exactly what you want to accomplish that session.

Reward yourself. One way to get yourself motivated to do something you may not want to do is to plan how you will reward yourself for getting the job done. Often students find this is a good way to begin a long hard task. The reward doesn't really have to be anything too extensive—maybe going out with friends or watching a movie. It just needs to be something you can look forward to doing or having after you study.

Seek help if you need it. If you use all of these strategies but find that you are still unmotivated, it may be that you need some help with the content. Often we meet students who say that they have no motivation when in reality they just do not understand the course content. Sometimes the best way to get motivated is to find someone who can help you understand the information or find some interest in the topic. Don't just give up. Most colleges offer tutoring (often for free), so you can get a tutor, talk to the professor, or ask a classmate to help you. You just might find your motivation.

And Staying Motivated

Once you get motivated, the key to success is being able to *stay* motivated. We know that motivation ebbs and flows; what motivates you one day may not motivate you the next day. So use the following suggestions to help maintain your motivation to learn.

Use both intrinsic and extrinsic motivation. You probably have heard somewhere that only intrinsic (or internal) motivation is good and that extrinsic (or external) motivation, such as money or even grades, is not. We believe that this really oversimplifies the complex concept of motivation. Usually people need *both* kinds of motivation to make it through school, and you need to use both to your advantage. For example, if you are enrolled in a class you don't really find interesting, you may initially focus on the external forces (testing, grades, and rewards) to get you going, but as you read and learn more about the topic, you may find yourself increasingly focused on the material. By the end of the semester, you may consider taking another course in the topic because now you are internally motivated to learn. Internal motivation is always more desirable because you usually learn more deeply, but extrinsic motivators can often lead you on this path.

Add variety. Change how long you study or even where you choose to study. Change the order of the topics you plan to study if you find you are getting bored (don't always start with math, then do history, then literature). However, some people do best by *not* adding variety to their studying. If you find that changing things throws you off task, keep your current routine and add variety to your life in other ways—take a walk after studying, or phone a friend instead of turning on the TV.

Organize a study group. Working with others can be very motivating. Create a study group to help you reach your goals. You may want to start out with one study partner instead of trying to work with several people. Have a plan for what you will do when you meet—maybe working sample problems or predicting (and answering) test questions.

Keep a schedule. We discussed the merits of good time management in the last chapter, but a schedule can help your motivation, too. If you find your motivation slipping (this usually happens at least once a semester—around midterm or when the weather finally breaks), try hard to stick to your schedule. You'll find that it helps you recapture your motivation to get things done.

> **X FOR ADULTS ONLY**
>
> Returning students often find their motivation weakens as the semester goes on because they feel unconnected to college life (especially if they are attending part-time). Forming a study group will not only help your grades, but it can also help you feel part of the social scene at school.

Use positive self-talk. When you speak positively to yourself ("I can do this"), you are much more successful than when you speak negatively ("I'll never get through this"). Every time you find you are telling yourself negative things, stop yourself and try to turn them into something positive. Instead of telling yourself, "Everyone else is smarter than I am," say, "I know that with enough hard work, I can succeed on the next test." If you have gotten into the habit of speaking negatively to yourself, this process can take some time, but after "correcting" your thoughts for a while, speaking positively to yourself will become a habit and you'll find your motivation will increase.

Take breaks. It is easy to burn out in college. Combining a lot of schoolwork with an active social life can be disastrous to motivation. But it doesn't have to be. Try not to overextend yourself either academically or socially. Take frequent breaks while studying. Some people need a short break every 30 minutes and others can study longer before needing to rest. Know thyself. If you need to stop after 30 minutes, then stop. Don't just sit there wasting time for another 30 minutes if you can't focus. In general, try to study for an hour and then take a short break (five to ten minutes) before getting back to work. Don't plan to study for three hours with no breaks—you'll find that you can't keep it up.

Maintaining your motivation is something you will need to think about again and again. Unfortunately, there is no quick fix for motivation problems, but using the strategies we've discussed should help you keep the motivation you've got.

Reviving Your Motivation

What if you are already unmotivated? How can you get yourself back on track? First, you need to think about what the problem might be. A lack of motivation does not necessarily mean that you are lazy. There are lots of barriers to motivation.

SAD BUT TRUE

Recently one of our students came to talk to us about her lack of motivation. Shelly was concerned about her grades and felt that if she could just get more motivated everything would be fine. As we talked to her we discovered all of the pressures Shelly was under. She lived at home and had an hour commute to school and back every day. She felt she was missing out on a social life at school because her parents expected her to be home each night and every weekend. She also had a part-time job, which was cutting into her study (and free) time. In addition, Shelly had been arguing with her boyfriend (whom she could not even tell her parents about because they did not think she should be dating, even though she was eighteen years old and in college—really). Is it any wonder that she felt unmotivated? But motivation, or lack of it, was not really Shelly's problem. We helped her set up an appointment with a counselor on campus to talk about the stress these other issues were causing in her life. Once she could see that other issues were getting in the way of her schoolwork (and once she started working through them with a counselor), she began to be able to separate out her school life from her home life—which helped her make it through the semester.

Think about things that may be hurting your motivation, such as procrastination, low self-esteem or self-confidence, bad study habits (or no studying at all), stress, fears and worries, or lack of interest. Are these getting in the way of your reaching your goals? Use the following suggestions to recharge your motivation.

Reevaluate your goals. Have your goals met the criteria we stated earlier in this chapter, or are they unrealistic or too vague? If so, this lack of direction could be causing you to feel unmotivated. Sometimes you can reclaim your motivation just by reworking your goals to be more specific and realistic.

Add more choice to your life. Are you feeling negative about college in general or the tasks you are required to do? How can you add more choice to your life? A lot of what you have to do in college is prescribed for you—the courses you need to get your degree, the tasks you must do to pass those courses, even when the classes meet. But you usually have a choice of professor, and you can always choose how you will approach learning in your courses (sometimes students choose not to study at all). Consider the choices you are making. Are the choices you are making getting in the way of your success?

Relate schoolwork to your life. Does what you are doing now seem unconnected with your future goals? How can you relate your schoolwork with your personal interests? The better you can do this, amazingly, the more interesting the topic will

---

🔊 LISTEN UP

We often hear students saying, "Why do I need to learn this? I will never use this in my life." When students feel this way, they are not able to connect what they are studying to their everyday life. But at the risk of sounding like your professors, let us assure you that you *will* use the information you learn (even in the courses you don't like) in ways you cannot even imagine today. For example, if you pay attention in statistics class today, you will be better equipped to evaluate the information you hear on the news about some implausible-sounding medical breakthrough. In addition, college teaches you the process of learning, so although you may not have to use calculus in the field of nursing, you will have to use the ability to problem-solve. That skill will serve you throughout your life.

become. You might even want to go talk to the professor to find out more about how his course relates to life—the prof may be able to discuss some links between his course and the wider world that you'd never think of.

> There are no uninteresting things, there are only uninterested people.
>
> —Gilbert K. Chesterton

Seek professional help if you need it. Are personal problems interfering with school? Are you feeling depressed? If you think that is what is making you unmotivated, seek some help from a counselor or psychologist on campus or talk to your friends or family. There are usually a lot of folks you can talk to who can really help you. But the worst thing you can do with a personal problem is just ignore it, hoping it will go away.

Don't hibernate. Often when we feel unmotivated all we want to do is curl up under the covers hoping it will all go away. However, the best way to overcome a lack of motivation is to do just the opposite. Instead, try to get more involved. Go out with some friends, join a campus group, go to a concert or a movie. Do something that gets you out and about. And by all means attend all of your courses. Skipping classes will just compound the problem.

Prioritize. Sometimes motivation slips because there are just too many things that need to be done. Students can feel overwhelmed and lose their motivation to get any of it accomplished. One good solution to this problem is to make a list of what needs to be done and then rank-order the tasks. Which ones need to be finished first? Which ones can wait until next week? By writing them all down, you can prioritize the tasks, put your workload into perspective, and get it all done in a timely fashion.

Try to recognize when your motivation breaks down. What kinds of things lead you to become unmotivated? Once you are able to see what affects your motivation, you will be better able to make adjustments (sometimes these will be very minor changes) to keep your motivation up.

Quick and Dirty

○ You are always motivated to do something during every moment of your life. The trick is to become able to be motivated to do the right things at the right time.

○ Set goals to help you get motivated. Set short-term and intermediate goals to help you reach your long-term goals. These goals should be specific, measurable, realistic, and flexible.

○ Use both intrinsic and extrinsic rewards to help you stay motivated. Although internal rewards are best for lifelong learning, external rewards (going shopping, seeing a movie, hanging out with friends) can help you stay motivated.

CHAPTER 9

ARRRRRRRGH! AND OTHER WAYS TO HANDLE STRESS

There are two times I feel stress—
day and night.

—Anonymous

This week you have two papers due, one quiz, and you have to read an entire novel for literature class. To top it off you just had a fight with your roommate and got a letter from the bank that you bounced a check that they're going to charge you $30.00 to "process" it. You feel so stressed out that you are about to explode. Could anything else go wrong?

There are many new kinds of stresses that you face in college, including social demands, academic pressures, financial responsibilities, and career anxieties. One thing you need to be aware of is that some stress is good for you. Yes, that's right. Without any stress at all life would seem dull and we would hardly be able to drag ourselves out of bed each morning. However, too much stress can be damaging. What you need to be able to do is figure out when you are experiencing too much stress and then find ways to cope with it.

THE INSIDE SCOOP

Researchers have found that students who have good social support networks from family and friends perceive and handle stressful situations more effectively. So when you are feeling stressed out, call home or talk to a friend. It may not solve all of your problems, but it will help you begin to feel better.

Good Stress/Bad Stress

Stress is defined as a response made by your body to a demand placed on it. It is impossible to live through even one day stress free. But not all stress is bad for you. Some stressors actually make life worth living. For example, you can feel a great accomplishment after running a 5K race or passing a difficult exam. Stress allows you to be creative and expand your experiences. However, stress becomes bad when it results from an overload of demands placed on you.

😀 GOOD STRESS	😟 BAD STRESS
feeling slightly nervous before a big exam	forgetting all the information you learned as soon as you enter the classroom to take the test
joining a sorority or fraternity or playing intramural sports	freaking out because you have a club or team meeting every single night and no time to do schoolwork
keeping up with your work for each class every day	having to read the book and write the paper the night before the assignment is due
planning a weekend road trip with friends	goofing off with friends all weekend and feeling like you'll never get all your schoolwork done

What Causes College Stress?

There is no doubt that college students feel stress. When you are new to college, you may feel stress about new responsibilities or living away from home. Returning students may feel stress about the time away from their family or balancing a full-time job with schoolwork. You may feel stress because it seems like all of your professors got together to schedule exams and papers for the same week (or worse, the same day).

> Make haste slowly.
> —Latin proverb

One of the most common reasons college students are stressed out is because they are having trouble dealing with all of the changes they have experienced in such a short time. Think about it. You are in a new place (maybe even away from home for the first time), you have new responsibilities (like paying your phone bill on time or dragging yourself to class at 8 A.M.), you are meeting new people, and you are dealing with a lot of schoolwork. You may not know one person on campus. Compare this situation with the comfortable setting you're used to. It is no wonder you may be feeling a bit stressed. Stress is caused by all sorts of things. Read on.

Academic Stress

There are several kinds of academic stress. You may feel anxiety when taking a test, giving a speech, or writing a paper. Or you may feel a general level of stress all the time because you are anxious about doing well in your classes. A little stress is probably good for your performance on these tasks. If you feel no stress at all when going in to take an exam, you may not be gearing yourself up enough to do as well as you could. But (and this is a big one) if your stress is getting in the way of your academic performance (for example, you know every word of the speech you are about to give, but you are too nervous to say it in class), you need to take action. Here are some common academic concerns.

Test taking, writing, or public speaking anxiety. Some students get so stressed before taking a test or writing a paper that they can't even remember what they've learned. Their palms get sweaty and their hearts beat faster. They may even get terrible headaches or colds every time they are placed in a testing situation. Usually these students do not do as well as they could on exams because they are too anxious to truly let the exam reflect what they have learned.

Procrastination. Some professors think that students who procrastinate just don't care about getting their work done, but we have met many a student who cares but just can't seem to get it together. These students feel more and more stressed as the semester progresses and they get more and more behind in their work.

High academic standards. Still others experience academic stress because they want to be the best. Maybe you were one of the top students in your high school. You always did well and the teachers expected a lot from you. Now you are in college and realize that you are *surrounded by top students*. Suddenly you feel even more pressure to succeed at much higher levels.

You may experience other academic stresses, and these stresses may change throughout any given semester (and throughout your entire college career). This stress may stem from dealing with relationships (not being compatible with your roommate or breaking up with your boyfriend or girlfriend) to drug or alcohol issues to money problems. Find out what these stresses are, because academic stress is different from other stresses you will experience.

Nonacademic College Stress

In addition to wanting to do well in classes, there are several other common concerns that college students have that can influence academics.

Financial stress. Money, money, money! College costs can really send students into a tailspin. Besides tuition, the costs of books, rent, food, and other, unexpected things (like parking tickets) can really cause sticker shock. Some students feel financial stress because they have just maxed out a credit card or have a $200 phone bill their first month away from home.

Social stress. Meeting new people can be overwhelming for some people. Could this be what is stressing you out? Suppose you are at a party with people you have never met before. Do you (1) find someone who looks interesting and start a conversation or (2) ease back into a corner and try to be invisible. The *b*s find it difficult to cope with situations where interacting with new people is involved.

Unfortunately for them, college involves lots of interaction with lots of folks. However, the *a*s are not off the hook: they may feel social stress because they have overbooked their schedules with social obligations. One look at their daily planners is enough to send us all into full anxiety mode as we try to think about how they will manage to study given all of their social tasks.

> ## DO YOUR HOMEWORK
>
> Ever tell yourself, "If I ignore it, it will go away"? Many students choose to ignore the enormous social stresses that are placed on them. However, research has indicated that students who feel an overwhelming sense of social stress are less likely to complete their college degree. Take action to change the situation rather than drifting along hoping it will change by itself.

Family stress. This may be the first time you are away from home, making decisions and taking responsibility for yourself. This can be stressful. But family stress can also occur because you want to make your family proud. Maybe you are the first in your family to ever go to college, or perhaps you have a brother who just graduated cum laude from some great school. Maybe you've left your full-time job to return to school for your college degree. Whatever your situation, chances are some pressure from family is involved.

The first step toward dealing with your stress is to recognize what is causing it. Consider your current situation. How would you rate your stress level on a scale of 1 to 10? If you're pretty stressed (say, a 5 or higher), what kinds of things are bothering you? Is your stress mostly academic or nonacademic, or is it a generous dose of both? Do academic stresses affect you differently than nonacademic ones? Once you know what kinds of stress you are facing, you will be much better able to cope with it.

What Does Stress Do to You?

Stress gets your body and mind to pay attention. You may have heard of this as a "fight or flight" response. Your heart pumps blood faster, your hearing and vision become more

😟 SAD BUT TRUE

Robert, a math education graduate student, was under so much stress as he finished his dissertation that one side of his face became temporarily paralyzed (a physical reaction to stress). Of course that was the week that Robert had a big presentation at a national conference, and he had to present his paper in this condition (adding to his stress, we are sure). Robert met with a counselor and learned to use deep breathing and visualization methods to reduce his stress levels. He eventually regained control of his facial muscles and learned to take his initial stress symptoms more seriously. What a wake-up call!

acute, and your body releases hormones such as adrenaline to meet the challenge. Although this might have been a great response in prehistoric times to being chased by a wolf, it is actually an overreaction for many of the daily stressors we face in modern life. And too much stress can wreak havoc on your body and your mind.

There are four general categories of stress reactions. You may find that you primarily experience stress in one or two of these ways. The good news is that once you identify how you react to stress, you can do something about it. Consider your own reactions to stress. Which categories best describe how you feel under stress?

THOUGHTS
loss of confidence
fear of failure
trouble concentrating
worrying about the future
forgetting things
inability to stop thinking about all
  you have to do

BEHAVIORS
acting impulsively
becoming withdrawn
using drugs or alcohol
grinding your teeth
sleeping too much or too little
eating too much or too little
crying for no apparent reason

PHYSICAL REACTIONS
sweaty palms (or general perspiration)
increased heart rate
dry mouth
feeling tired
headaches
susceptibility to illness
nervous tics
nausea
"butterflies" in stomach

FEELINGS
anxiety
irritability
moodiness
feeling scared

Do you recognize yourself in one or more of these categories? Some people react to stress strongly in one category (for example, thoughts), while others experience stress in several ways.

If you are having trouble figuring out which types of stress reaction you exhibit, the next time you are feeling stressed take a few minutes to think about how you are responding to the stress. Do you have a headache (physical reaction)? Are you just plain irritable toward everyone around you (a reaction through feelings)? In order to reduce your anxiety levels, it helps to know how you experience stress.

Reducing Stress Levels

You probably already have some ways to handle stress. Maybe you take a hot bath, call a good friend, or hide out and read a juicy novel. However, once you experience the added stresses of college life, you may find that these old strategies just don't cut it anymore. Maybe you have had one illness after another all semester. Maybe you have developed a strange facial tic. Or maybe you have mild anxiety attacks that affect your breathing. Instead of abandoning the way you used to handle stress (or giving in to stress altogether) we suggest you try some (or all) of these suggestions.

Exercise. If you experience physical reactions to stress, this may be the best solution for you. Exercise allows your body to cope with the physical symptoms of stress (such as an increased heart rate) in a healthy way. If thoughts or feelings are the way you experience stress, exercise releases hormones that will actually make you feel better and will take your mind off of your troubles. You don't even have to do very vigorous exercise to reap the stress benefits—a short walk will often do the trick.

URBAN LEGEND

A student was extremely stressed out under the pressures of final exams. He was at his science final and he just couldn't take it anymore. He sat straight up in his chair, stuck a sharpened pencil in each nostril, threw his head back, and slammed it onto the desk, thrusting the pencil points into his brain. He died almost instantly. Although this story is not true, the moral of it is that you should control your stress level.

Find a hobby (or rediscover one). Basically, do something just for fun. Check out the flyers posted on campus to see if there is something you might find interesting enough to pursue as a hobby.

Focus on your strengths. Each time you feel stressed or like you can't make it, try this little activity. Instead of thinking about all of the things you can't do, think about all of the things you can do. You might even want to make a list of these things to help you remember.

Relax. Take a few minutes each day to really relax—no TV, computers, or even conversations. Just some quiet time for yourself without any distractions. You'd be amazed at what just a short quiet time can do for your stress levels.

Eat well. Some people can't eat at all when they are stressed and others tend to overeat. Recognizing your own eating patterns in relation to stress can help you make changes. Above all, don't turn to junk food (or worse yet, alcohol) to soothe your stress, because the lack of proper nutrition can send your stress levels even higher.

Sleep well. When you are stressed you may not be able to sleep, or you may be the type of person who *only* wants to sleep at the first sign of pressure. Either way, try to get enough good sleep every day, but don't sleep too much: wasting time can lead to greater stress levels.

Study smart. Throughout *College Rules!* we will offer you strategies and tips for becoming a better studier. In general, the better prepared you are for the academic tasks you have to do, the less stressed you will feel. There is no better cure for test anxiety than knowing that you really know the information.

There are two ways of meeting difficulties: you alter the difficulties or you alter yourself meeting them.

—Phyllis Bottome

Just say no. Sometimes we create our own stress by becoming overcommitted. And it is amazing just how fast this can happen. A favor for a friend, an added responsibility with a social organization, and poof—suddenly you don't know how you will find the time to cram it all in. Our best advice is to pick and choose your commitments carefully. Do the things that you will really enjoy and learn to turn down the things that will get in the way of achieving your goal (getting that college degree).

Practice deep breathing and visualization. These techniques really work. The next time you are feeling stressed, close your eyes and focus on your breathing. Take ten nice deep breaths of equal length (your breath in should be as long as your breath out). With each breath out think, "relax." Then, think about a time when you were truly relaxed. Where were you? What did it look like? What time of day or year was it? What did you hear and smell? Who (if anyone) was with you? Try to fully visualize the situation with as many details as you can.

Listen to soothing music. Put on a set of headphones, close your eyes for a few minutes, and let soothing music take you away. Some students find that classical music, light jazz, or new age music is just the thing to help them relax. Even if you don't usually enjoy these types of music, they can be great stress reducers.

THE INSIDE SCOOP

If you practice visualization often, when you are stressed you need only think about your relaxing memory and your body will automatically begin to relax, because it has been conditioned to react that way to the memory. So make a habit of taking a mental trip to the beach, the mountains, or your grandma's house.

Put things in perspective. Don't build up tasks to disproportionate levels. After all, it's only a test, right? Will you even remember the grade you made on it in five years? The things that seem huge now may not seem so important later on. Knowing this can often help you get through the stressing event faster.

Confide in someone. Use your support system. Talk to your family or friends about how you are feeling instead of bottling it all up. Sometimes just sharing your concerns can help you overcome them.

See a counselor. Visiting a counselor gives you a chance to talk to someone who is trained to help people in your situation. Usually there is a counselor available on campus for a small fee (or even for free). Some colleges even offer group sessions for reducing stress levels. Our advice is to get help earlier than later. Don't wait until your stress levels have caused you a lot of trouble to get the help you need.

The best plan for controlling and reducing your stress is to use as many of the strategies we discussed as possible. If you rely on only one or two, you may find that they don't work in really difficult situations. The key is to be flexible and try several ways to attack your stress.

Quick and Dirty

○ Stress comes in a variety of flavors. You may find that you experience academic stress (test anxiety, procrastination, or perfectionism) or nonacademic stress (financial, social, or family)—or both—in college.

○ People react to stress in a variety of ways. These include thoughts, feelings, behaviors, and physical reactions.

○ Reducing your stress levels requires that you know both what is causing your stress and how your body reacts to stress. You need to have several strategies for coping with stress handy to help you through difficult times.

WHAT'S IT ALL ABOUT? UNDERSTANDING HOW YOU LEARN

> Some people never learn anything
> because they understand everything
> too soon.
>
> —Alexander Pope

Have you ever stopped to think about what it means to learn? College students learn every day, yet few really think about what it means to learn and how people go about learning things. According to Webster's dictionary, learning is "modification of a behavioral tendency by experience." Huh? Simply put, learning equals a change in behavior. Some things take a long time to learn (like calculus); other lessons we learn immediately (like when a child touches a hot stove). But whether the learning takes a long period of time or short period of time, we know that LEARNING = CHANGE.

Learning occurs in many different ways. Some people talk about learning styles and say that they are "auditory learners" meaning that they learn best when they hear something. Others say they learn best visually, and still others say that they learn best kinesthetically, or by doing things. Although we won't go as far as saying that this is a bunch of hogwash, we will say that this way of classifying how people

⚡ GET WIRED

If you are interested in finding out more about your own personal style of learning, there are several assessments available on the Internet. Go to one of the major search engines and type in "learning styles." You should find several sites that offer information and assessments. You also might try to see what the learning center on your campus offers. Most centers offer online assessments of learning styles for free.

learn is far too simplistic to be helpful. Think about it: if you were truly only a kinesthetic learner, you would be in big trouble in most college classes, where the majority of teaching is done through lecture. Everyone learns through using his or her senses (through seeing, hearing, touching, smelling, tasting), but this is just part of the picture. Many other things influence how you learn. This chapter talks about the stuff that learning is made of.

🏠 DO YOUR HOMEWORK

Think back to something that you learned very easily. It may have been a sport, like playing golf or tennis, or it may have been something academic, like learning the ins and outs of computer use. Now think about something that was hard for you to learn. Why do you think it's easier for you to learn some things than others? As you begin college, it's important that you think about this. No matter what your major, some courses will always be easier for you than others.

Profiles of Amazing Students

The fact that a change occurs as a result of learning indicates that the learner is involved in some way in a complex process. Learning just doesn't happen magically, nor by osmosis. Learning can be easy or a struggle, and you're not always even conscious of the fact that you are learning something.

Although no two students are exactly the same when it comes to learning, there are some general traits that lead to more effective learning. When students have these characteristics, learning can be a fun-filled journey with more long straight highways than bumps in the road. So what does an amazing student have that a mediocre or poor student doesn't? Read on to see how well you fit into the amazing student profile.

AMAZING STUDENTS ARE WILLFUL

Willfulness is perhaps the most important of all the characteristics of amazing students. Students who are willful have an enthusiasm and zest for learning. They may not love learning everything, but they have the motivation to persist, even in courses they may not like or that are particularly difficult for them. No matter the course or the topic, they see something of value in it. Willfulness also implies effort. Although we may learn lots of life's lessons without even realizing it, most school learning doesn't simply "happen." Classroom learning requires conscious effort (what is usually called studying), which in turn requires you to be an active participant—you know, be willing to do your part.

SAD BUT TRUE ☹

Everyone knows at least one person like Chad. In high school, he was the guy who never cracked a book but managed to pull decent grades in spite of it. He was care-free, loved to laugh, and prioritized his life so that the fun stuff was always done first. His teachers called him smart but lazy, and prodded him to put more time into schoolwork. His parents did the same. They knew that he was smarter than his grades reflected. Chad knew he could do better too, but he just couldn't bring him-self to put more into his schoolwork. He knew what he needed to do, and he had the skill, but he lacked the will.

When he applied for college (because there's no better place to go for contin-ued fun), his SAT scores were top-notch, but his grades only so-so. He did, however, get accepted to the school of his choice. It was a university that challenged students academically, but also one that rated high on the "party scale." Chad was in paradise. At least at first. So many parties, so little time. "There will always be another test. Who knows when another party will come along?" was his motto. It didn't take long for his lack of willfulness to catch up with him, however. By midterm, his grades in all of his classes were in the toilet. He went to class most of the time; he asked good questions and occasionally contributed to discussions. He would even chat with his professors after class, particularly about topics he was genuinely interested in. But he couldn't bring himself to study. Not at all. Once again, his teachers called him smart but lazy. His parents did the same. Chad man-aged to rally and pull all Cs his first semester. This pattern pretty much continued throughout his college career. And to his credit, he did graduate—with a 2.3 grade point average.

AMAZING STUDENTS ARE SKILLFUL

Skillfulness is the ability to know what to do and how to do it in any given learning situation. Being skillful means that you're more than a one-trick pony. You approach each learning task by consciously asking yourself, "What skills and strategies should I use to be successful here?" Skillfulness involves having the ability to plan your time, set learning goals that you can reach, monitor and evaluate your progress, and know a variety of ways to approach lots of different kinds of knowledge and ways to learn. In short, skillfulness involves a lot. When students are making the transition to college, they may approach every course, test, or learning task the same way, using what we like to call "the rubber stamp approach." Think about it this way: Would you wear a tuxedo to a baseball game? A strapless dress to a funeral? A bathing suit to religious services? Probably not. You know that there's appropriate dress for different occasions and settings. Skillful learners know that "putting on the same clothes" won't work for every class. They are flexible learners. They have different strategies and know when to use them. They know that you study for multiple-choice tests differently than you study for essay tests. And they not only know what to do, they also know how to do it.

AMAZING STUDENTS ARE CURIOUS

Curiosity. Without it we'd still be carrying clubs and living in caves. An astronaut wouldn't have walked on the moon, certain kinds of cancer wouldn't have cures, and it would take weeks instead of hours to cross the ocean. There would be none of the things that have come to be dear to lots of college students' hearts—cell phones, computers, the Internet, and TV. Curiosity is what makes learning fun and discovery possible. It's what makes you keep searching for the solution for a difficult problem.

As we move from childhood to adulthood, we seem to lose much of our curiosity. If you've spent any time around small children, you know that they ask endless questions. But as children grow into adolescents, they seem more and more reluctant to search for answers or to ask

> Some problems are so complex that you have to be highly intelligent and well informed just to be undecided about them.
>
> –Laurence J. Peter

questions. Sometimes the spark of curiosity can be reignited in college. If that happens, doors open, learning becomes a quest, and college becomes a life-changing experience.

AMAZING STUDENTS ARE OPEN-MINDED

Open-mindedness is the ability to try new things, listen to the ideas of others, and possibly change your own views. When freshmen arrive on college campuses, they generally have already formulated strong opinions on certain issues, particularly those that have been discussed around their dinner table over the years or those that are community related. For example, you may have very strong opinions on controversial issues such as a woman's right to choose, political preference, evolution, or censorship. These opinions are very difficult to change, and we're certainly not suggesting that you should. However, one of the ways for you to get the most of your college experience is not only to listen to the views of others but also to evaluate why you have the opinions you do. Students who are able to support their views with something more than "That's just the way I was raised" stand a better chance of leaving college with the ability to look at all sides of an issue and appreciate the importance of diverse viewpoints.

LISTEN UP

The idea of open-mindedness struck home with our students on September 11, 2001, the day the World Trade Center and the Pentagon were struck by terrorists. We were putting the final touches on *College Rules!* and our students were gearing up to take their first exams of the semester. In our classroom discussions about what had happened, it became clear that students were having to do some heavy-duty thinking about what all of this meant and how it might influence their daily lives. Many freshmen were struck by the diversity of the opinions they heard, because they were used to being in settings where everyone had similar views. Some didn't know where to begin to sort it all out. But after a bit of time passed and the rawness of emotions gave way to more rational thought, most students found the different perspectives on the tragedy helpful as they tried to form their own opinions. It pays to listen to others, to evaluate what they say, and to keep an open mind, especially about events and issues that few of us understand very well.

AMAZING STUDENTS ARE SELF-DISCIPLINED

The ability to do the right thing at the right time regardless of what you really want to be doing is called self-discipline. When you're in college, you're in charge of your actions. No one is going to check that you go to class or that your homework is done. No one is going to ground you if you stay out all night. No one is going to prevent you from piercing any body part that you want pierced. You have to discipline yourself to take care of business, whether that business is academic or personal.

So what does it mean to be self-disciplined? It means having the ability to read your biology assignment when everyone else on your hall is going to get pizza. It means going to the library to do research for a paper when you would rather spend the afternoon playing Frisbee on the quad. It means making an informed decision not to abuse alcohol or your body. It means understanding the consequences of the choices you make. It means setting reasonable goals for yourself and then doing what it takes to meet them. Self-discipline is just plain hard.

Learning Matters

X FOR ADULTS ONLY

Adults who are thinking about going to college after they have been out of high school for several years often experience problems with math. They may not have taken college-level math in high school, and even if they did, it's long forgotten. If you fall into this category, you may want to see what refresher math courses your college has to offer. In most instances, you probably wouldn't receive credit for taking such a course, but it's better taking that route than jumping into a course that is way over your head.

You can probably think of a gazillion things that influence how you learn—everything from how you feel when you get up in the morning to whether you like the course material or the teacher to how things are going in your personal life. That's why there's no prescription—no one best way to learn. However, we do know that there are some general mindsets that freshmen students bring to college with them. Mostly these are things that you haven't thought much about in high school, so you may be kind of surprised that they will make a difference.

WHAT YOU ALREADY KNOW

What knowledge and information are you bringing to college with you? Are you a math whiz? Can you write poetry in your sleep? Were you a member of the debate team? Are you an American history buff? You may have been able to take tons of advanced math classes in high school, so you are well prepared to compete in higher-level math courses at the beginning of your college career. Compare yourself with someone who attended a very small high school where there were no advanced math courses offered. Which of you has more knowledge about math? Which could be predicted to enroll in higher-level math courses in college, and which could be expected to do better?

But there is a difference between having knowledge and having information. Students who are knowledgeable can make connections between pieces of information. They can apply information in new situations, thus creating knowledge. Students who know information—who can spout off lots facts but fail to see how things fit together—are certainly ahead of those who don't, but behind those who have figured out the knowledge thing.

Two of the major factors that influence the knowledge you bring to college are the quality of the high school you went to and the level of courses you took there. Although it differs from state to state, most high schools have a "college prep" curriculum that prepares students for introductory college courses. The curriculum dictates the number of courses (or units) you need to take in high school. For example, most college prep curriculums state that you need four units of English, which means that you would need to take English in each of your four years in high school. And you can't just take any English: business English wouldn't count. You would need college prep English, honors English, or AP (advanced placement) English. In addition, if you do well in AP English, you may even be able to use that class for college credit.

Being able to take increased knowledge with you to college is one of the reasons it's important to take more advanced courses in high school, rather than simply taking a course because you know it's an easy A.

> The test of a first-rate intelligence is the ability to hold two opposed ideas at the same time, and still retain the ability to function.
>
> —F. Scott Fitzgerald

Marlene was a pretty conscientious student in high school. She always did her homework (most of the time correctly), she studied for tests, and she made high grades. But she made one tiny mistake that came back to haunt her when she started college. In fact, she made the same mistake that lots of college-bound students make: she took the easy way out. At the advice of her older brother, Marlene decided not to enroll in the more challenging high school English classes, even though her teachers encouraged her to do so. Her brother told her it was her grade point average that mattered, not the courses that she took.

She was accepted at the college of her choice, so she was sure that she had done the best thing. Everything was going fine—that is, until she went to freshman orientation and took placement tests. To her surprise (actually, to her horror) she placed into a remedial English course. According to her test results, she was not prepared to enroll in English 101. Flashback to brother's advice!

This story is repeated often on college campuses. The level of your high school courses does matter. It's important to get as much out of those high school years as possible. Don't take the easy way out. Challenge yourself in high school and you will continue to do the same in college.

WHAT YOU BELIEVE LEARNING TO BE

What do you believe learning is? How do those beliefs match up with those of your college professors? By "beliefs about learning," we mean both the attitudes you have about what learning is and how you study based on those attitudes.

Do you believe learning either happens quickly or not at all? If so, it will be difficult for you to keep at studying, especially in courses that are difficult or that simply require more time and effort of you. If you find yourself slamming your physics book shut after trying to work one problem and saying, "I can't do this," after only ten minutes of effort, you may believe that learning should be quick.

Do you believe that your teachers or other authority figures have all the answers? If you go to class each day and dutifully read your textbook but don't question what you read and hear, you probably suffer from "empty vessel syndrome." Simply put, this means that you think of learning as something that is done *to* you. It is your professor's job to "fill you up" with information, not your job to actively participate in learning. After all, what are you paying for, anyway? Students who have empty vessel syndrome find it easy to let themselves off the hook when things aren't going well. They will often blame their lack of success on the teacher, saying things like "He was a really bad lecturer" or "She taught chemistry in a way I could not understand." Now don't get us wrong. We're not saying that all professors do everything right and that when students don't do well it's always their own fault. What we are saying is that having the belief that learning is a shared experience where you too bring something to the situation is important.

Do you know how long the average high school student persists at figuring out answers to algebra problems? According to the experts, it's about two (that's right, two) minutes. If he can't solve it in two minutes, he gives up. Sometimes he moves on to another problem; sometimes he gives up totally. Shuts the book. End of story. Even teachers get caught up in the idea that things should happen quickly. What happens in class when your teacher asks a question and no one volunteers an answer? Usually she'll answer the question for you if more than ten seconds go by. For some reason, even a short period of silence in the classroom is too long. But we know that some things can't be accomplished at lightning speed. When you find yourself giving up, take a deep breath and try again.

Do you believe that learning means memorizing facts or conceptualizing information?
Many students equate learning with memorizing. If you believe that all you have to do is to memorize the boldfaced terms in biology or the battles of the Civil War in history, you may be missing the boat—especially if the task requires you to really think about the material. Of course some memorization is necessary. Where could we go in math without having memorized all of those times tables? How would we look words up in the dictionary efficiently without memorizing the alphabet? How would we know that NaCl is ordinary table salt or that Abraham Lincoln was assassinated by John Wilkes Booth in 1865 without having memorized those facts?

But memorization is not the be-all and end-all of learning. In many classes in college, your professors will expect you to conceptualize—take the information you have memorized and put pieces of it together in a way that makes sense. In biology, for example, if you memorize the terms in the genetics chapter—genotype, phenotype, homozygous, heterozygous, and so forth—but you can't understand how these terms interrelate using the concepts of Mendelian genetics, you will probably run into difficulty.

It's easy to see that students who believe that learning is only about memorization will select different approaches to learning than will those who understand the importance of conceptualization. Although both groups of students might use similar strategies to learn, perhaps by making flash cards of the definitions of terms, the memorizer would stop there. The conceptualizer might go beyond flash cards by making up genetics problems to solve, talking through the problem-solving process with a study partner, and making sure he understands the logic behind Mendelian genetics.

WHAT YOU ARE WILLING TO INVEST

How much time, discipline, and motivation will you put into learning in college? Have you ever heard the saying "You reap what you sow"? Nowhere does this ring truer than in college. Those students who are willing to make a big investment in their college experience will have learned considerably more than those who are satisfied to just get by. And we don't just mean academics. That's only part of the investment. Granted, students who graduate magna cum laude have invested time and are obviously disciplined and motivated. But if you talk to students like this, they have probably also invested heavily in other aspects of the college experience. They have been active in clubs and organizations where they made connections with students and professors with similar interests. They have written for the campus newspaper, conducted research with a professor, held offices, or been active in the residence hall where they live or in community projects. All of these activities have a big payoff down the road when you seek employment. It often doesn't matter to employers what you have done beyond the classroom, just that you have done something. To land the really good jobs after graduation requires considerably more than good grades.

WHAT YOU WANT AS AN END RESULT

What degree do you want to earn, and what experiences are important to you? Earlier we talked about the difference between a major and a career. Remember that some majors lead to specific careers; for instance, a degree in education usually leads to a teaching career. Others prepare you more generally for a variety of careers. It may surprise you to know that some companies just want you to have a degree; they really don't care what it's in. For example, one of the authors has a daughter who is a talent agent. The firm that hired her wasn't interested in what her degree was in, although she had to have one. They were just as concerned with her ability to deal with people, her social skills, and her other work experience in dealing with the public. Had she not developed those skills as a college student, she probably would not have been offered the position, no matter how good her grades were. The point is, at some point in your college career, you need to have an idea of the skills and knowledge you'll need to be successful once you graduate. If you want to spend the rest of your life developing computer software, the kinds of experiences you might want to have in college will differ greatly from those you would want if you want to be a journalist for the *New York Times*.

As they head off to college, students rarely consider the importance of the factors that influence their learning, but these things do make a difference. Those who think about the big picture of learning and the more subtle things that influence it are those who are on the right track to becoming amazing students.

Quick and Dirty

○ Students who are amazingly successful in college are willful, skillful, curious, open-minded, and self-disciplined.

○ To be the best student possible, you need to consider how you would answer these questions: What information are you bringing to college with you? What do you believe learning is? What are you willing to invest? What do you want as an end result?

CHAPTER 11

A MOMENT OF SILENCE, PLEASE: CONCENTRATING WHILE YOU STUDY

Learning without thought is labor lost.

–Confucius

L earning and studying are not the same thing. In the last chapter we talked about how sometimes learning can happen unconsciously (for example, that song on the radio that you hate yet somehow know every word to), but studying should *never* be unconscious. If it is, you have probably fallen asleep. Zzzzzz. Remove the textbook from your face and read on.

Sometimes students tell us that studying makes them tired. It's true that studying can make you tired: if you are doing it right, studying takes an enormous amount of concentration. But has the following ever happened to you? You are reading your biology (or history, or accounting) text and you look up after a few pages—and have absolutely no idea what you've just read. If so, you weren't really concentrating and that time you spent looking at those pages was, well, wasted. Finding ways to concentrate is one of the toughest challenges facing many college students. The first step toward achieving better concentration is setting up an environment that is favorable for learning.

Creating a First-Rate Learning Environment

Take a look at the place where you do your studying. Are you somewhere that allows you to really focus on your work? Would you recommend this type of learning environment to your friends? Or are you in a place that may actually detract from your ability to concentrate, such as on your bed or, worse yet, on your bed with the TV on? Sometimes students don't give much thought to where they are studying, but if you can't focus, you probably are not getting much real studying done.

THE INSIDE SCOOP

Research has shown that students who study in a similar environment to where they will take their exam tend to do better on the exam. This phenomenon is called state dependent memory, which means that you will do better on a test if you take the test in the same "state"—the same mental state, that is—you were in when you did the learning. This is because your environment gives your mind cues that help it more easily access the information. So try to create an atmosphere like that in your classroom: make the lighting, temperature, and comfort level similar to those you will experience during testing. You may even want to find an empty classroom to use, if possible.

Use the following chart to help you think about and assess your current learning environment. Check all that apply.

My studying location	My concentration level in this location rated from 1 (poor) to 10 (excellent)									
Bedroom	1	2	3	4	5	6	7	8	9	10
Living room	1	2	3	4	5	6	7	8	9	10
Kitchen	1	2	3	4	5	6	7	8	9	10
Library	1	2	3	4	5	6	7	8	9	10
At work	1	2	3	4	5	6	7	8	9	10
Other_____	1	2	3	4	5	6	7	8	9	10

My studying area	My concentration level in this location rated from 1 (poor) to 10 (excellent)
On my bed	1 2 3 4 5 6 7 8 9 10
At a desk	1 2 3 4 5 6 7 8 9 10
On my sofa	1 2 3 4 5 6 7 8 9 10
At a table	1 2 3 4 5 6 7 8 9 10
Outside	1 2 3 4 5 6 7 8 9 10
Other_____	1 2 3 4 5 6 7 8 9 10

My environment	My concentration level in this location rated from 1 (poor) to 10 (excellent)
Quiet	1 2 3 4 5 6 7 8 9 10
Music playing	1 2 3 4 5 6 7 8 9 10
TV playing	1 2 3 4 5 6 7 8 9 10
Roommates / others talking	1 2 3 4 5 6 7 8 9 10
Other_____	1 2 3 4 5 6 7 8 9 10

If you found that your studying location, area, and environment were all good to excellent (at least 7s or above) in terms of concentration, then congratulations! You are well on your way to learning success. If, on the other hand, you have found that you are not currently in a good situation for learning (less than a 5), then your homework for tonight is to try out some different locations until you find one or two that work for you.

LISTEN UP

Some students believe that they should make themselves as comfortable as possible while studying and choose to study on their bed or on a cushiony sofa. However, it turns out that people concentrate better when they are not entirely comfy and relaxed. You will find that you are able to focus better if you choose a straight-backed chair, such as a desk chair or kitchen chair.

DO YOUR HOMEWORK

Many students find that they concentrate better with a little noise in the background (like a radio playing softly or the white noise of a fan humming), but no one can concentrate with the television on, because you will quickly find yourself engrossed in whatever is on the tube. So if you are having trouble concentrating while studying, turn off the TV.

> I took a speed reading course and read _War and Peace_ in twenty minutes. It involves Russia.
>
> —Woody Allen

Getting Rid of Distractions

Think about a time when you were really engaged in whatever you were doing. In fact, you were so into it that you lost all sense of time and space. Perhaps you were lost in a good book, or maybe you were in the zone in your basketball game. There is a term for this type of engagement—you were "in flow." That is, you were able to rid yourself of all distractions and focus completely on the task at hand.

Now picture yourself studying. What image do you have? Are you in flow, or are you sitting with your books and notes open but your mind is a million miles away? Think about the noises you hear. Is there someone talking? Music playing? Clocks ticking? Phones ringing? Visualize what you are focusing on. Is it the chapter you are reading? A noisy roommate? A sudden urge to clean your room? A growling stomach? About 100 things that you are currently worried about? Whatever things you picture hearing or seeing are the distractions you need to get rid of before you study. We know that this is sometimes easier said than done.

> The finest words in the world are only vain sounds, if you cannot comprehend them.
>
> —Anatole France

Adam, a sophomore English major, lived in a house with two roommates. Unfortunately for Adam, one of the roommates found the need to practice his electric guitar every time Adam sat down to study. To add to Adam's troubles, his other roommate continually had friends over at all times of the day or night. Adam found it hard to concentrate if there was any noise while he was studying. So, needless to say, he didn't do so well on his first round of exams and—shock—he blamed his roommates for his failure because they were always making so much noise. Adam failed to realize that it was his responsibility to fix these problems. Rather than becoming angry with his roommates, he needed to work out the problems. In fact, the roommates didn't even realize there was a problem until Adam brought it up. The point is that you need to take responsibility for your own learning and if something or someone is getting in the way of your ability to concentrate on your studies, you need to do something about it.

When you sit down to study we want you to be able to focus on what you are doing (sometimes it is hard enough to just get started, right?). So let's identify those things that can distract you while studying.

The distractions students face while they study come in two flavors: external distractions and internal distractions.

If you are returning to college after having a family, then you know that it is not always easy to "get rid of distractions." Our best advice is to carve out some study times in the evenings when you are off-duty or to plan to study when your family is sleeping (either early in the morning or at night). This strategy has worked for both of us (in fact, as Jodi is writing this very sentence at 5:30 A.M., her family is sound asleep).

EXTERNAL DISTRACTIONS

External distractions include noise, other people, light, TV, snacks, phone calls, and so on. Some of these distractions are fairly easy to fix because you can simply move to a better location. Go to the library or another quiet place to get some serious studying done. Other distractions can be a little more difficult to deal with. You may have noticed that there are a lot of fun things to do on your campus and that there is always someone around to talk to or to do something with. So if you are not study-ing because a friend offers something better to do, then you can quickly find yourself in some trouble, because there is *always* something more fun to do than study. But part of being a college student is learning to prioritize. And because you are a stu-dent, studying should always be close to the top of your list of priorities. Besides, you will be able to (1) have a better time when you play and (2) concentrate better on your schoolwork if you get it out of the way first.

INTERNAL DISTRACTIONS

Internal distractions are more complex than the external ones. There are several dif-ferent types:

Physical distractions. These include feelings of hunger, sleepiness, or illness. If you find that you are always tired or hungry when you plan to study, you may have to move your studying sessions to a different time of day. Or try taking a quick walk or eating a light snack before you study. If you find that you always feel ill when you study (for example, you get a headache every time you read) you may want to get a physical to make sure nothing is medically wrong, or an eye exam to see if you need to wear glasses while reading.

THE INSIDE SCOOP

Eye doctors have found that students who have trouble concentrating in school often can be cured of this problem by wearing glasses (or contact lenses) while reading. Some students just need a reading lens that will help their eyes relax even though they can see just fine. If you have always had trouble concentrating, you may find the solution through a simple eye exam.

Internal anxieties. These can include worrying about test performance, personal problems, or other responsibilities you have. If these concerns are keeping you from getting your work done, try to put the problems that are worrying you into perspective. Is it something that can wait, or something you need to deal with before you can study? If you find that you are never able to concentrate because of your anxieties, you may want to talk to a friend or a counselor and come up with a plan of action.

Boredom. You may be feeling bored or disinterested in some of your classes, or you may even have an intense dislike for certain courses. However, you need to be able to make it through all of your courses. So how do you concentrate on courses you don't really like? One way is to tell yourself that the semester lasts only 15 weeks (give or take a week or so). You can do anything for 15 weeks, right? A better approach is to find something about the course that interests you. Anything, no matter how small, may make it easier for you to get through the course. You might also try studying with others. Sometimes this can give you just the push you need to make it through the course.

SAD BUT TRUE

Janet thought she would have more fun in college. She loved her new friends, but found all of her courses boring. Really boring. In fact, there wasn't one she liked at all in her first term. It seemed to her that she hardly had time to think about anything before the class moved on to another topic. So she found herself tuning out during lectures. She didn't read her texts too often because they were also pretty dull. Janet came to us after her first round of exams (after cramming to get through five weeks' worth of material in all of her classes) to learn some better time management skills.

Although this was a concern and we did talk to Janet about time management strategies, we focused more on addressing the boredom issue. We asked Janet to interview her professors to find out what they liked about their fields (surely there must be something, otherwise why would they spend their time on it?) and to talk to students majoring in the subjects she was studying. The hope was that she would find something of interest in each course that she could latch on to (we also sent her for some tutoring and met with her several times). Janet needed to overcome a mindset that she was learning for someone else (the teacher); she needed to believe that she was learning for herself. This is a process that takes some time, but it can be done.

Daydreaming. Daydreaming while studying can become a habit for some students. And some may not even be aware that they are daydreaming until they close their books and realize that they don't remember an iota of what they've just read. The first thing you need to do if you're a daydreamer is learn to recognize when you are beginning to drift off. Then you need to be able to separate studying from daydreaming. When you find yourself dreaming, stop studying and allow the thoughts to come, then regain focus and start studying again. Or push the day-dreams out of your mind by writing them down, and then resume studying. But your goal is to be able to separate the dreaming from the studying.

Perfectionism. Sometimes students find themselves paralyzed by perfectionism or the need for everything to be done exactly right. Although this may sound good in theory, spending a lot of time perfecting things unnecessarily can actually hamper your ability to concentrate. Try to make the distinction between the things that need to be letter-perfect and those that just need to be good enough.

Identifying the things that keep you from concentrating is not always easy, and you may find that they vary from day to day. Our best advice is to monitor yourself, and when you find your motivation for studying is slipping, ask yourself what is getting in the way of your ability to focus. Once you can recognize the problem you can begin to use strategies to fix it.

Six Ways to Improve Concentration

Once you get down to studying, do you find yourself thinking about everything in the world except the task at hand? Here are some strategies that will help you focus—they may actually cut down on the time you need to study because you will get so much more accomplished.

Keep a jot list. Have a pad of paper where you can write down your "worry list"—all of those thoughts you have (about calling home, doing laundry, or cleaning your room) that keep you from concentrating on your studying. Some students find it helpful to jot this kind of information into their daily planners so that it becomes their to do list.

Set a purpose. Before you study, know what you want to accomplish in the session. Be as specific as possible—"studying science" is not really a purpose, but "understanding the concepts in chapter 7" would be a good studying purpose. It is also a good idea to set a purpose for reading. Think about what you already know about the topic and ask yourself questions that you will answer while reading. This is a great way to keep focused.

Take an active role. If you have ever read a chapter in your text and then realized that you have no idea what in the world you just read, then you know how important it is to really concentrate while studying. Otherwise you are simply wasting time. One way to take an active role in your studying (instead of passively turning pages) is to take notes while you read. We will talk about this in more depth later, but for now, note-taking simply involves writing down all of the key information in your own words as you read.

Study in the same place and at the same time. Some students are very easily distracted by a change of scenery. If they study outside, they end up playing with the grass or watching people walking by. If they study in the library, they end up browsing the stacks instead of getting their work done. If this is you, then plan to study in the same place—preferably a place that you know well (such as your room) so that you are not distracted by new things. However, some get bored quickly when studying in the same place and find that their concentration improves when they have a few places to choose from. So figure out whether you do better in the same place every time or whether you should plan to have several places where you can get studying done. You should also plan your study sessions for the same time each day. This helps you work when you can concentrate best and it helps make studying a habit—if it's 7:00 P.M., then it's time to study.

Have a set start and end time. Many students tell us that they just set aside two or three evenings per week for studying. They plan to study for as long as it takes to get the work done. However, these students often find that without a start and end time for studying, they end up wasting a good deal of the evening without getting too much accomplished. They say things like "I studied for seven hours last night." But when you talk to them about how much of that time was really spent studying, it is often more like an hour and a half. If you set a time limit for your studying you tend to get more work done, because you have imposed a deadline for yourself. The trick is to plan enough time in your schedule to get everything done.

Be here now. If you find your attention is a million miles away from your studies, you need to pull yourself back. Every time you find your mind wandering, repeat this phrase until you find yourself focusing again: "Be here now." Try it—it really works!

Think about the strategies you use to help you concentrate on things you like to do (like playing a sport or exercising). You probably use some of the techniques we've discussed. How do you think you can apply these techniques to reading and studying?

Quick and Dirty

O   Create a study space where you can focus. We suggest sitting in a straight-backed chair in a room with good lighting. Try playing some quiet background music if it helps you concentrate.

O   Get rid of distractions. Remember to consider both external (noise, roommates, room temperature) and internal (hunger, test anxiety, daydreaming) influences on your concentration.

O   Have a plan for getting your concentration back. Set studying hours and studying goals to keep yourself on track.

CHAPTER 12

YOUR COURSE SYLLABUS IS YOUR FRIEND

Knowledge is of two kinds; we know a subject ourselves, or we know where we can find information upon it.

—Samuel Johnson

In high school, you probably showed up to class each day with little or no idea of where the course was heading, what topics you'd be covering, or when all of the exams were going to happen. Only the teacher had this knowledge. In college, however, professors provide you with a lot of this information in their course syllabus, which is usually distributed at the beginning of each term. A syllabus can be as simple as one sheet of paper listing reading assignments and test dates. Or it can be as thick as the Sunday newspaper, chock full of detailed course information. Some professors consider the syllabus to be a contract with their students: if you successfully complete the tasks described in the contract, you will pass the course. Other professors consider their syllabus to be a work in progress. These professors tend to make minor changes to the syllabus throughout the course (though major tasks like exams and paper assignments usually don't change).

One of the steps to becoming a successful college student is to know how to read your syllabus for important information about the course—information that other students might miss. For example, your history professor may tell you in the syllabus that he believes that history is not made up of "facts," but that it is a story that is continually changing as new information is discovered. This simple statement tells you an awful lot about the type of test questions you can expect from this professor. We'd bet that you wouldn't be asked many questions about names and dates. Instead, you probably will be asked questions that require you to make interpretations of and think critically about events.

DO YOUR HOMEWORK

After the first day of classes, go through your syllabi (the plural of syllabus) and highlight all the important information such as exam dates, due dates of papers or projects, and key information about what is expected of you in class. Then *put them somewhere safe and don't lose them!* We'd suggest you keep the syllabus for each class in your notebook for that class so you can refer to it often. This is one way to monitor your learning.

Anatomy of a Syllabus

Here are the first few pages of a typical syllabus—read over the sections, then we'll discuss the sorts of things you can expect to find in a syllabus.

This section tells you what to call your professor, where to find her, and how to contact her.

This section also tells you what you need to buy for class. Note that this class requires more than just a textbook.

LEARNING TO LEARN

Professor:	Dr. Smith
Office:	225 Land-Grant Hall
Office Hours:	M 10–1, W 12–4 and by appointment
Phone:	555-0000
Email:	smith@bigu.edu
Text:	Nist, S. L., & Holschuh, J. P. 2000. *Active Learning: Strategies for College Success.* Allyn & Bacon.
Supplies:	Schedule book
	Email account
	Folder with pockets
	(These supplies are not optional; purchase them when you purchase your books.)

GENERAL INFORMATION

The purpose of Learning to Learn is to teach students how to become better learners by developing efficient and effective studying behaviors. Learning to Learn helps students learn and apply more mature study strategies and select strategies based on the text, the task, and their own characteristics as learners.

It is important for students taking Learning to Learn to understand that successful completion of the course demands practice. As strategies are taught, students are expected to apply them to college-level materials presented in class as well as to other courses in which they are enrolled.

> In this section you find information about the professor's philosophy of the course as well as what is expected of students.

EXPECTATIONS REGARDING ASSIGNMENTS

You are responsible for assignments whether or not you are in class the day they are assigned or the day they are due. If you are going to miss class for any reason and wish to receive credit for the assignment due that day, you must get the assignment to me at the beginning of class on the day it is due.

> After reading this section, you will know not to ask Dr. Smith if you can turn in work late. She simply won't accept it.

GRADING

As with other courses, grades depend primarily on how well students perform on exams and other course requirements. Exams will consist of objective questions, essay questions, and scenarios based on problem-solving activities. Grades will be determined using a point system and will be weighted as follows:

> This section explains how grades are computed and weighted.

Exam 1	20%
Exam 2	20%
Project	10%
Practice and quizzes	20%
Final exam	30%

By using the word *tentative,* Dr. Smith is telling you to expect changes to the schedule. It also tells you that she will be some-what flexible about covering the topics.

In this section you also find daily discussion topics, daily assignments, and important dates for exams and projects.

TENTATIVE COURSE SCHEDULE

(Note: Reading assignments are due on the day they appear in the syllabus. This means that on August 21 you should have read chapter 1 before you come to class.)

8/16 Syllabus; introduction to the course
Differences between high school and college

8/21 What is an active reader?
Starting out on the right foot
Reading assignment: chapter 1

8/23 Active learning
Four factors that influence learning
Reading assignment: chapters 2 & 3

8/28 Motivation
Studying cycle
Gearing up for class
Reading assignment: chapters 5 & 12

8/30 Figuring out the task
Annotation
Reading assignment: chapters 10 & 13

9/4 Time management
Assessing your learning
Reading assignment: chapter 4

9/6 Exam 1

Although syllabi differ depending on the course content and instructor, the following features are present in most. Check out your syllabi and make a mental note of which of these elements you find. Spending a little time getting to know your syllabi can help you a great deal in the long run.

It is always a good idea to let your instructors know when you are coming to office hours so they can be sure to be there. Most professors try to keep their schedules free during office-hour time, but take it from us—things crop up all the time. If you do not let your professor know you are coming, you may find an empty office. And nothing is more frustrating than actually hiking across campus to see your professor and not finding him there.

How to reach your instructor. This information is very important to know. Generally the syllabus will tell you the instructor's office hours, office phone number, and, often, email address. Sometimes your instructor will tell you her preferred mode of communication: "Students may find it difficult to reach me in my office because I am usually working in the lab, so my advice is to contact me by email."

Some students assume that curving scores is a way to help students raise poor grades. But in reality, curving is based on the notion of creating a grade distribution that follows a bell-shaped curve. So if your professor is using a traditional curving method, this means that some high scores need to be curved downward in addition to some low scores being curved upward.

The grading policy. You will find several pieces of information about how you are being graded that should answer the following questions: What counts as an A? Ninety

Craig was taking intro to chemistry. He was very relieved when the professor announced that all grades would be curved for each exam because he'd always heard that curving helps student grades. After each test, students were given an answer sheet so they could figure out their score, and grades were posted about a week after each test (the curved grades, however, were not calculated until the end of the term). Craig figured that he was making a low A based on his point scores for each exam. He was pretty angry when he found out that the curve actually dropped his grade to a high B. We are not sure if curving is the fairest system, but many professors continue to employ it.

GET WIRED

Most textbooks have a resource page on the publisher's Web site. Even if your instructor does not require you to use these resources (or even tell you that they are available), it is a good idea to check out the Web page to find more information about the text, other links, and even a bank of test questions about the material.

percent or above? What happens if you get 89.55 percent? Are grades calculated using a point system? Are exam scores curved? If you are writing papers, is there a grading rubric or some set of criteria that the instructor follows? Are your assignments graded by the professor or by a teaching assistant? All of this information should be found somewhere in the syllabus.

Texts and materials. Your syllabus lets you know what you need to purchase for the course. Most courses require you to purchase at least one textbook, but many also

DO YOUR HOMEWORK

Most professors do not offer any type of extra credit work (and get irritated at students who request extra credit work), so if it is not stated in the syllabus, don't even bother asking. Instead, focus on doing well on the assigned tasks.

require other supplies, such as calculators, art supplies, lab equipment, or computer software. In addition, the syllabus will tell you about supplementary materials you may need to find in the library, on a Web site, or elsewhere on campus.

Special policies. Some instructors have attendance policies wherein you lose points for each absence (or gain points for perfect attendance). Others have participation policies wherein you earn course points for becoming involved in class discussions. Your instructor may even offer extra credit for participating in a research study or doing some extra work.

Course requirements. Your syllabus will contain information about what you will need to do to demonstrate your learning in the course. This includes schedules and descriptions of tests, papers, reports, projects, presentations, homework assignments, or anything else you will need to do. The course requirements section should also tell you if there are any prerequisites for the course (for example, you must successfully complete Math 101 before taking this course).

Sara was taking an introduction to music course and knew that she would be graded over three exams. Sara did fairly well on the exams and was sure there was an error when she received her grade at the end of the term. She had earned a C for the course. When she contacted the professor, he told her that she did not complete all of the course requirements. Sara told the professor that she had saved her old exams and that, according to her calculations, she was making an 83 percent. The professor agreed with these calculations, but said that she had lost points because in addition to the exams, students were required to attend three music concerts, and Sara did not turn in tickets to prove her attendance. Sara did not even know that this was a requirement, but when she looked at the syllabus, there it was in black and white.

Instructor's philosophy. Contained within most syllabi is some insight into how your professor views the content she is teaching. Consider this statement from Dr. David Zehr's history of psychology course at Plymouth State College: "This course is not designed to merely teach you the 'facts' of psychology's history. Anyone can memorize names and dates. And if that's all we did, then even I'd be tempted to cut class on a regular basis! To the contrary, it is my hope that this course will provide a framework that will help you better understand the complexity and diversity of contemporary psychology; understanding the present is inherently easier if one possesses a perspective on what has come before." This professor spells out his view of what history is and why he thinks it is important to learn history. If you were a student in this class you would know from reading the syllabus that memorizing names and dates would be a waste of time.

The absent are always in the wrong.
—English proverb

Course objectives. Your syllabus should contain several statements about what the instructor hopes you will learn as a result of the course. For example, Dr. Deborah Martin of the University of Georgia, a professor in human geography, states the following objectives:

- to enhance your knowledge of the world by comparing and contrasting patterns of culture, population, political, and economic systems in various parts of the world

- to foster geographic thinking and analysis through critical examination of spatial patterns of human processes

- to stimulate greater interest in understanding the world geographically

After reading these objectives you would know that you would be expected to think critically about different populations through comparing and contrasting different geographical patterns.

Study tips. Your syllabus will often contain helpful hints, such as "be sure to read the text before coming to class" or "previous classes have noted that it is much easier to study this material in a group setting." Explore your syllabus for this type of information; it will really help you know how to prepare for the course requirements.

Course calendar. The course calendar provides information about the order of the topics to be covered and also about exam dates and other deadlines. Note these important dates by highlighting them in the syllabus and by putting the dates into your schedule book. If you have homework requirements in the course, other smaller assignments, or special events such as a field trip or a visiting speaker, note them as well so you don't forget about them. In addition, if your professor revises the original calendar, note that information as well.

What Can Your Syllabus Do for You?

We don't think we can stress the importance of your syllabus enough. When you start any new class you should carefully read the syllabus. Then you should put it in a place where you can easily access it and won't lose it (like in your class notebook). After you have been in the course for a week or two, you should read your syllabus again. It is amazing how much more you will get out of the second reading once you are familiar with the professor and the expectations of the course.

Your syllabus will help you study for your class. Check the syllabus for the topics you need to cover for each exam, but look at more than just the chapter numbers. Often your professor will list discussion topics for each class meeting. These are the most important ones to cover in your studying. In addition, reading over your professor's course philosophy can give you an idea of the kinds of questions that will be asked. For example, if your biology professor states that "there are no truths in science" then you know that when your book presents several theories for a science concept, your professor will ask you to evaluate all of them rather than memorize just one.

Your syllabus can help you organize and think about course material. Use it to help you plan your weekly schedule. Check out your assignments for each week and plan accordingly. Suppose you find that you have three chapters of history, two biology chapters, and 30 precalculus problems to work this week. You can use this information to help you plan out your studying sessions. In fact, information on your syllabi is one of the most important resources at your disposal. So get the most out of each syllabus by referring to it at least once a week.

> I fear explanations explanatory of things explained.
>
> —Abraham Lincoln

Quick and Dirty

○ Syllabi contain a wealth of information. Use your syllabus to find information about how to reach your instructor, grading and special policies, texts, and requirements for the course.

○ Examine your syllabi for information about preparing for the course. Take a look at statements about your professor's philosophy, course objectives, and information regarding studying for course exams.

○ Keep your syllabi handy. Use the information you find to help you plan your weekly studying schedule.

WHAT'S UP, DOC? UNDERSTANDING YOUR PROF'S EXPECTATIONS

> Don't play what's there,
> play what's not there.
>
> —Miles Davis

One of the keys to being successful in college is the ability to get inside your professor's head and try to understand the way he thinks. No way, you say. Don't even want to go there, you think. All those "stories" inside your history professor's head. The excitement your botany professor gets from explaining why some flowers are white and others are lilac, even though they come from two purple parents. Two purple parents? Yeah. Right. The fact remains, however, that if you can figure out how your professors think about their content areas, you'll understand how they want you to think about that content. When you know how you're supposed to think about the information, then you can also anticipate how your professors will test you. Actually, it's not too hard once you get the hang of it.

Professors have you do stuff in their courses. We call this stuff "tasks." Tasks can be things like knowing what kind of tests you'll have and the level of thinking that is required on these tests. Tasks can be in-class essays or out-of-class papers. They can be multiple-choice tests that ask you to memorize a bunch of facts, or critical reviews that make you think till it hurts. Tasks can be carried out on the computer, in class, or in the privacy of your own room. You may think this all sounds pretty simple. You go to class; your professor tells you that you will have a multiple-choice test on Friday. Bingo. Task known. Sometimes, however, it's not that easy.

Have you ever studied for a test really hard but then couldn't figure out where your professor's questions came from? Mars maybe? If that's happened to you, chances are you didn't understand the task. So knowing how to prepare for exams is one reason it's important to know what a course's tasks are. Why else is it important to know the tasks? How do you figure it all out? And what if you can't figure it out? What do you do then? Read on.

Why Bother Figuring Out the Tasks?

Part of being successful in college is figuring out what others expect of you, especially your professors. When you were in high school, you had your teachers for a longer period of time, often for the entire school year. You were taught in smaller groups and, therefore, you got to know your teachers fairly well. You were evaluated through homework, quizzes, and frequent tests. Chances are you earned a gazillion points in any one grading period. In addition, your teachers may have given you lots of supports—study guides, terms to know, questions to think about—before each major test. All of these things helped you to figure out the type of questions and information that your teachers might ask you. You knew what you had to do, perhaps without having to think much about it. You made good grades on your tests and report cards. And you probably were able to earn extra credit to boot. Life was easy then. In college, figuring out what you have to do—the tasks, that is—can be more of a challenge, but it is a key skill to have if you want to be successful. Why, you ask?

> **URBAN LEGEND**
>
> A university professor gave an examination question in which he asked, "What is the difference between ignorance and apathy?" A professor had to give an A+ to a student who answered, "I don't know and I don't care." Trust us—it's not quite that easy to earn an A+.

● If you can figure out the task, you'll know how your professor wants you to think about the material. Some professors may ask you to think about information in a superficial way. They may simply want you to memorize information rather than to apply it. But most want you to think beyond what is in the book and lecture. They expect you to make connections between ideas. Once you understand how to think about course material, half the battle is over. Okay. Only a quarter of the battle is over.

● If you can figure out the task, you can select the appropriate learning strategies. If you use the wrong kind of strategies when you study, you're just spinning your wheels. Wasting time. Getting nowhere. In situations where you put lots of time into studying for a test and still did poorly, your strategies probably didn't match the task.

SAD BUT TRUE 😞

Kevin was enrolled in Introduction to Anthropology. There were so many boldfaced words in the text that he was sure he knew what he had to do to prepare for the multiple-choice exams—in a word, memorize. For the first test, Kevin made about 150 flash cards to learn all of the new terms. He'd flip through them waiting for the bus, before class started, any time he found a few free minutes. He also put in a good deal of study time at home and felt prepared because he had every card memorized, front and back, before the exam. Imagine Kevin's surprise when he couldn't answer the majority of the questions because they focused on synthesizing and applying all of the terms he had dutifully memorized. He realized that although he knew definitions, he really did not understand what they meant in the big picture. He began to get a handle on the fact that he needed to make a change in his study approach before the next test.

● If you can figure out the task, you can earn good grades on the exam. And (following this line of thinking), if you score high on the tests, you'll make a good grade in the course and even learn some cool information in the process. It's important to

A moment's insight is sometimes worth a life's experience.

—Oliver Wendell Holmes

think about what you are supposed to do in each of your college classes. Once you know the task, you should be able to choose the right strategies.

⊕ THE INSIDE SCOOP

There's a link between figuring out the task and being successful in college. It has been shown on several occasions that students who can figure out what their instructors expect from them do better in college. In fact, even if you start out not understanding the task, but figure it out after the first exam and make adjustments in your studying, you will end up doing well.

Figuring It Out

Occasionally you will have a professor who is easy to figure out. That's not saying you'll earn an A. We simply mean that she's straight up about what she expects from you. She may even say things such as "This is what you have to do to be successful in here" or "I want you to think about the material in this way" or "Here are some studying tips for this class. Do these things, and you'll do well." But most of the time, it takes a little more maneuvering. More often than not, figuring out the task is like putting together the pieces of a puzzle where each piece comes from a different place. If you're having problems figuring out what it is your professor expects, you have several sources to tap. Remember that you may have to get bits and pieces from most or all of these sources in order to have a complete picture of the task.

> Results! Why, man, I have gotten a lot of results. I know several thousand things that won't work.
>
> —Thomas A. Edison

READ YOUR SYLLABUS

At the very least, your syllabus should outline your professor's expectations. It should tell you if you will have multiple-choice or essay tests. You should also find information on how many tests you will have and the approximate dates they will be given. There also may be hints on the syllabus about the type of thinking your professor expects. For example, if your syllabus states something to this effect: "In this course, you will be expected to read your text, take detailed notes both in lecture and in your discussion group, and then make connections between what you read and what you hear," you can be fairly certain that you will have to synthesize the information and think about ideas at deeper levels.

THINK ABOUT HOW YOUR PROFESSOR LECTURES

After a while, you'll catch on to the idea that professors have different lecture styles. Some profs will make a general statement first ("All dogs have fleas") and then fill in the details ("Some dogs have more fleas than others. Indoor dogs have fewer fleas than outdoor dogs...yadda, yadda, yadda"). This is an *inductive* style of lecturing: the key point is given, then followed by details. Other professors will provide the details first ("Some dogs have more fleas than others. Indoor dogs have fewer fleas than outdoor dogs...yadda, yadda, yadda") and then finally get to the big picture statement ("All dogs have fleas"). This is a *deductive* style of lecturing: details are given first and followed by the key point. Most students prefer the inductive style because they at least are aware of the big picture and can get that in their notes. Sometimes when a professor is throwing lots of details out there first, it becomes harder to figure out the main point. Professors can also lecture in a storylike fashion, something that is very common in the humanities, particularly history. Or there may be little lecture and more discussion or demonstration or problem-solving.

Besides the lecture style, we suggest you pay attention to the type of information the professor stresses from the textbook. History profs will often stress the order in which things happened (chronology), political science profs will stress charts and flowcharts, and science profs will stress diagrams. The point we want to make is that sometimes students aren't aware that thinking about how their professor lectures gives them some important insights into the way questions will be asked on the exam.

😟 SAD BUT TRUE

Sonja was enrolled in a botany class that she enjoyed very much because she was thinking of majoring in landscape architecture. She had taken advanced biology in high school along with other life sciences, so she felt very comfortable and confident about doing well in the course. But her professor taught quite differently from her high school teachers. Both lectured and had students work through computer modules, but her college prof used loads of diagrams during his lectures. Sometimes they were similar to those that were in the textbook, but other times Professor Wilson seemed to produce them out of thin air. Not only did he know botany, he could also draw! Because Sonja could hardly draw a stick figure, she never put any of the diagrams in her notes. Few students did. Instead, they just wrote down the lecture material—that is, until after the first test. Sonja couldn't believe it. She studied long and hard for the test, but because she had never been tested over diagrams in the past, she ignored them. And the test was full of them. Almost every question referred in some way to one of the diagrams. By using diagrams as a big part of his lectures, Professor Wilson was sending a message, a message that Sonja and many others in the class didn't even recognize.

TALK WITH PAST STUDENTS

👂 LISTEN UP

As you are working on figuring out the task, it's important to make sure that you are very clear what you will be expected to include when you're answering identification questions. On our campus, for example, most history professors give tests that require students to answer identification questions in addition to essay questions. In order to get full credit on the identification items, students must first define the item and then explain the significance of it. Students who give only the definition receive only half credit. So ask rather than lose half the points.

It really doesn't matter if they made an A or an F in the course. The purpose of talking to former students is to get as much information as possible about how the professor tests. And we don't mean the exact questions she asked, because the same items usually aren't used from term to term. If the tests you will take are multiple-choice, try to find out if the questions on past tests focused on facts (who, what, when, where questions) or on higher levels of thinking, asking you to recognize examples or apply information to new situations. If you will have essay exams or other kinds of exams that require you to write, ask former students how the exams were graded and what kinds of information you would need to include in order to maximize your score.

If your task involves writing—essays, short answers, or identification items—be sure to find out if your professor subtracts points for spelling, grammar, and usage errors. A few professors we know do, because they see it as their task not only to help you learn their discipline, but also to encourage you to improve your writing skills. Actually it is a trend now on college campuses for courses to have goals beyond teaching basic content. Improving writing skills and developing critical thinking skills are two popular targets.

TALK WITH CLASSMATES IN THE KNOW

There will always be students in your class who seem to hang on every word the professor says, ask thought-provoking questions, take notes that look as though they were professionally done, and, in general, have it together. If you don't have much of a clue about what you're supposed to be doing, chat with those who do. Ask them how they are studying and the types of strategies they are using in order to prepare for the exams. Be honest and tell them that you're having a hard time figuring out what the professor expects, but don't give them the idea that you are trying to get out of doing the work on your own. For example, saying something like, "Hey dude. Can I copy your notes?" after you have slept through class will probably not endear you to the student who has taken some time to figure out the task and then does what he needs to do.

LOOK AT RETIRED EXAMS

Depending on your campus, you may or may not have access to old, "retired" exams. Some campuses keep test files in the library where students can check them out. Some professors will let you look at retired tests—or at the very least provide you with examples of questions that they have used on previous exams. Another resource for old exams is students who have taken the course in previous terms. Sometimes even campus groups, such as Greek organizations and student governments, keep test files. If you have access to retired exams, don't make the mistake of trying to memorize answers to the questions or just studying the information required to answer questions on this particular test. The purpose of looking at old exams is to give you an idea of how the professor tests.

LISTEN FOR "IN YOUR FACE" COMMENTS

We are always amazed at the kinds of information students *don't* attend to or put in their notes. We have been in classes where professors give students very clear signals about the task, in some cases almost hitting them over the head with information that they will have to know. All too often such signals go unheeded by students, particularly if these pearls of wisdom are thrown out right at the beginning of class when students are settling in or in the last couple of minutes when the prof is winding down his lecture and students are already putting away their notebooks and thinking about something else. So be smart. When your professor makes a really profound statement like "Gee, that would make an interesting essay question," write it down in your notes with a big *TQ* (for test question) in the margin. Such statements are another piece of the puzzle of determining the task.

TALK TO A TUTOR

Because campus tutors work with and talk to lots of students, they often have insight into what is expected of you in the courses you are taking. Even if you are not having trouble with the content, you can make an appointment to run your studying approach by the tutor. If you are memorizing when you should be synthesizing, the tutor can usually set you straight.

> **LISTEN UP**
>
> It's good advice to verbalize the task, or what you think the task is, as you are trying to figure it out. Talking yourself through it sometimes helps you see if your reasoning is faulty and realize what you do and don't understand about the task.

But What If You Still Don't Get It?

If you have exhausted all of your sources and resources and still can't figure out what your professor wants, don't give up. There are still a couple of things you can do.

Most students who have difficulty figuring out the task don't realize it until after the first test. They think they know what they are doing, and they put time into studying, but they earn a disappointing score on the first test. Now is not the time to throw in the towel. Now is the time for regrouping and action. Rather than shoving your exam or paper inside your backpack, spend some time going over it to see if you can figure out the kinds of things you did wrong. If you took a multiple-choice test, what types of items did you miss? If you took an essay exam, why did you have points taken off? If you did poorly on a paper, why? Take some time to see what you did right and what you did wrong. Look for patterns. Ask yourself: How does Professor Smith want me to think about this information? Just what is the task? How can I change my test preparation behaviors to match what she wants? We have found that most students who spend time evaluating their test performance end up improving their grade significantly on the next exam, paper, speech, and so forth.

Another alternative is to make an appointment to talk with the professor. Take your test or paper along (unless your prof keeps them) and ask him to go over it with you. Make notes about what he says; these comments may help you as you continue through the course. Students tell us that having a conference with their professor after a poor performance may be a bit intimidating at first, but that they gain information that will help them do better. As we have said earlier, most professors want their students to succeed and they are willing to meet with them if they are having problems. Sometimes it's enough just to say to your professor something like "I thought I was on the right track. These are the things that I did…. What am I doing wrong? How should I be thinking about this material?" Questions such as these show her that you are serious about learning in her course.

If you realize right from the start that you're lost and clueless about what direction to take in learning the material, don't wait until after the first test. Go—run—to see your professor as soon as you realize that you don't know what the heck is going on. If you are hesitant or really nervous about talking with

URBAN LEGEND

After learning about conditioning, a psychology class decided to train their professor using positive reinforcement. In order to pull this off, the class only paid attention when the professor stood in one specific corner of the room. When he wandered from that spot students started shuffling papers, talking to each other, and generally looking disinterested. The story goes that eventually the professor was "trained" to stand in that one corner for the entire lecture. Yeah. Right. This one has been around for a while. "Training" your profs really isn't this easy.

your professor face-to-face, see if it's possible to use email. A word of caution, however: No matter how lost and confused you are, try to articulate your difficulties. Telling your professor that you don't know what your problems are—or worse yet, blaming your lack of understanding on him—will not get you anywhere.

Recognize that even if you are having trouble figuring out what you're supposed to be about, there are alternatives to doing nothing. Talking with your prof is the best place to start.

Smart Strategy Selection

Although we will discuss specific test-taking strategies later in *College Rules!*, it's important to understand that the strategies you use to study should match the task. Remember, you can't choose the most efficient and effective strategies if you don't know what it is you're supposed to do. Here are just some of the tasks that professors may expect from you:

- a multiple-choice test that mostly asks you to memorize information

- a multiple-choice test that asks for "higher-level" thinking, perhaps including questions focusing on examples or the applications of ideas

- an essay test that asks you to analyze, synthesize, or critique theories, events, and so forth

- a paper that asks you to provide support for your stance

- identification questions that ask you to define a term and also give examples of the item or explain its significance

- problems where you have to show your work, even though it's a multiple-choice test

- a speech or presentation

Although this is a rather short list of different tasks (there are lots and lots of other alternatives), how you would approach each of them would differ, in some cases pretty dramatically. For example, if you have a multiple-choice test that just asks you to memorize, making a bunch of flash cards with the terms and definitions would probably get the job done. But if the multiple-choice test has questions that ask you to provide examples or link ideas, you might want to ask yourself how and why questions, use strategies that help you visualize how the ideas are connected, and work with a study group.

We have found that a good number of students tend to categorize tasks too broadly to be of much help. They can tell you if the task is a test or a paper and, if it is a test, whether it has multiple-choice, matching, essay, or short answer questions. But that's about it. If you can only identify the task in the broadest sense, you're probably going to have some difficulty deciding on the right strategies and approaches for studying.

Quick and Dirty

○   When you have defined the task, you have figured out what it is your professor expects from you. Defining the task involves knowing not just the type of test or other activity you will be facing, but also the level of thinking necessary to complete the task.

○   It's important to figure out the task so that you can think about the material in the way your prof wants you to, so that you can select the best strategies to use, and so that you earn good grades on tests and papers.

○   To figure out the task, use your syllabus, think about your professor's lecture style, talk with students who have taken the class before and with current classmates, look at old exams, listen carefully for hints, and meet with a tutor.

○   If you still don't get it, meet with your prof or regroup after the first test, analyzing it to see where you went wrong.

CHAPTER 14

TAKE NOTE!

When I give a lecture, I accept that
people look at their watches, but
what I do not tolerate is when they
look at it and raise it to their ear
to find out if it stopped.

—Marcel Achard

"What will be on the lunch menu?" "What's going to happen today on my favorite soap?" "This guy (girl) sitting next to me is kind of cute. Should I talk to him (her)?" These are some of the burning questions that may run through your mind as you sit in yet another lecture. Because taking lecture notes seems like such a passive activity (you have to just sit there, after all), many college students find it difficult to pay attention for the entire period, especially if the professor is, well, dry, dull, and boring.

Taking notes is an everyday occurrence in college so it's something that you need to do well. As a matter of fact, you need to do it extremely well. Students who take good lecture notes and know how to use them to their advantage usually do better on tests. Plain and simple. And we all know that

DO YOUR HOMEWORK

We're going to warn you right up front that we have found that, for some reason, students are more reluctant to change their note-taking habits than just about any other studying practice. But the information in this chapter may be some of the most helpful in the entire book. Try out the suggestions. You just might find that you'll have a set of notes that will be an awesome study tool.

doing better on tests leads to good grades, an excellent GPA, a great job...the Presidency. Good lecture notes are the meat and potatoes of learning.

Write On: Some Terrific Note-Taking Tips

No matter how you take lecture notes, there are some general tips that cut across all formats. Your goal here is to get to the point that these behaviors become routine, no matter what class you're in.

BE THERE—ON TIME

Nothing is worse than plopping down in your seat, out of breath from rushing up five flights of stairs, right when the professor is beginning to lecture (or worse yet, after she has started), and finding that your pen has fallen somewhere into the bottomless pit of your backpack. By the time you've found your pen and are ready to take notes, the professor is already wound up and going full steam ahead—and you, my friend, have missed some really important stuff. So move it. Get your butt in gear. Try your best to get to class a few minutes before it starts so that you can be ready to go when your professor starts lecturing.

SIT IN FRONT

Don't be shy. Let the prof see your smiling face—especially in large lecture classes. Students who sit in the front of the classroom tend to listen better, ask questions, take better notes, and even perform better on tests than students who hide in the back. It's especially important to sit in the front if the visuals the professor uses are of poor quality (things like overheads, PowerPoint presentations, or material written on the board) or if the acoustics are bad. On our campus, even some of the smaller

Q THE INSIDE SCOOP

Students who sit near the front of the classroom perform better than those who sit in the back. In fact, the closer to the front you sit, the better you'll tend to do. Those who sit closest to the front tend to make more grades of A and B, those in the middle, more Cs, and those near the back...well, you figure it out. The message here: The nearer to the front the better, especially in large lecture classes.

lecture rooms in major classroom buildings have such poor acoustics that students in the back of the room have to strain to understand what we are saying.

BE PREPARED

Have everything out and ready to go when the lecture begins. As soon as you get to class, get everything out that you think you will need. Take out your notebook and pen and have clean sheets of paper ready to go. Once you're set, if you still have time, take a few minutes to read over your notes from the last lecture. It will get your mind ready for the lecture to come and will help you keep up your attention better.

DO YOUR OWN THING

Outlines or other visuals provided by your professor are a great way to help you organize your notes, but think of them as only a place to begin. It has been our observation that when professors provide students with an outline to frame their lecture, or when they put terms and definitions on the board, students will copy the professor's notes and then drift off...zzzzz. Keep in mind that most outlines are just that—something brief meant to help you organize your notes and give you the key points. As your professor lectures on each point, include the additional explanations in your notes. We can guarantee you that your prof will expect you to be able to fill in the details on test day.

USE A BINDER, PLEASE

We're not sure why binders fell out of favor with college students. Perhaps it's because they are a bit more bulky to carry around. Whatever the reason, binders are much better for holding your notes than spiral-bound notebooks (and they're cheaper in the long run since you can reuse them). Using a binder makes it easier to organize your notes. If you miss class, you can easily insert notes that you copy from someone else; class handouts are also easily inserted. Gone is the worry that you'll lose important handouts because they fell out of your notebook. And if someone wants to borrow your notes for a particular class day, you don't have to give them your entire notebook, just the pages they need.

WRITE LEGIBLY

Because you'll have to use your notes to study from, write as legibly as you can while still taking notes at 100 miles per hour. You'll be upset with yourself if you can't even decipher your own handwriting. No scribbling allowed.

KEEP AT IT

Write for the entire period. It's much better to get too much information in your notes than too little. Because listening to a lecture is a relatively passive task, you need to do something to keep active. If you're not writing, your mind will wander or, worse yet, you'll nod off and drop your pen, which will clatter loudly on the floor. But if you are actively listening and writing, the chances are you will attend better.

HEADS UP

Listen for cues during the lecture. Some professors lecture in an organized manner. Their lectures tend to flow, and they provide you with cues as they talk. If you are fortunate enough to have professors like this, listen for words or voice changes that alert you to important information. For example, professors may cue you to important lists ("There are three explanations of why people forget information. First..."), definitions ("Psychologists define repression as..."), examples ("Examples of schizophrenic behaviors include..."), or rhetorical questions that they then proceed to answer ("Why are there several explanations of how memory works?"). They may also throw out very obvious cues ("This is really important for you to know, so be sure to get it in your notes"). Also listen for voice changes. The more important the information, the greater the tendency for professors to talk louder and slower. Finally, don't forget about visuals. When a professor presents visuals, especially diagrams, that can be a cue that you will be expected to know that material at test time. Some students even keep their text open while taking notes so they can make notes on the diagrams in the book as the instructor is explaining them.

Nothing is a waste of time if you use the experience wisely.

—Auguste Rodin

Brian hated history. And so when he had no choice but to register for an introductory history course to round out his schedule the first term, he was not a happy camper. To add insult to injury, his professor talked a mile a minute and, in Brian's mind, lectured in a really bizarre way. He started every lecture with a bunch of facts, facts that were hard to connect together. Brian was certain that he wouldn't be tested on these facts so he never wrote them down. He always used this part of class to zone out or to work some of his math problems. He figured he would wait until the important material came and then just write that down. No use in wasting paper and cluttering up his notes. But by the time his history professor got to the "good stuff," Brian was off in la la land. If he did catch anything, he had a hard time making sense of it since he had effectively tuned out a big part of the lecture.

By the time the first exam came around, about four weeks into the term, Brian had about ten pages of notes—total—and most of them weren't in any shape he could use to study from. After he failed that test, he decided that he'd better rethink his approach to note-taking. Even though it was like torture, he began to listen more attentively and to write down all those facts that the prof spouted out. Pretty quickly he realized that when his prof did discuss the important stuff—the big picture—those facts served a purpose: they outlined the key points of the professor's forthcoming lecture. Brian still hated history and still found it difficult to stay focused during the lectures, but he discovered that he could take notes from professors who lectured this way. Brian didn't exactly ace the class, but even after his awful performance on the first test, he managed a C+ in the course.

LISTEN, THINK (FAST), AND THEN WRITE (FAST)

Accept the fact that you are not going to be able get down every word the professor utters. Students who try to get down everything that is said in lecture usually wind up getting half thoughts. If you have ever found yourself trying to take notes and getting half a phrase written before the teacher is on to another idea (which you have already missed) then you know how frustrating taking notes can be. But actually, it is not that important to get down every single word. Instead, try listening to the entire thought, quickly paraphrasing what was said, and then writing that information in your own words. Remember, ideas that simply go in your ears and out your pen, without going through your brain, are not going to be well remembered later.

REVIEW YOUR NOTES REGULARLY

You don't want to wait until a day or two before a test to start reviewing your notes. We suggest that you go through at least the notes for the previous class as soon as possible after class. Do it whenever you have small pockets of time. In addition, try reviewing your notes from the previous day while you are waiting for class to begin.

COMPARE NOTES WITH A CLASSMATE

One of the best strategies for making sure your notes are complete is to set aside some time to compare your notes with someone else's. We suggest you choose someone from each of your classes who seems on the ball—it can really help you clear up confusing points or missing ideas.

⚡ GET WIRED

If you know how to type and if you can afford it (two big ifs) buy a laptop computer and use it to take notes in your classes. The advantages: (1) you can organize your notes as you type; (2) it's easy to reduce or add to the notes you have taken; (3) your notes are always legible; and (4) it helps you concentrate and pay closer attention to what is said.

Taking a good set of lecture notes that can stand the test of time takes more than just showing up. You need to come to class prepared to take notes for the full period, and you need to review your notes on a daily basis.

Be Creative: Use the Split-Page Method of Note-Taking

The best method of note-taking we have found is called the split-page method. It's called this because you divide (or split) your paper into two columns, as shown in the figure on page 159. You take notes on the wider right-hand side and then use the left-hand side (which will have a two- or three-inch margin) to write questions or annotations once the lecture is over. You can buy special notebook paper, usually called law paper, that has the wider margins already set for you, but this paper often costs three times more than the regular stuff. So we suggest splitting your own paper. To split your page, you can either draw lines on several sheets of paper before you go to lecture, or you can simply fold the narrower margin back.

Once you have your paper ready, keep these tips in mind:

- Date your notes in case you need to refer to notes given on a specific day.

- Number each page so that if you take pages out of your notebook to study or to lend to a classmate, you'll be able to get them back in the right place.

- Take notes in the larger right-hand space. (You'll write in the left-hand margin later.)

- Write in pen rather than pencil. Pencil fades, smudges, and smears. This can be a big problem if you have cumulative exams and you can't read your notes from two months ago.

At last you are ready to take some notes. Here are some guidelines to taking notes in an organized way:

- Write in simple paragraph form. Don't try to make detailed outlines. Students who outline tend to leave out lots of important information and often concentrate more on the outline itself than on the material that should be included.

- Indent or underline key points. This will help you distinguish main ideas from details.

- Skip a line or two between those key points. This way you will know at a glance when there is a shift in ideas.

- Identify examples. Marking them with an X or in some other way alerts you that the info is important to study.

- Number lists. Often tests will ask for "three causes of acne" or for "four reasons why you shouldn't squeeze pimples." If you know how many reasons or causes there are to study right from the start, you will do better.

- Write in phrases. Don't attempt to write in complete sentences, but be sure to get enough information so that you understand the point.

Use abbreviations. It saves a considerable amount of time. For example, if your professor is lecturing on President Kennedy, it's much quicker to abbreviate it as "JFK" rather than to write it out each time.

LISTEN UP

Although taping lecture notes may sound like a good idea, in most cases it's not. Think about the negatives. If you tape, you're probably going to pretty much ignore the lecture during class. Also, you'll have to listen to the lecture again (not a very efficient use of your time) and you'll still have to take notes at some point. Even in difficult courses, we recommend taking notes during class and using the time you would have used to listen to your taped notes to rehearse and review the notes you have taken.

To see how your notes should look, consider the example opposite. It shows you how a page of notes taken in the split-page method might look.

You've taken notes in the larger right-hand side of your notebook paper but you're not quite finished yet. (We warned you that there was a lot to this note-taking business.) Now it's time to do something with that smaller left-hand side. As soon as possible after the lecture, take 10 or 15 minutes to read through your notes (it's a great way to review while the information is relatively fresh in your memory). As you read your notes, you can do one of two things. You can either

1. write questions in the margins that you can ask yourself as you study or

2. annotate key words and then verbally turn those key words into questions when you study.

When you get to this stage, the important thing is to think about information that your professor will ask *and* the way you think she will ask it. Think back to what we said earlier about understanding the task. We said it then, but hey, it never hurts to repeat the good stuff: the key to doing well on exams is to figure out what your professor wants you to know. As you are writing your questions or annotations in the margins of your lecture notes, what your prof

> Examine what is said, not him who speaks.
>
> —Arabian proverb

wants becomes crucial. If there is not a match between the types of questions you pose in your notes and those that your professor asks, you're sunk.

title of lecture

11/10/01	Memory Lecture Notes

3 types of memory   3 DIFFERENT MEMORIES

annotations or questions

key point

What is sensory store?   1.   Sensory Store (SS)
                                 —lots of info comes in that
                                 we don't pay attention to

What function does   —sometimes called a "gatekeeper"
STM serve?   —only info that's processed (gets
                             attention) can go into

supporting info. indented and organized

How does info get
into STM?   2.   Short-term Memory (STM)
                           —limited capacity (7 + or - 2)

Define and give an ex.   but
of chunking   —can be expanded by
                             → chunking

What are the   def grouping things
characteristics   together into units in order
of STM?   to remember more
                           ex Soc. Sec # is

2- or 3-inch margin

                           remembered as 3 "chunks"
                           rather than 9 indiv. pieces
                           of info
                      —is short
                      —only lasts ~30 sec unless info
                        is rehearsed

There is a small business in our town, strategically located near campus, that sells notes from a variety of core courses offered on campus. They hire students who are taking the classes to be their note-takers. Then before exams students can purchase packets of notes (they are generally pretty expensive). The notes are typed and printed on a dark red paper that cannot be copied. Hordes of students buy these notes, and often they get shortchanged. Some of the note-takers are hardly stellar students themselves (we know of one instance where the note-taker got a C in the course). Information in the notes is at best incomplete and at worst incorrect. Although this business is certainly enterprising and we are sure the owners make buckets of money, we think it's important for students to learn to take good notes themselves. The message here is, buyer beware.

You're Almost There: Self-Testing Using the Split-Page Method

One of the key advantages of taking notes using the split-page method is that it allows you to do what we call blind self-testing. Think about the way you normally study from your notes. The scenario may go something like this: you open your notes and study by "reading through" them for a period of time. And you probably spend equal amounts of time on everything—things you know well are given the same amount of time as things you are struggling with. When you "feel pretty good" about what you know or you simply run out of time, you quit studying. Does any of this sound familiar?

Although this procedure may have worked fairly well for you in high school, it may not be so successful in college. So we offer you a better way, a way that will help you use your studying time a bit more wisely. Try this approach:

1. Begin by doing what you perhaps have always done: read through your notes a couple of times to review and familiarize yourself with the major topics. But don't stop there.

2. Fold your notes back so that all you can see is the narrower left-hand margin where you have your questions or annotations.

3. Now ask yourself the question or turn your annotation into a question.

4. Try to answer the question without looking at your notes. Say everything you know about the concept, providing explanation and examples when appropriate. Be concise and accurate, but thorough.

5. Now look at your notes. How much of the information did you remember? Was what you said earthshakingly brilliant and accurate, or do you still have a way to go?

6. Continue asking yourself questions as you plow through your notes. Find some way to distinguish the questions you know from those you need to spend more time on. For example, you might check off those that you know or highlight those that you need to study more. Then you will only put in additional time on those questions that you have not checked off.

Self-testing not only is a more efficient way to study your notes, but it will also make you feel more self-confident going into your exams. If you are self-testing correctly, when exam day rolls around, you should know the material and feel confident that you will ace the test.

Different Strokes for Different Folks: Modifying the Split-Page Method

There may be times when you want to modify the split-page method somewhat depending on the types of tests you will have and the type of course you are in. Every course is not a lecture course, after all. In addition, there may be parts of this method that you simply want to modify and personalize. We encourage that! In fact, good students are flexible in the way they use strategies; they change strategies to suit themselves as learners. The one element we strongly suggest you keep, however, is the left-hand margin of your paper for your questions or annotations. This feature allows you to self-test. Here are some ways our students have modified the split-page method to suit their needs.

CONSOLIDATING TEXT WITH LECTURE

In courses where there's lots of overlap between lecture and text, some students like to use the back of their paper to add material that is related to the lecture but is only found in the text. If you are in a course that is taught in this manner, take your notes in the split-page method as described above, but take them on the front of the paper only. Then as you read your text, write notes on the related material on the back of the page. As you study, you will have everything in one place and won't have to bounce from lecture notes to textbook.

DISCUSSION CLASSES

Some classes have discussion sessions once a week, and some rely heavily on discussion all the time. Our students often tell us that it is difficult to take notes during discussion because it's hard to figure out which ideas to include. For discussion classes we suggest a three-column approach to note-taking. In the narrower left-hand column, write the question that is posed by the professor or discussion group leader. Divide the larger space into two columns. In one, jot down student responses. You can jot them all down and sift through them later, or just write down those you think are worthy—ideas that you think would be good to include on an essay exam, for example. In the last column, write any additional comments that your professor makes. Be sure to get down (in brief paragraph form, of course) all of your prof's important points.

LISTEN UP

In many discussion classes, professors create their exam questions based on class discussion. By taking notes during such a class, you are creating a study guide that many of your classmates (those who are not taking notes) will lack. So rather than tuning out during discussions, tune in. There could be lots of good stuff here to use come test time.

VISUALS GALORE

It's common for some professors to lecture using diagrams, particularly in the sciences. The prof will put up a cross-section of a root or a diagram of a cell and wax eloquent about it for 30 minutes. If you have a professor who teaches using diagrams, get reasonable replicas into your notes. It is also important that you get down the lecture notes that go with that diagram. If you have both, you can better determine what your professor wants you to learn and why he has used a diagram to make his point. You might want to draw each diagram on the top of the page and describe it below or divide the larger side of your paper into two columns—one for the diagram and the other for the explanation. When you go back to review your notes for the day, check your textbook for a similar diagram. If one is present, make a note of the page number in your notes so that when you study, you can refer to a visual that may be clearer than yours. This step is particularly important if you're artistically chal-lenged, like we are. (Also remember to write questions or annotations in the margins of your lecture notes to use for self-testing.)

LECTURE NOTES ON THE WEB

With more and more professors using Web-based components as part of their courses, notes on the Web are becoming common. We know several professors who have student workers scan in their notes after each class. Although we believe that this actually may encourage some students to take the easy way out—you know, skip class and then download the prof's notes—they can be very helpful if you compare your notes with your professor's as a way to make sure your notes cover all the important points. If you have access to notes on the Web, go to class everyday and take the best

SAD BUT TRUE 😞

Jen's professor put his notes on the Web for students to use. Because he wanted students to take notes on their own, however, he waited until a few nights before each exam to post his notes. Jen never really took notes in class because she fig-ured she would just rely on what the professor posted. After all, she thought, he is the expert, right? So why should I go to all the trouble of taking notes—lousy ones at that—when I can just copy his great notes? But the unthinkable happened and Jen found herself in a heap of trouble. Two nights before the first exam there was a tremendous thunderstorm that knocked out power on campus for an entire day. Jen was unable to download the notes until a few hours before test time. To make matters worse, with no electricity she couldn't email her classmates to get their notes. Because she hadn't taken any notes of her own, she didn't have much to review and had to make a last-ditch effort to learn some of the material by going back and rereading the text (by candlelight to boot). Jen learned a valuable lesson, but at quite a cost.

possible notes you can. Once your prof's notes are posted on the Web, download them and compare yours with his. Insert important information you may have missed into your own notes, then read through the expanded notes to review. Remember, though, that having access to your professor's notes (or anyone else's) does not take the place of taking notes yourself.

Taking good notes and being able to use them efficiently and effectively is one of the keys to being a successful student. It's a skill you should develop early in your college career.

Quick and Dirty

○ Some note-taking behaviors should be routine. For every class, you should be ready to take notes when the prof begins lecturing, write legibly, keep at it for the entire period, listen carefully, write in simple paragraph form, and review your notes regularly.

○ In order to take notes in an organized way, use the split-page method, annotating or writing questions based on the information in your notes.

○ Self-test as a way of reviewing for your exams.

○ Know how to modify your note-taking for situations other than straight lecture classes.

CHAPTER 15

GETTING IN GEAR: PREPARING TO READ YOUR TEXTS

There is an art of reading, as well as an art of thinking, and an art of writing.

—Isaac Disraeli

P reparing to read is really good for students, yet we have a hard time convincing most to do it. However, we are not going to let our prior failures prevent us from telling you about the amazing benefits of warming up for reading. So...read on.

For most things in life you warm up in some way. You stretch before you work out, run your car for a few minutes before driving it on cold days, and tune up your guitar before you play. But students rarely think about warming up before learning—they just go into it cold. Really, this is how you were taught to do it during your entire school career. You were expected to go from literature class to math class to Spanish class without doing anything to help you switch gears from one subject to another. But you will find that you are a much more effective learner when you take the time to warm up before you start to read—or before you go into a lecture, for that matter.

Preparing to read your texts doesn't have to take long. All we are asking for is a few minutes of your time—five to ten minutes in most cases. Basically, you just want to get a sense of what the text will cover. You also want to think about what you already know about that topic. That's it. We know it sounds pretty basic, but it is a crucial step that many students skip.

THE INSIDE SCOOP

Students who take the time to warm up before reading remember more of what they've read. As an added bonus, these students are also able to concentrate better and make stronger connections between ideas—this can really come in handy come exam time.

Get to Know Your Textbooks

Before you begin to read anything in your texts, take a few minutes to familiarize yourself with their contents. Why? Your textbooks are one of the key components of learning. In fact, about 85 percent of all the learning you do in college involves text, so becoming familiar with the contents of each book helps you better use one of the most important tools for learning. Each textbook is written with some overarching plan in mind, but this organizational design is not immediately noticeable to most students, who usually just open up to the first chapter and start reading. By previewing a few chapters before you start to read, you can get a sense of the author's purpose as well as the format, structure, and design of the book.

SAD BUT TRUE

Marcus, a first-semester freshman, was having some trouble. The college did not receive his student loan check. After many, many phone calls he thought he had finally straightened things out. But he also didn't get the money he needed to buy books. He was getting way behind, but there was nothing he could do about it, or so he thought. During the third week of class, one of his instructors noticed that he didn't have the text and told him about a service offered by the university whereby he could borrow up to $200 interest-free for buying books, paying bills, and so on. This was just what he needed until his loan came through. The moral to Marcus's story: Find out about the services offered by your college—no one wants to see you going without your books.

How do you preview the text? Follow these suggestions.

1. **Start with the table of contents.** The questions below will help you identify the organization of the material. They will also get you thinking about what you already know about the topic.

   - How many chapters are there?

   - Are the chapters grouped by idea or unit? If so, what are these ideas or units?

   - Does the table of contents contain detailed information about the headings and subheadings in each chapter?

   - What do you already know, if anything, about the ideas contained in the text?

2. **Read the preface or introduction.** It's amazing how much helpful advice is contained in these sections. The following questions will help you pull out hints for reading and thinking about the content.

   - What is the author's philosophy of the topic?

   - What advice does the author have about reading or studying this material?

   - What motivated the author to write this book?

3. **Examine the material at the end of the book.** There are usually several aids contained at the end of a textbook. These questions will help you identify what is available for you there.

   - Is there a glossary of terms? If so, skim some of the words. How many are somewhat familiar to you?

   - How is the book indexed? Are there both general and specialized indexes? Are there appendices or activities?

   - Are there answers to problems or questions?

   - What other features appear at the end of the text?

4. **Preview a couple of text chapters.** Previewing will allow you to become familiar with the structure and format of each chapter. The information you will find in response to these questions will help you see the "big picture."

- How difficult to read does the writing in the book appear to be?

- How are the chapters organized?

- Are there headings and subheadings?

- Are there boldfaced and italicized words? If there are both, on what occasions is each of these two font types used?

- Do the chapters begin with objective questions or statements?

- Are there introductions to each chapter or text section? If there are, what do these introductions tell you about the units or chapters you will be reading?

- Do the chapters contain figures, diagrams, pictures, or other graphics? If so, what kind of information is depicted (is it key information or supporting information)?

- Do the chapters end with summary paragraphs, thought questions, problems, or exercises?

> As knowledge increases,
> wonder deepens.
> —Charles Morgan

🔊 LISTEN UP

Many students buy used books to save some money. We suggest you skim through the text and select a book that has not been written in or highlighted. We've heard that some students actually look for highlighted books, figuring that someone has already done the work of selecting key information for them. But what if the previous owner failed the course?

Warming Up

Think about the last time you studied. Did it take you a good five or ten minutes to begin to focus on your reading? If so, you were getting yourself ready to read in that time. You were getting rid of distractions and getting your mind ready to learn. But if you did not warm up and you were trying to really read or study during this time, those five to ten minutes were wasted because you were not really concentrating.

One of the best reading warm-ups that can actually help you learn more during your reading is called prereading. When you preread, you go over the text chapter before you actually read it. We know this sounds like extra work, but stick with us. We would never suggest anything that would *waste* your time, and we guarantee you that it will be a good thing in the long run. There are several benefits to warming up, or prereading, before you start studying.

- It gets you pysched up. Many students tell us that the way that they prepare for reading is looking through the book, not to see what the chapter is going to be about, but to see how many pages they have to trudge through (and how many pages are made shorter by pictures or figures). But knowing what you are about to read actually makes you more interested in learning the topic. You should find yourself much more motivated to learn about the topic at the end of your warm-up.

- It makes your mind ready to learn. By prereading the chapter, you are giving yourself the time you need to be ready to focus on what you are about to learn. This means you will be able to concentrate on your reading and get more out of it. No more wasting time at the beginning of studying: now you have a purpose the minute you sit down at your desk.

SAD BUT TRUE ☹

Meg could never get herself to study her sociology book. All those boldfaced words. Ugh. Every time she tried to read, her mind would wander, to the point where she just decided that she was no good at sociology and never would be. She even started to question her ability to finish her college degree. But the problem was much simpler. When Meg studied sociology she would just sit down, open her text, and attempt to start reading. If she couldn't focus after ten minutes, she would get up, take a break, and plan to come back to it at a later time (a tip she learned at her freshman orientation). What Meg didn't realize is that without warming up in some way, it can take much longer than the ten minutes she gave herself just to get going. Adding a five-minute prereading time could really get her ready to focus.

● It helps you organize. Prereading the text gives you clues to how the author thinks about and organizes the material. As you go through the chapter, you may make an observation such as "Oh, I see. This political science book is set up by decade, but within each decade the author discusses domestic policy, then foreign policy, economic policy, and social policy." During your prereading you are creating a mental outline that you can follow when you read the chapter.

● It creates better comprehension. When you preread, you are figuring out the key ideas in the reading. This will help you understand what you are reading—it sets the groundwork for efficient studying.

We think you'll find these benefits to be worth the little bit of effort required in prereading.

Ready...Set...Read!

You have gotten the big picture of your text and you know how the book is organized. And it really hasn't taken you that long. Now it's time to preview the chapter you are about to read to learn more about the ideas contained within it. There are several steps involved in this stage of prereading, though they should not take you more than a few minutes.

1. **Look at the chapter title and think about what you already know about the topic.** This activity helps you set your purpose for reading and starts helping you get your mind clear of other thoughts and ready to focus on the topic at hand. This will also help you set your reading purpose when you start to read. For example,

THE INSIDE SCOOP

Thinking about what you know about the topic, or activating your prior knowledge about that topic, helps you to be able to connect new information to what you already know. According to research on learning, the ability to relate new information to previous knowledge will help you remember that new information come test time.

in a psychology course you might encounter the chapter title "Aging." Just this one word can get your mind ready to think about the process of growing older.

2. **Read the chapter headings and subheadings.** This information can tell you a lot about the subject. The headings and subheadings point out key concepts and ideas presented in the chapter. They also help you determine the overall organization of those concepts, which makes it easier to see how these ideas relate to one another—the big picture. In our "Aging" chapter, perhaps there is a heading "Sex after 60": something you don't even want to picture, but helpful in understanding some of the concepts the chapter will cover.

3. **Look at the figures, charts, pictures, and graphs.** Graphical aids often tell you about the key points of the chapter, so don't just skip over them. Be sure to read the captions below each graphic during your prereading. We have found that some texts (especially in the sciences) discuss the most crucial points in figures, and by previewing the figures before you read the chapter, you will be better able to connect the text information to the information contained in the figure. Our "Aging" chapter may have a table listing the number of times on average couples have sex from ages 20 to 80. This information can help spark your interest and personalize the material. (Ugh. My grandparents still have sex?)

4. **Scan the boldfaced or italicized words.** In most classes, you will find a lot of new content-specific vocabulary; that is, words that are specific to the subject matter. Usually, knowing the meaning of these content-specific words is key to understanding the material you are about to read. Reading the definitions during your previewing will help you remember their meaning as you read. One word you might learn in our "Aging" chapter would be *geriatric*.

5. **Check out the end of chapter materials.** A summary or some reading questions may appear at the end of the chapter. Knowing what type of information is contained in these materials can help you focus your attention on the key points when you read the chapter.

6. **Make a plan for reading the chapter.**

   Think about these questions as you plan
   your approach:

   - Will it be helpful to read the chapter
     before you attend the lecture? It is usually
     helpful for most classes, but in some
     courses (especially mathematics), students
     get more out of the reading by previewing
     before the lecture and reading after class.

   > Great minds have purposes, others have wishes.
   >
   > —Washington Irving

   - When and where will you read the chapter? It is best to read as soon as
     possible after previewing.

   - Will you need any special materials, such as a calculator, dictionary, and
     so forth?

   - What kind of information will you be looking for? Are there cause and
     effect or compare and contrast relationships? Are there a lot of new terms?
     Is a chronology of events described? Are a variety of viewpoints represented?
     Are several theories discussed?

   - How long do you estimate it will take you to read and understand the chap-
     ter material?

   Try to make prereading a part of your studying routine. The more you practice
   this strategy, the more you will come to value its usefulness.

DO YOUR HOMEWORK

Try this activity at home. Divide the reading for one of your courses in half. For the
first half, just read it like you always do. For the second half, read it after using the
prereading technique. Which section do you remember better? That's all there is
to it. Give it a try tonight. A few minutes of your time and you are on the road
to success.

Quick and Dirty

○   Familiarize yourself with your textbooks. Look at how the information is organized and how the chapters are set up. This type of information will help you see
the big picture that the author had in mind while writing the text.

○   Prereading helps you warm up for reading. Warming up for a few minutes before
reading will help you concentrate better. The big benefit for you is that you will
actually remember what you've read.

○   Preread by reading headings, subheadings, boldfaced words, diagrams or
charts, introductions, and conclusions. It should not take more than a few minutes, and then you will be ready to read.

CHAPTER 16

ACTIVE READING

It is possible to store the mind
with a million facts and still be
entirely uneducated.

—Alec Bourne

Okay. You've sat down to read your anthropology text. You are in a comfy chair dutifully highlighting the pages of the chapter. Armed with a handful of colorful markers, you highlight everything that seems important. How about pink for today? Once you have made it through, you close your book, pat yourself on the back for completing your reading, and breathe a sigh of relief. But wait...what do you remember? Anything? Aghast, you realize that you just wasted another 45 minutes.

No active reading going on here. Active reading requires more than just highlighting. What you want to do is read in a way that will help you remember the information. When you highlight, you tend to read passively. You probably won't remember what you have read five minutes later because instead of learning from what you've read, what you did was mark the information that you wanted to come back to learn later. However, in college you can average over 250 pages of reading per week if you are taking a full course load. This means that you will barely have time to get through the material once, much less go back and reread everything. Now you are thinking, "I just bought a whole bunch of highlighters—one in every color they make. Are you saying that I need to throw them out?" No. You can use them for other things that we'll talk about later. But there are more effective ways to handle the tons of reading you will be faced with.

Active reading feels different than reading passively. Your mind is engaged and you are actually interested in the material. To get a sense of what it means to read actively, try this activity.

1. Choose something to read from either a textbook or a magazine (but make it a nonfiction piece). It should be something you are somewhat interested in, but also something that you don't know a whole lot about. Try to pick a piece that will take you at least five minutes to read.

2. Brainstorm and write down everything you know (or think you know) about the topic. You don't have to be sure of your facts at this point. You are just trying to remember all you know about it.

3. Now, read the article. As you read, check your knowledge. Make some mental notes, or use these marks in the margin of the text:
   + This is information I knew already.
   – This is information I thought I knew, but it turns out I did not.
   ○ This information is new to me.
   ? This information is confusing to me.
   ! I'd like to know more about this piece of information.

4. Check your comprehension. What new information did you learn from this reading? How much information did you already know? Was there some information that you had misconceptions about (you thought you knew something, but the text said otherwise)?

You probably noticed that you read this piece of text differently than you normally read your textbooks. But keep in mind that this was only an activity to help you read actively. We really don't want you to mark your books in this way (though if you have siblings or children in middle school, it would be a great strategy to show them). Why did it feel different to read this way? Because you had a task. You were checking your knowledge as you read. This is a process that good readers use all the time. In fact, when you are reading something in which you have a lot of interest (a novel, an article about a hobby), you probably already use this process without even thinking about it. Basically, you are continually checking the new information with what you already know about the topic and making modifications to your knowledge as you learn new ideas. So how do you create this atmosphere of active reading while you are reading your textbooks? Read on.

> Grace dutifully read her textbooks every night. She was very careful to keep up with assignments because she didn't want to fall behind. So, armed with a pile of high-lighters, she would read and mark. Blue for definitions, yellow for examples, green for details—you get the picture. When she was finished, she would note with satisfaction that she had made quite a few marks. In fact, Grace marked just about everything. Grace was in for a big shock when she started studying for her exams and realized that she didn't remember one thing from her reading. Horrified, she began to read over her highlights (which covered almost all of the text) and found much of the information to be downright confusing. She had the right attitude toward getting her work done, but what Grace needed was a new strategy to help her read for learning.

Reading for Learning

How many times have you sat down to read with your only goal to get the mind-numbing assignment finished? You really had no intention of learning anything from your reading (though that might have been nice). Rather, you were focused on getting it done: "I have to read these 20 boring pages of biology tonight." If this describes you, then you were not really reading for learning. To read for learning you must set a reading purpose, just as you did in the activity above.

Reading for learning from your texts is a three-step process:

1. Ask questions about the headings and figures.

2. Read actively by staying engaged in what you are reading by answering the questions you posed and by taking notes as you read.

3. Review and rehearse the information so you remember it. (This will be discussed in the next few chapters.)

Did you ever notice how your textbooks have those blue (or gray) text boxes? The publisher and author who created that text box are saying, "This information is so important that we will pull it out of the text and highlight it in another color so all the readers will be sure to see it." What do most students do when the come across a text box in their reading? You guessed it. They skip over that section—even though it may contain the key to all of the important information presented in the text. Instructors know that students tend to skip text boxes and will often ask questions about that material. Our advice? Read the text boxes, of course.

Strategies for Active Reading

The best strategy we have found to help you set and keep your reading purpose is annotating, that is, taking notes in your text. Unlike in high school, where writing in your books was punishable by death, you own your textbooks in college. You have spent a lot of money on your books and they are yours for better or worse, so make the most out your reading by writing in them.

Some students use underlining or highlighting as a shortcut to learning. They read and highlight what they will come back to later when they are studying for the test. But this method is much less effective than reading to learn the first time because, in reality, highlighting is a passive activity. Annotation, on the other hand, helps you think about and learn the information as you are reading. Then, when you go back to study, you have done a lot of the hard work already.

Annotation is a strategy for active reading wherein you write the key information (such as major points, definitions, and examples) in the margins of your text. You are looking for and marking all of the information you will need to remember from each chapter. Because it gives you a purpose, you'll find that annotation helps you concentrate while reading and actually helps you learn from the text.

Students who annotate their texts perform better on exams than students who did not. (We know. We've done some of this research ourselves.) In addition, students who annotate actually spend less time studying because they have been learning the material as they annotated rather than leaving it until they reviewed for the exam.

Text annotation works because it:

- gives you a purpose for reading

- improves your comprehension

- provides an immediate test of your understanding

- increases your concentration

- keeps you from having to reread the chapters over again

- creates a study tool that will help you prepare for exams

The Nuts and Bolts of Annotation

Before you annotate, you need to get a sense of what the chapter or section is about. That's why we suggest you read brief portions of text—at least a paragraph or two—before you annotate it. If you try to read and annotate at the same time, you will end up writing way too much information, because you think everything is important. Of course, you also might annotate too little because you don't yet know what is important, nor do you have a sense of the big picture.

READ BEFORE YOU WRITE

Read at least one paragraph before you write anything down. The amount you need to read ahead will vary. In some texts, you may be able to read an entire section before annotating; in others, only a paragraph. For example, you can probably read more about "television violence in popular culture" than you can about "the lifespan of the nematode worm" (though we have some good friends who would argue that nematodes make for a fascinating read). It depends on the difficulty of the material and on how much you already know about the topic. So use your best judgment.

THINK ABOUT THE IDEAS YOU'VE READ

If you were going to talk to someone else about the information, what would be important to tell them? This is the material you will annotate. In fact, some of our students take this idea one step further by imagining that they will need to tutor someone on the material. They tell us that their goal is to annotate enough information to be able to teach the topic.

WRITE KEY IDEAS IN THE MARGINS

Your annotations shouldn't be longer than the text itself. Be on the lookout for:

- **Definitions.** These are usually the boldfaced or italicized words in your text.

- **Examples of the main ideas.** Examples often find their way onto your exams. But don't get caught up in using only the text examples. If you can think of an example from your own experience, write it down—you'll be more likely to remember it.

- **Details or characteristics of the main ideas.** You need to annotate this information to get the full picture of each concept. If you just annotate the key ideas, but leave out the details, you won't have enough information to use for studying and will find you need to resort to rereading everything (a big waste of time).

- **Lists.** If your book states, "Scientists have discovered five types of...," be sure to note that information. In fact, even if your text does not explicitly state that the information you are reading is a list, but you notice that it can be summed up in a list, annotate it in this way. For example, if you were reading about procrastination and noticed this list of information, you would annotate it like this:

  > 3 causes of procrast.
  > 1. lack of time mgmt skills
  > 2. lack of topic interest
  > 3. habit

Making your own list will help you organize the information in your memory.

- **Names, dates, and events.** It is not enough, however, just to note the dates; instead, focus on why the dates or events are important. Why do we care about this event? Use dates to provide a chronology of events, but don't use them to memorize facts.

- **Cause and effect or comparison and contrast.** This kind of information is not always obvious in your texts, but it is frequently what professors ask about (especially on essay exams). Whenever you see these kinds of relationships in your texts, you can mark them with a C/E or C/C in the margin.

- **Possible test questions.** Put a big *TQ* in the margin whenever you see something that strikes you as a point you will be tested on.

- **Confusing information.** If there is information you don't understand while you are reading, mark it with a question mark. Then be sure to ask about it in class the next day.

> Do you know the difference between education and experience? Education is when you read the fine print. Experience is what you get when you don't.
>
> —Pete Seeger

REVIEW YOUR WORK

Check your annotations to be sure they make sense. If you had only your annotations to study from, would you have enough information marked? If not, go back and fill in any gaps.

LISTEN UP

Are small margins an excuse for not annotating? Of course not. Then what should you do if your texts have really small margins? Invest in some larger-sized sticky notes to write on, or cut strips of notebook paper and insert them in the binding of each page. We do not suggest taking notes in a separate notebook. It is important to keep the annotations with the original text so you can refer to the text if there is something you do not understand and so you can review important diagrams and figures as you study your notes.

A SAMPLE ANNOTATION

We include this sample for two reasons. First, we want to show you how annotations are organized—to give you a sense of what kind of information to note and how to note it. Second, we actually want you to read about how people remember things. So in addition to examining it for information on how to annotate, read the passage to learn a little bit about how memory works. We will be referring to this information as we show you other strategies later in *College Rules!*

Human Memory System

3 types of storage: SS, STM, LTM

Though every person thinks and remembers information, scientists do not fully understand how the human memory works. Many of the ideas and theories about memory are quite controversial, but most scientists agree that memory involves three different types of storage: sensory store, short-term memory, and long-term memory.

3 MEMORY PROCESSES:
1. Encoding -getting info in
2. Storage -keeping info
3. Retrieval -getting info out

In addition, there are three processes that enable memory storage: encoding (getting information into memory), storage (keeping the information in memory), and retrieval (getting the information back out).

Info enters thru SS -acted on or lost -filters info -info process in SS moves to STM

According to this theory of memory, information enters through the **sensory store** (SS), where it is either acted upon or forgotten. An individual is bombarded with information nearly all the time, much of which is not attended to. Right now as you are reading this passage, you might not be aware of the clock ticking or the hum of a fan or the people talking quietly around you because you are paying attention to your reading. The sensory store can be considered a gatekeeper for the mind. You would become quickly overloaded if you had to attend to all the stimuli around you. The information that is ignored by the sensory store is not processed, or "forgotten." The information that is processed by the sensory store can be encoded into short-term memory.

STM: Limited capacity 5-9 items

Bell phone co. research -phone # 7 digits

Short-term memory (STM) cannot handle much information at one time. In fact, research has indicated that the capacity of short-term (or working) memory is seven plus or minus two items. This means that you can keep anywhere from five to nine ideas in your working memory. The Bell Telephone Company conducted a good deal of this research; thus it is no wonder that your phone number is seven digits long. One can expand the capacity of STM through a process called chunking. **Chunking** is a type of organization in which letters, digits, or words are grouped into some psychologically meaningful or familiar sequence. Consider your social security number. At ten digits, it is beyond the

def chunking -grouping ideas meaningfully to expand capacity of STM (ex) soc. sec #

capacity of STM. However, when the information is chunked into three groups of numbers (186-888-0000), one can easily remember them.

Besides having a limited capacity, short-term memory also suffers from decay after about 30 seconds. That is, information becomes inaccessible after a relatively short period of time. However, information can be renewed in STM through maintenance rehearsal. **Maintenance rehearsal** is the act of mentally repeating the information to be recalled. An example would be looking up a phone number in the phone book then repeating that number to yourself several times as you walk over to the phone to dial it.

Although this process works well for keeping information alive in short-term memory, **elaborative rehearsal,** or adding meaning to the information you are trying to remember, is necessary for storage in long-term memory. For example, if you were introduced to a new person (let's call her Joan), you could say to yourself, "I have an aunt named Joan and this person has blue eyes like my aunt." By connecting meaning with the name rather than merely repeating the name several times, you are more likely to recall it.

Long-term memory (LTM) stores an unlimited amount of information for an unlimited amount of time. LTM holds many different types of information, such as factual knowledge, events, motor skills, perceptual information, beliefs about ourselves and others, and knowledge about familiar environments.

The information contained in LTM must be retrieved before it's used, but unlike in STM, where all the available information can be scanned, LTM information must be recalled using **cues.** This process is similar to using a call number to find a book in the library. LTM also differs from STM in the way information is stored.

Information is usually stored in STM in terms of the qualities of the experience (what was seen, heard, touched, smelled, or tasted) and is often remembered through sound. Information in LTM is stored primarily in terms of meaning (we associate the great taste of grandma's apple pie with the smell of her house and the wealth of experiences we shared with her) rather than sensory images. Although memory does not decay from LTM, there are many theories on why it is often difficult to recall. When we say we can't remember something we are actually saying that we can't access the information from our long-term memory.

Margin notes:

Info lost from STM after 30 sec.

def
maintenance rehearsal—renews info in STM by repeating info. ex. looking up phone #

def
elaborative reh. —adding meaning to info to store in LTM
ex remembering Joan by my Aunt Joan

LTM—unlimited storage of info for unlimited time —many types of info—facts, events, beliefs, etc. —info must be retrieved using cues (unlike STM where info is scanned)

LTM—info stored by meaning
ex grandma's pie

STM—info stored by qualities or senses

Many theories on why we can't access info in LTM—not really forgotten

C/C STM & LTM
T.Q.!!!

Sometimes, returning students tell us that they wished they had the memory of an 18-year-old. They say that when they read, they feel like the information doesn't "stick" like it would if they were younger. If this describes you, then annotation just might be your best strategy for leveling the playing field. When you annotate, you create a permanent record of the key information you'll need to study and you'll be more apt to remember what you've read.

Notice how the information is organized in this example. Definitions and examples are labeled, as are key ideas. Text questions are noted, as are comparison and contrast relationships. In addition, notice how the information in the annotations is abbreviated as much as possible. When you annotate, use any abbreviations you would normally use when taking notes in class. Here are some common abbreviations used by students, but don't feel that you need to stick to these. Be creative and come up with some of your own.

Remember to create and use abbreviations for content-specific terms, such as STM for short-term memory in the passage above. But be careful not to overabbreviate.

ABBREVIATION EXAMPLES

w/	with
b/c	because
b/4	before
w/in	within
$\triangle$	change
$\uparrow\downarrow$	increase or decrease
h'er	however
ex	for example
*	most importantly

☹ SAD BUT TRUE

Scott, a sophomore management major, learned annotation in our course and thought he could do it and save time by utilizing abbreviations. So Scott abbreviated every term in his history text: IR for industrial revolution; MP for the Marshall Plan; 3CoVW for three causes of the Vietnam War. Though this was a great idea in theory, he abbreviated to the point that he couldn't understand what he had written and ended up needing to reread his entire text before his cumulative final. The moral of Scott's story is to read over your annotations to make sure they will make sense the next time you read them. Good annotations stand the test of time.

Studying Your Annotations

When you annotate, you create a study guide you can come back to again and again, which is really useful if you have cumulative finals. Gone is the need to reread your texts. You have already pulled out all of the information you will need to study and (most importantly) you have written it in a way that you understand. And if you find you have to reread something, you can do it selectively.

To study your annotations, use the following steps as a guide:

> **LISTEN UP**
>
> Many students believe that rereading is the best way to remember information from their texts. In fact, rereading is the number one strategy reported by college students. But as you probably learned by reading in the memory passage, simple rereading is less effective than using a strategy that helps you elaborate on the information in a way that makes it meaningful for you.

1. **Cover up the text**. You don't want to reread entire pages, just your annotations.

2. **Read your annotations and rehearse the material**. Ask yourself questions. Do you understand all of the key ideas? Do you understand how all of these concepts relate to each other and how they relate to the larger concepts?

3. **Reread selectively**. If you find a section that is not entirely clear to you, uncover the text and reread only that section.

4. **Test yourself**. Once you are comfortable with the material in the text, try to self-test. Look at chapter headings and subheadings. Cover up the text and the annotations then try to say the information to yourself.

> The man who does not read good books has no advantage over the man who can't read them.
>
> –Mark Twain

Once you have tested yourself several times on the information, you may want to compare what you've read with the information in your lecture notes. This will help you start to pull the ideas together.

If you have a mild case of test anxiety, there is no better cure than feeling confident that you know the information. Self-testing is one of the best strategies to determine what you do and do not know.

Quick and Dirty

o   Good readers are active. Active reading means that you are focused on the text and learning as you go. Highlighting your books does not usually lead to reading actively.

o   Annotation encourages active reading. Gone are the days of reading and not learning. To annotate, you summarize the key ideas of the text in the margins using your own words (a good test of your understanding).

o   Use your annotations to study. Annotations provide a way to test yourself on the information you'll need to remember for the exam.

CHAPTER 17

THREE RS AND AN M: REMEMBERING WHAT YOU HAVE READ AND HEARD

An education isn't how much you
have committed to memory, or even
how much you know. It's being able
to differentiate between what
you know and what you don't.

–Anatole France

Warning! Warning! If you don't read and reflect on any other chapter in this book, do so with this one. There are piles of important stuff in here, some of which is hard to make exciting or fun to read. So here's the point where you need to suck it up, read on, and learn the *real* secrets of academic success in college.

Have you ever spent a considerable amount of time reading a textbook or "studying" your notes only to find that you remember little of what you have read? Have you ever looked up a number in the telephone book to make a call, been briefly interrupted (even for a few seconds), and then find you can't remember the number? Do you find yourself thinking, "My grandma has a better memory than I do"? If any or all of these things have happened to you, you may feel frustrated or even stupid. Fear not! It happens to everyone, or at least everyone who doesn't know about the three

Rs and an M. No, that's not readin', ritin', and 'rithmetic. Our three Rs stand for reflect, rehearse, and review, and the M stands for monitor. Got that?

We've found that many students skip the 3RM step when trying to study and learn information. In fact, when we ask students how they studied for an exam, they often say (with pride), "I read the text." We respond (with encouragement), "That's a good start, then what did you do to study?" They reply, "What do you mean? I read the book." We shake our heads, saying, "But reading and studying are not the same thing!" "Huh?" they say (feeling confused). We assure them that a student who only reads the text, but doesn't reflect, rehearse, review, and monitor will have trouble remembering information later. No wonder so many students chalk it up to a bad memory!

> ## THE INSIDE SCOOP
>
> Students who rehearse and review information remember up to three times more than students who just read. Three times! That means there's a big payoff in reviewing, especially in courses where cumulative final exams include material from the entire term. So we suggest that a portion of your study time each day be spent rehearsing and reviewing.

Reflecting: Thinking about Information

You have probably already figured out that successful college students are active readers and critical thinkers. They become involved in their work as students by reflecting on the information they come in contact with. Rather than reading just to get the job done or attending class just to be there, they engage in activities that keep them connected to the tasks, and they think about the material as they go along. That's what reflection is. It's making sense of what you are trying to learn rather than simply skimming over it.

Earlier you learned about annotation. You know, writing all that important stuff in the margins of your texts. Annotation requires a considerable amount of reflection because you have to think about what you've just read before you annotate it. If you simply copied the exact words in your textbooks, you wouldn't be reflecting. Reflecting requires that you put the material in your own words as a way of making sense of what you are reading or hearing.

Carl had always done well in chemistry in high school, so he decided to take intro to chemistry to meet his lab science requirement. He figured that since he never had to spend much time studying it in high school and he always aced the tests, the same would hold true in college. The first week or so of class reviewed material he'd already learned, so he didn't read his much of his text nor did he take very good lecture notes. What little he did read and hear didn't sink in, because he really didn't think about it. As a matter of fact, Carl continued to tune out and lag behind even after the material got more difficult to follow. Before he knew it, the first test was upon him and he was totally lost. But Carl still had confidence that he could pull it out. After all, he had done it in high school without too much effort. He decided to devote the weekend to studying for the test, which was on Monday. He got up early Saturday morning, got out his textbook and his notes, and set to work...for about 45 minutes. He skimmed through a chapter without really thinking much about the material and was stunned that he could not work the problems at the end of each section. Rather than reflecting on the information and trying to make sense of it, he simply slammed the book shut, threw his notebook across the room, and decided it was a lost cause. He spent the rest of the weekend trying to get his friend who was also in the class to explain things to him. But that didn't go very well either. Carl learned the hard way that there is no shortcut to learning difficult material.

If you don't take time to try to make sense of information by putting it in your own words or by talking about it with other students—in other words, by reflecting— you may have a difficult time making it through your classes, particularly classes in which you have to work a little harder in order to be successful. And you're certainly not going to learn very much if, like Carl, you slam your book shut and throw your notes against the wall.

The mind is like the stomach. It is not how much you put into it that counts, but how much it digests.

–Albert Jay Nock

Rehearsing: Getting Information into Your Memory

You've reflected on a chapter that you have been assigned to read, so you pretty much understand it. Now you're ready to learn it in such a way that you can store it in your memory and get it back out again when you need to. In order to do this, you need a crash course on memory. Think for a minute about how memory works. Why can you remember some information fairly easily and other information seems not to "stick" no matter what you do? Since you've already read something about memory, let's do the very brief version of the memory crash course, just to give you some time to reflect.

Basically, you have two different memory systems: short-term memory, or STM, and long-term memory, or LTM. Both are important. Short-term memory holds information for a short period of time, up to about 30 seconds. And it holds only a small amount of information—seven plus or minus two pieces of information, to be exact. This means that STM can hold somewhere between five and nine pieces of information at one time. STM is the part of your memory you use when you look up a phone number, close the phone book, and immediately call the number. STM holds information when there is no need to remember it for very long. In addition, phone numbers (without the area code) consist of seven digits, well within the range of the number of pieces of information that can be held at one time.

Your long-term memory (as its name implies) holds information for a longer period of time, up to a lifetime, even. That's why you can remember stuff that you learned years ago: the alphabet, the multiplication tables, the name of the puppy you had when you were three. LTM also allows you to drive your car to the mall without getting lost and to remember stories that your grandparents told you when you were young.

Think how difficult learning would be without a long-term memory. But how does information get from your STM to your LTM, and how do memories in LTM become "permanent"? Why does some information get into LTM while other information doesn't? Let's go back to the phone book example we used earlier. You look up the number, close the phone book, dial...and the line is busy. You hang up the phone and start to dial again only a minute later, but you

Unless we remember we cannot understand.

—E. M. Forster

can't remember the number. Why? The answer is simple: you haven't rehearsed. Simply defined, rehearsal is acting on information, doing something to it in some way so that it moves from STM to LTM and so that you can remember it later. If you wanted to remember that phone number in case the line was still busy when you tried again, you could have said it several times or you could have written it down. (Actually, in this particular example, you could have simply used the redial function on your phone, but you get the point.)

Knowing a little bit about how memory works makes it easier to understand why reading alone, or simply listening to a lecture, isn't enough. After all, if you can't remember a seven-digit phone number after a minute without rehearsing it, how can you expect to remember the information contained in several textbook chapters and three weeks' worth of lectures? It's not that you have a poor memory; it's simply that you need to learn some ways to rehearse information so that it gets into your LTM where you can use it later.

There are two basic ways you can rehearse: repeat it aloud or to yourself several times, or write it down.

REPEAT THE INFORMATION

You can say it to yourself or out loud. Just like actors rehearse their lines by saying them over and over again, you can learn information by repeating it until it's fixed in long-term memory. The problem with simply saying information, however, is that there is no record for you to study from later on. In addition, this type of rehearsal sometimes leads to rote memorization, so you may have trouble remembering the information after a short period of time. Rote memorization really only works when learning tasks that you will do automatically (such as driving a car), but does not help you make connections that will allow you to get back to the information once it is no longer fresh in your mind.

WRITE THE INFORMATION DOWN

Writing gives you a more permanent record from which to study, so we suggest writing information first and *then* saying it as the better way to rehearse. In addition to being permanent, there are lots of different ways to organize information when you use writing as a way of rehearsing. Some alternatives include the following.

Concept Cards

You probably have made and used concept cards without knowing it. You may have called them "flash cards" and used them to learn vocabulary words or in courses where you had to learn definitions. Although our concept cards may look a little different than those you have made, the purpose is the same. Look at the example below of the front and back of a concept card for short-term memory.

1. On the front of the concept card, put the term that you want to learn (in this case, "short-term memory").

2. Under the term, put the page in the text where more information can be found.

3. In the upper right-hand corner, put a word (or phrase) that helps you organize the information by providing a larger concept (in this case, "short-term memory" would be subsumed under the general concept of "memory").

4. On the back of the card, write all of the important information you need to remember about short-term memory.

5. Make your cards as you read rather than annotating—but only use this technique in courses where learning terms is the main focus—or you can use your annotations to make your cards. Either way, you have a written record from which you can now rehearse.

6. When you rehearse, look at the front of the card, say the term and all of the information you should know about it (here's where the talking part comes in). Then flip the card over to see how much you remembered. Concept cards are good to use in classes where you have to learn lots of definitions or formulas. Students also find them useful for studying a foreign language.

Concept Maps

Concept maps are actually outlines that are constructed in such a way that you can see how information is related. When you make traditional outlines, it's often difficult to see how all of the information connects, so we rarely recommend outlining as an effective strategy. However, when you make concept maps, the relationships among ideas become clearer. There is no one best way to map, and it may take you a bit of time to figure out what will work best for you. It would only be on a rare occasion that you would map an entire chapter. Rather, mapping works well for concepts where it's important to see relationships. Look at the example of the two concept maps below. This gives you an idea about the variety of forms that mapping the same information can take.

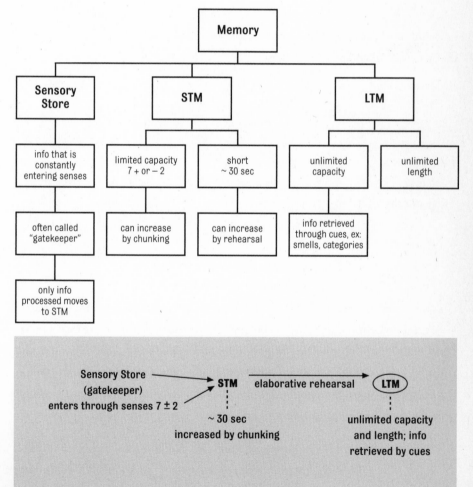

🦻 LISTEN UP

Many students tell us that they are visual learners. If this describes you, then concept mapping just might end up becoming your favorite strategy because it allows you to be creative in visually depicting how the concepts are related. Or if you like the idea of outlining, mapping nets the same results, only in a more organized way.

Charts

Charts are a good rehearsal strategy to use when you know that you will have to compare and/or contrast information. For example, you may be asked to compare and contrast the presidency of Lyndon Johnson with that of John Kennedy. The hardest thing about constructing charts is coming up with descriptors to compare and contrast on.

For example, in the chart below, we contrast short-term memory with long-term memory. Note that our descriptors are purpose, length, capacity, and role of rehearsal. It's important that the descriptors are terms that can apply to *all* concepts that you wish to compare or contrast.

	STM	LTM
Purpose	Stores info for brief periods	Stores info for long periods—a lifetime, even
Length	~30 sec.	Unlimited
Capacity	7 ± 2 items	Unlimited, never fills up
Role of rehearsal	Maintenance reh.—"refreshes" info in STM	Elaborative reh.—necessary to get info to LTM

Questions and Answers

Questions and answers are sort of like the study guides your high school teachers may have given to help you prepare for a big test. Our version asks you to create your own study guide by writing questions and answering them in a way that allows you to test yourself. The secret is to make up good questions—questions that match the task—and then to write out concise yet complete answers. Because objective questions are generally narrower in focus, questions and answers work best for objective-type tests.

● Begin with the traditional question words. If you know that your test will focus mostly on memorizing information, concentrate on questions that begin with who, what, where, and when.

- If the test questions will be more thinking and synthesis questions (as is more common), write quite a few why and how questions.

- Use the right format. Put your questions on the left-hand side of your paper and the answers on the right.

- When you study, cover up the answer to the question, and talk through the information.

- Uncover the answer and check to see how accurate and complete your talk-through was.

- Use a highlighter to mark questions that you need to spend more time on. Your questions and answers should look something like this:

Questions	Answers

1. Define and give an example of chunking.	Chunking is the grouping of items together so that you can increase the capacity of STM.
	    Ex. Telephone number (706) 555-1212
	    Soc sec # 111-11-1111

2. Why would you have trouble remembering this sequence of letters in your STM: imagoodstudent?	Because 14 pieces of info exceeds the capacity of STM. It only holds 7 ± 2 pieces of info.
3. How could you move the string of letters above from STM to LTM?	You could chunk the letters into words and then use some elaboration to remember it. Notice that it spells "I'm a good student." Now if you connect that to your own knowledge ("Hey, I *am* a good student") then you will remember that information.

If you find yourself writing questions that you can answer in one word (it takes you longer to write the question than it does to answer it), you probably need to put a bit more thought into your questions. Remember, this strategy works best when the questions you pose really make you think about the concepts. In almost all cases, you will need to write questions beginning with "how" and "why" rather than all "what" questions.

Reviewing: Keeping Information in Memory

Now that you have gotten information from your STM to your LTM, you want to keep it there. Unless you engage in activities that help you keep the ideas you have learned in your LTM, you are likely to forget them. Reviewing helps you hold onto what you've learned.

When we talk with students about how they review, a common answer is that they read over the material, either from their text or from their notes, a couple of times. Although this is a good start, it's not enough. It's important to do more than simply read over things. Each time you review, you should pare information down to its essentials, both so you have a reasonable amount of information to remember and so you can focus on the most important information. About two-thirds of what you read in texts and at least some of what you hear in lecture is filler—material that is there but that is not particularly important for you to remember. Your first task when you review is to figure out what is most important to learn and then to concentrate your reviewing on that.

TALK-THROUGH CARDS

One of the best ways to review is to make talk-through cards, like the one below. Here's how to make and use one.

● Use an index card (a piece of paper will do in a pinch) and list the key pieces of information you need to remember in an organized way. How much information you will put on your card depends on the topic. For a very difficult concept, you might just talk through one or two pieces of information. But in some courses, you may be able to talk through an entire chapter (or more) with one talk-through card. Notice that on our card you can tell which bits of information are the key ideas and which information supports each key idea. Cues are also provided to help you remember when you need to know examples.

- After you have read through your rehearsal strategies (concept cards, concept maps, and the like), annotations, and lecture notes, use your talk-through cards to cue you to important information. This is one of the last things you will do before you take the exam. Start with the first major idea on your card and then say (aloud) what you know about it without looking at any other materials. Make connections between and among this idea and other key ideas. Be precise.

- Say the information out loud because when you don't (or if you just say it to yourself), you can fool yourself into thinking you know stuff when you really don't.

- If you get stuck on something you have written on your card, go back to the source—text, lecture notes, or written rehearsal pieces—and read through the rocky part again. Be sure you understand the material before you go back to your talk-through card and proceed.

Once you make your talk-through card, reviewing will be easy. Remember, the information should already be in long-term memory. The goal of reviewing is to keep it there. Here's an example of a talk-through card:

STUDY GROUPS

Another good way to review is to join or form a study group. The best study groups meet for weekly review sessions, perhaps more frequently as test dates become closer. Productive study groups tend to have these characteristics:

- They are relatively small. Five members are about the maximum any group should have.

- All members pull their weight. When you become part of a study group, you should make a commitment to come to each session prepared. If you organize a study group, try to invite classmates who you know are interested in staying on task.

- The groups don't take the place of reflecting and rehearsing on your own. You need to do much of the work on your own and use your study groups as confirmation that you know and understand the material.

- Study groups are best used for reviewing information, for troubleshooting difficult material, and for testing each other.

- If you have a regular study group, meet at the same time and place each week. This tends to lessen the confusion about where and when to meet and encourages you to stay on task from week to week.

It's important that you understand the purpose of reviewing. You have reflected and rehearsed; for the most part, you know the material. You're reviewing to keep that information in long-term memory so that you can retrieve it accurately on test day or for future courses (or even after you enter the workforce). Reviewing can be done for 10 or 15 minutes here and there, at points in your day when you might otherwise waste time. Our students are always

DO YOUR HOMEWORK

Usually when students form a study group, they choose a few friends and voila! An excuse to party. So don't study with friends. Instead, we suggest you look for students who are doing well in the course or generally seem to be with it.

amazed at how much difference it makes to use small pockets of time for reviewing. Even ten minutes a day every day yields big rewards.

LISTEN UP

All of this reflecting, rehearsing, and reviewing stuff sounds like loads of work, doesn't it? It does take time but it doesn't have to be an insurmountable task, and the payoffs are huge. If you create a studying cycle wherein you are reading and annotating for one course and rehearsing and reviewing for another, it's much easier to stay on top of things. The only people who think college is a cakewalk are those who have already graduated, and they may have forgotten just how much work it was.

Monitoring Your Learning

Have you ever thought you did really well on a test, only to get it back with a big, fat D (or worse) on it? Or have you thought you understood a theory or how to solve a problem only to get an item on a test you swore you had never even heard about? If you have been in this situation (and most students have been) you may be having difficulty monitoring your learning. We think monitoring is one of the greatest difficulties college students face, right after time management and staying motivated.

Monitoring is generally a problem for college freshmen because they haven't had to do much monitoring in high school. Your high school teachers may have explained everything from your textbooks clearly enough that you never really had to figure things out on your own. They may also have given you study guides (or even told you the exact information you would be tested on). As a result, you really did not need to monitor your learning. They did it for you. What a deal.

In most college classrooms, however, things operate a bit differently. Your college profs expect you to know when you're having problems understanding something and to ask for help when you need it. That's another reason why it's so important to keep up with your reading and studying. If you put it off until right before the exam and then find that you are totally confused about some of the material, you won't have time to get the help you need, and you won't feel confident going into the exam.

To monitor your understanding during reading, make notes about ideas that confuse you as you read your textbook. During lecture, do the same. If your professor's explanation isn't clear, ask her to rephrase it or articulate what you don't understand. If you are in a very large classroom setting where it's impossible (or intimidating) for you to ask questions during class, see the prof after class, send your question by email, or talk it over with classmates. Whatever method you choose, monitor your learning as you go along. It should be part of a continuous cycle: reflecting, rehearsing, reviewing, monitoring.

Monitoring is also very important as test time becomes closer and as you are studying. We might go so far as to say that if you leave monitoring out of the studying formula you will not have an accurate perception of how well you will perform. Before you take a test, you should have a pretty good idea of the concepts you know very well, those you know fairly well, and those that may pose problems. Certainly after the test you should be able to predict with a high degree of accuracy how well you did. If you leave with a feeling that you aced the test only to discover that you made a low C, or if you feel as though you didn't do well at all when, in fact, you end up earning a B, you need to work on monitoring your learning. Students who consistently overpredict their performance tend to be disappointed when they receive their grades at the end of the semester. Students who consistently underpredict never muster the confidence they need in testing situations. Here are a few tips to help you monitor your learning:

● Keep up with your reading and other assignments.

● Think about your understanding of the concepts as you complete each assignment and hear each lecture.

> **⚡ GET WIRED**
>
> One of the best ways to monitor your learning and to get immediate help with a question you have is to exchange emails with a couple of other students in your class. Another idea is to participate in chat rooms and bulletin boards if your professor has made such supports available to you. Many professors encourage students to help one another by forming virtual study groups.

- Evaluate your learning at the end of each studying period by quickly talking through what you have learned.

- Be honest with yourself. If you don't understand something, don't ignore it. Get your questions answered as they occur.

The secret to monitoring is to do it as you go along. Monitor as you read and annotate, during lectures, and as you are making concept cards or using other rehearsal strategies. If you realize your understanding is breaking down, reflect on the information some more or ask your professor or students in your study group. Monitoring during test preparation is also important, but if you haven't monitored all along, it may be too late to do it well when it comes time to prep for an exam.

Quick and Dirty

- When you reflect, you think about the information, making an effort to make sense of it.

- When you rehearse, you use strategies that help get information into your long-term memory. Strategies such as concept cards, concept maps, charts, and questions and answers, which involve writing, are good ways to set information in your memory.

- When you review, you work to keep information in your memory. Talking through the information in a planned and organized way lets you review it.

- When you monitor, you stay on top of what you know and what you don't know. Monitoring should be an ongoing part of your studying routine.

CHAPTER 18

STUDYING SMARTER

If someone had told me I would be Pope one day, I would have studied harder.
                                —Pope John Paul I

As a general rule, your profs do care about you. They want you to be successful and will work with you to make that success a reality. But frankly, most professors really don't know how to tell you to change your studying behaviors other than by telling you to study harder...or longer. And, as you have probably realized by now, it's not necessarily studying harder or even longer that makes the difference. (We don't even know what studying harder means, but it sounds painful!) The key is studying smarter. Studying smarter means knowing and using the strategies that will work in particular learning situations. It means having a pocketful of approaches that you can use depending on the course you are taking, the kind of test you are studying for, and how you learn best. Studying smarter means being flexible. It means knowing that you study for chemistry differently than you study for history or French. That's why having lots of strategies to choose from makes learning in college easier. Sometimes it even makes learning fun.

Mara made an appointment to see her statistics professor after totally failing the first exam. This was a positive move on her part, but unfortunately, the meeting didn't go particularly well. The chain of events went something like this:

- Mara arrived at Professor Olson's office on time.
- Mara sat down and wove a tale of woe about studying really hard, harder than she had ever studied in her life.
- Mara also lamented the number of hours she put into studying for the course.
- Mara cried.
- Professor Olson smiled and nodded his head.
- Professor Olson asked Mara what she did to prepare for the first exam.
- Mara said, "I studied really hard. I put in a lot of time."
- Professor Olson smiled and nodded his head.
- Professor Olson said, "Study harder. Study longer."
- Mara nodded her head and left feeling very frustrated.

Being Flexible: Selecting and Modifying Strategies

❌ FOR ADULTS ONLY

If you are a nontraditional student, you really have to study smart. Because you may have a family and job to deal with beyond your college responsibilities, it's particularly important for you to study as efficiently as possible. Use small pockets of time to study with index cards—on the bus, while you're cooking dinner, during a break at work. If you have kids, get them to quiz you. You'll be spending some quality time with them, they'll feel grown-up, and you'll be reviewing. Everyone wins!

Throughout *College Rules!* you have read about a variety of strategies. If you use them, you can learn and remember information better. But not all of these strategies will work in every class, for every student, or for every professor. In addition, not every strategy will end up being carried out in the exact way we have presented it. In fact, one of the most important ideas that you should learn about using strategies is that you need to be flexible and modify your strategies to fit both the task your prof gives you and your own personal preferences as a learner. Try things out. Make strategies your own. Don't be afraid to experiment. Students we know who do well in college consciously consider their approaches to studying and have a variety of tricks up their sleeves to make learning easier, less painful, and more successful.

One of the misconceptions that students often bring with them to college is the idea that if they put time into studying, they should gain big rewards in terms of good grades. But that is not always the case. Think of Mara. She said, "I'm putting in a lot of time," but she still was doing poorly in the course.

> ## LISTEN UP
>
> Recently one of our students realized that making to do lists helped her remember things that she had to get done. But the problem was that she kept losing her lists. To solve this problem she started writing her lists on her bathroom mirror using washable markers. Every time she went into the bathroom, she saw what she still needed to get accomplished and could mark off what she had done. We think this is what strategy modification is all about. She solved her problem by creating an effective technique that worked for her.

Although it's important to put time into studying—you'll never be a member of Phi Beta Kappa by putting in only enough hours to get by—what you do during that time is equally important.

Students who put in what they consider to be "a lot of time" but still aren't reaping the rewards of good grades, are probably are making one of two mistakes:

1. They're not being honest with themselves about the actual amount of time they are investing (an hour break does not count toward study time).

2. Or they actually are spending a lot of time in course-related activities, but they are using inappropriate or inefficient study strategies (like memorizing definitions when they need to apply the concepts).

Now let's get down to the nitty-gritty and talk about ways to study in a variety of disciplines. Our goal is to help you realize that one size does not fit all. Different courses require different approaches because they have different types of content, exams, requirements, and lecturing styles. Different students use different approaches since no two students are alike. What we present are guidelines to think about as you decide which strategies you will select. We'll talk a little about each discipline, the kinds of tests that are generally given, and which strategies students in the discipline often see as good matches for studying smarter. Although courses are traditionally divided into three groupings—sciences, social sciences, and humanities—we have taken the liberty to further divide them so that we can be a bit more specific about studying foreign languages and mathematics.

Acting Like Einstein: Studying in the Sciences

The sciences can be broken down into subcategories, each with several courses as part of that subcategory. These subcategories and examples of the different disciplines that fall under them include:

- exact sciences: chemistry, physics

- biological sciences: biology, medicine, forestry, botany, zoology, agriculture

- physical sciences: geology, astronomy

- engineering and computer sciences: electrical engineering, industrial engineering, information technology, information science

WHAT'S THE FOCUS?

Science courses tend to focus on basic principles and well-researched, but not necessarily proven, theories. They stress the relationships among ideas and are usually taught in a sequential or hierarchical manner. For example, in biology you would learn about the structure of cells before you learned how cells group to form organs and systems. Science courses usually involve a "hands-on" element in the form of a lab. In the lab, you'll probably engage in discovery learning. You might examine different types of cells under a microscope so you can better learn to differentiate plant from animal cells (in a biology lab) or you might examine different types of rocks (in a geology lab).

They know enough who know how to learn.

—Henry Adams

Science textbooks and lectures are loaded with new terms and definitions, which are usually introduced at warp speed. In fact, a term that is defined in one paragraph may be used to define another new term in the next paragraph. These terms often represent key concepts and are also interrelated. In science, most professors rely heavily on diagrams for teaching purposes. Diagrams will be everywhere—in your textbooks, lectures, and computer modules.

FOR ADULTS ONLY X

Students who have been out of school for a while may need to bone up a bit on scientific concepts and problem-solving before returning to college. Basic principles and laws of science may be long gone from memory. Science courses that require you to use math, such as chemistry and physics, may also require some additional work. If you fall into this category, think about joining a study group or getting tutoring right from the beginning to help you fill in the gaps.

WHAT SHOULD YOU ALREADY KNOW?

At the very least, your professors will expect you to have some knowledge of the scientific method—how basic laws and principles are discovered and researched. They also assume that you can understand the relationship between scientific principles and the proofs that support them.

WHAT CAN YOU EXPECT?

Tests in science courses tend to be objective—multiple-choice, true or false, matching, and some diagram labeling or interpretation. In the exact sciences, you will be required to solve problems as well. Additionally, at least some of what you do in the lab part of the course will also be tested, although on some campuses course and lab testing are separate.

WHAT SHOULD YOU DO?

Because there are lots of terms to learn in science courses, concept cards are a good beginning point. But don't make the mistake of thinking that's all you should do, unless, of course, your prof just expects you to memorize. You'll need to use other strategies to help you see how ideas connect. If you're a visual learner, concept maps are great tools for learning science. You will also need to study diagrams. Some students like to copy them from their texts or notes and then talk through the important information. If you are in a science course that requires problem-solving, such as chemistry or physics, talking through the information, doing practice problems, and studying with others are all constructive ways of approaching these courses. With some modification, concept cards also work well for learning formulas. In science courses, it's also helpful to read before you go to class, since some of the same terms that are introduced in your textbook will also be use in the lecture.

🔊 LISTEN UP

Because information in the sciences tends to build on previous information, you will need to get a good foundation in the early chapters and lectures to be able to understand concepts presented later. So be sure you understand each concept as it is presented before you move on.

Beyond Freud and Mead:
Studying in the Social Sciences

Like the sciences, social sciences can be clustered into different categories. These categories include:

- social orientation: psychology, sociology, education

- study of cultures: anthropology, archaeology, human geography

- political orientation: political science, prelaw (Some include history in the social sciences, but we think it's a better fit under humanities.)

- business: economics, accounting, marketing

WHAT'S THE FOCUS?

Because it is difficult to prove much about people and social institutions, such as the legal and educational systems, social scientists rely on theories about what generally happens in society. The major problem students have in learning the social sciences is that they often confuse fact and opinion. Social science texts are usually arranged around particular topics, or in the case of history, chronologically. These texts tend to use an abundance of organizational aids—headings, subheadings, italicized words—to help you follow a chapter's organization. They also use lots of visual aids, usually in the form of tables, charts, and time lines that summarize information. Photographs are also often present, primarily to create interest.

Unlike science, there are not lots of new terms in social science, but there are terms that are used in ways that you may not be familiar with. In other words, terms like *family* or *class* take on new, specialized meanings that could require additional attention.

WHAT SHOULD YOU ALREADY KNOW?

Social science professors will expect you know something about people and how people and societies function. For example, they would expect that you would be able to understand their lecture on *social class* with only a brief definition of the term because you have lived and functioned in society. They also assume that you can distinguish fact from opinion, and in the case of history, understand that it is an interpretation of events rather than an objective recounting.

WHAT CAN YOU EXPECT?

Tests in the social sciences tend to require you to do more writing. This writing can take the form of papers, essay or short-answer tests, or group projects. You may have some objective questions on exams, but usually they are combined with some form of writing.

WHAT SHOULD YOU DO?

It's especially important in the social sciences to have a good grasp of the task, because there are a variety of ways that social science professors can test you. If the task is more heavily focused on writing, you will need to predict questions, talk through the information you would include in your answer, and even practice writing out the answer to a question or two. In the big scheme of things, concept cards won't help much in social science courses, particularly if you use them in traditional ways; there are not many new terms to learn.

The reverse side also has a reverse side.

—Japanese proverb

The Art of the Dance: Studying in the Humanities

The humanities include a wide range of disciplines, including:

- literature: classics, English and foreign literature, writing

- philosophy and theology

- fine arts: art; music, theater, drama

- history

WHAT'S THE FOCUS?

Humanities courses are perhaps the most difficult to generalize since they include a broader variety of courses and disciplines. For example, literature stresses points like the author's purpose, character development, tone, and mood, requiring you to think critically about and interpret what you are reading. Other types of humanities courses focus on historical events and are often organized chronologically or, in the case of the fine arts, by different movements or periods. Humanities texts vary in the amount of new terms that are included, from few in history to lots in philosophy and even in the fine arts. They also vary in the amount and types of visual aids used. Art and history courses rely heavily on photographs; other humanities courses may include time lines and occasional graphs or diagrams.

DO YOUR HOMEWORK

In the past few years we have noticed that students have become terrible spellers. We think this phenomenon may be partially due to a trend in elementary education a while back that encouraged children to write without the burden of worrying about correct spelling. It was called "invented spelling." Although this might have helped kids learn to write more creatively, now that these invented spellers are in college they simply can't spell worth a dime. If you fall into this category, know that professors for whom spelling is a pet peeve won't cut you much slack. So buy yourself a good dictionary or invest in a good spellchecker (maybe even one of the hand-held checkers) and be sure to read over your papers for spelling and grammar issues (or take them to your campus writing center) before you turn them in.

WHAT SHOULD YOU ALREADY KNOW?

Literature professors assume that you know something about the structure of stories, plays, poetry, and so forth. They also assume that you know how to interpret literature, that you can detect symbolism, extract themes, and recognize figurative language. Other humanities professors expect that you have some knowledge of historical chronology (World War II came after World War I, which came after the Civil War) or general movements in art (impressionism, dadaism). In most of the humanities, you will be expected to do a fair amount of writing, so your profs will expect you to have acquired decent writing skills and a working knowledge of grammar and spelling.

WHAT CAN YOU EXPECT?

In courses that focus on literature, history, and philosophy, there will be a heavy emphasis on writing. In literature, you may have to write essays that ask you to compare and contrast the works of different authors or interpret symbolism. In history, you may be asked to analyze the influence of historical events. In the fine arts, you may have to write papers or do projects about different movements, or analyze how historical events influenced art, music, or the theater. You may even have tests that ask you to identify pieces of music and works of art as well as their creators. But few humanities courses offer a steady stream of objective testing.

WHAT SHOULD YOU DO?

Because humanities courses are quite varied, you'll need a number of strategies to meet their wide-ranging demands. In general, however, annotation is a strategy that can be used effectively, with some modification, in most humanities courses. In history, for example, students often fall into the trap of annotating every little fact and lose sight of the big picture. But when you are annotating and reflecting on your history text and when you listen to lectures, you should concentrate on the key conclusions that are drawn. Then annotate only the most important supporting information.

Because most of the humanities have a heavy historical focus, creating time lines is a good strategy to help you put events or movements in an historical perspective. These time lines can then be used to predict essay questions and to be sure that you understand the course material's chronology. Questions and answers would work well for courses in which you have to answer identification questions.

In literature, it's very important to carefully read your assignments with a critical eye. Make brief notes in the margins of your books that will enable you to think about the issues your professor discusses in class. Mark crucial passages with sticky notes so that you can refer to them as you review for tests or prepare to write papers.

Parlez-vous Français? Studying Foreign Languages

Studying a foreign language is often considered part of the humanities, but because it offers different challenges, we will deal with it separately. Many students believe that studying a foreign language means learning vocabulary, grammar rules, and sentence construction. Although that is the main part of learning a language, there is also an emphasis on learning about the culture and the people.

One of the interesting aspects of foreign language courses is that the first course is generally fairly easy, especially if you have had a couple years of a language in high school. Initially, you learn words with high usage, regular verbs, and general grammatical sentence structure. Chapters are usually arranged by topics, such as going to a restaurant, planning a trip, or meeting new people. Each chapter offers dialogues for you to practice and activities where you can apply a particular skill you have learned. Most language courses also include the often dreaded language lab, where you listen and respond to conversations by native speakers.

But foreign language courses tend to get very difficult quickly, often without students even noticing it until they have fallen way behind. Let's face it, learning a language requires lots of memorization: memorization of grammar rules, verb tenses, vocabulary, and on and on. But very quickly, all of that memorization must be applied to reading, understanding, speaking, and perhaps even writing about longer and longer pieces of text. That's why it's important to commit some time each day to studying a language. Here are a few suggestions to help make learning a language a bit easier.

- Do all of the practice activities, even if they aren't all assigned.

- Have a "language hour" with classmates (or native speakers, if possible) to discuss problems and practice speaking.

- Modify the traditional concept card by putting the foreign word on one side and the English word on the other. Cards can also be used to learn grammar rules and irregular verbs.

- Never miss a lab. We know that you would rather do just about anything else, but listening to a native speak the language helps you develop an ear for the language and improves your speaking skills. Also, if your campus has an international coffee hour (or something similar), as ours does, attend whenever possible. You'll make new friends and be able to practice not only speaking the language but also developing an ear for it.

- Get into the culture. Nothing makes learning a language more fun than understanding cultural traditions. Check out local festivals or campus organizations.

- Plan a trip (even if it's for graduation) to the country whose language you are learning. If that's not possible, try visiting cities that have thriving enclaves of people from the country whose language you are studying. Planning a trip gives you a real purpose for studying because in your travels you will be able to actually use your language skills (in fact, you might even have to).

X + Y = What? Studying Mathematics

Like foreign languages, studying math requires some different approaches and a different mindset than studying other disciplines. Some students have the attitude that they just can't do math, which, in turn can end up being an excuse for not putting in much effort. The problem isn't so much that students don't have an aptitude for math as that they simply lack the background. And if you get to college and still don't have the background, you're going to have to work extra hard to be successful in math and math-related courses. But we are confident you can do it.

Another problem that gets in the way of learning math for many students is the idea that there are no practical applications of math. "When am I ever gonna need calculus?" you ask. Perhaps you won't ever use calculus per se, but you probably use the

Larry absolutely hated math. It had been a source of frustration for him since elementary school. He could almost pinpoint the day when it began: when his class started on percentages and fractions. He didn't get it in fourth grade and he did not get it now that he was headed off to college. Now he had to do fractions with letters in them (all that x and y stuff). What was that about? Larry was glad that at least there was now a term for his affliction: "mathematically challenged." That described him perfectly. During summer orientation, Larry met with his advisor, Ms. Mason, to discuss his course schedule for fall. Her suggested schedule included the first-level math course, freshman English, political science, and introduction to ecology. Everything sounded fine to Larry except the math. He informed Ms. Mason that he was going to put off taking his math requirement as long as possible. Then maybe his math anxiety would go away and he might be able to do enough to eke out a C.

Although Ms. Mason tried to convince Larry that he needed to take math sooner rather than later, he would not budge. She even suggested that he enroll in a preparatory class if he didn't feel as though he was ready to tackle the credit course: "You have nothing to lose and everything to gain by having some success. Get in at a level you'll feel comfortable with." Larry held firm and took a geography course rather than the math. And Larry held firm the next semester as well, and the next, and the next. In fact, he let it go so long that he had not only forgotten just about all of what he had learned in high school math, but he was also at the point in his coursework where his lack of math credit was keeping him from taking some other courses that he thought he would enjoy. The last we heard of Larry, he was still trying to find some way around the math requirement.

skills that underlie calculus more frequently than you realize. That's because math is about problem-solving, and we all know that life throws us one problem after another.

Because college math courses build on what you have learned in your previous schooling, it's important to begin at the right level. If you find yourself overwhelmed during the first week of class, you're probably in over your head. When this happens, you have choices to make. Are you going to withdraw from the course and take a lower-level one, even if it means sitting in on something you won't get graduation credit for? Or do you feel confident enough in your ability to do the work if you get tutoring or other assistance? Either choice requires you to put in some extra effort to do well in the course.

For those who are at the right level of mathematics and will be successful with some effort, try these tips.

• Stay current. Because math concepts build on one another, it's important to stay on top of things. Although you may be able to catch up with your reading in other courses, it's very difficult to play catch-up in math once you get behind.

• Read your textbook and annotate in the margins. Math textbooks have become more reader-friendly in the last couple of years (hooray!) and offer understandable explanations and study aids.

• Review daily. Don't wait until a day or two before an exam to review all of the concepts that you will be tested on. This point is so important that we will say it again—review daily.

• Take good lecture notes. Be sure to pay close attention to detail when your professor explains a problem. Mathematics requires attention to detail.

• Ask questions—lots of them. Failure to understand even a minor point can have grave consequences later on, so clear up problems as they come up.

• Talk things through by putting words to formulas. If you can talk about a problem, it shows you understand it.

DO YOUR HOMEWORK

One of the major problems that students have is that although they do fine when they work on the problems at the end of each section of the book, they don't know what to do when problems involving different concepts from several sections are put together on a test (which is often what you'll see on math tests). Make sure when you do your homework that you mix it up and practice different types of problems. Try combining some problems to come up with larger ones. By doing this, you'll be able to recognize when confusion sets in and get help for it early on.

• Practice, practice, practice. Do application problems even if they aren't assigned; do a variety of problems.

• Use concept cards to learn formulas and important mathematical principles. A good approach is to put the formula on one side of the card and a brief explanation of the formula on the other side. For math principles, put the principle on one side and an example problem using that principle on the other side.

- Always ask yourself: Does my answer or solution make sense? Professors tell us that if students would check to see if their answers made sense, fewer test items would be missed. One chemistry professor told us that students tend to confuse units of measure and that if they would just think through their answer to see if it made sense, they would be able to catch their mistakes.

- If appropriate, draw diagrams, especially for word problems. Diagrams can help you see relationships and information that may not be apparent from reading the problem alone.

Studying smarter. It's about being flexible and knowing which strategies to use in which situation. Those who study smart put time into learning (everything takes time, remember; usually longer than you thought it would). But they also learn efficiently and effectively by knowing and using a variety of strategies.

Quick and Dirty

- Strategies are not set in stone. Be flexible and modify strategies depending on the task and your own preferences as a learner. What works for one student won't work for another.

- All courses are not the same. You study humanities differently than the sciences, which in turn, are approached differently than the social sciences. It's important to know how to adjust and modify from discipline to discipline.

- Studying foreign languages and mathematics requires a very unique use of strategies.

CHAPTER 19

GETTING THE MOST FROM COMPUTERS

*My interest is in the future because I am
going to spend the rest of my life there.*
—Charles F. Kettering

Believe it or not, when we were undergraduates in college we didn't own computers (and it really wasn't even the dark ages). Today, however, having a computer is even more important than having a cell phone or a credit card on campus. Even if you don't own your own computer, professors will expect you to have an email account that you check regularly. And gone are the days of turning in a handwritten paper—you may be expected to turn in your finished paper via email attachment and in the proper style, to boot. In addition, you will need to use a computer for some course assignments (especially in literature, business, engineering, and mathematics classes) and may even take some exams on computer. If you want to find a book in the library, chances are you will need to get on a computer to locate it.

Most college campuses have computer labs that students can use free of charge (although many campuses now charge a "tech fee" for use of computers and other technological services). If you need them, there are often courses you can take to familiarize yourself with how to use computers in general or how to use the computer services offered by the school (check your college's bulletin or Web site to find out where you can get this kind of training).

Surfing Strategies

The Internet can be a wonderful source of information. However, searching for information on the Internet can be difficult (and darned frustrating) for a multitude of reasons. There is an enormous amount of information, but no central place where it is all catalogued. Often when you search for a topic, you find thousands and thousands of sites of which only a handful are useful at all. In addition, Web sites are constantly changing addresses or just closing down without warning. So you can't count on the information you find today to be there in the weeks and months to come. Web sites also offer information of varying quality—some good, some bad, and some ugly. So where do you start?

USE GOOD KEYWORDS

The most common difficulty people face when searching Internet sites is that they use terms that are too general. For example, if you wanted to find out about Bill Clinton's presidency and you typed in "Clinton," you would get information about every Clinton out there (including several towns). So start out as specific as possible; you can always expand your search if you need to.

USE THE RIGHT SEARCH ENGINE

There are numerous search engines, but they generally fall into two categories: those that are sorted by people and those that are sorted automatically.

Human-sorted sites have some advantages in that presumably some thought has gone into the categorization of the information. These search engines (like Yahoo!) are good for general searches of information. But because their scope is limited to descriptors (and not the actual words on the Web page), you may not find all of the sites about your topic.

Automatically sorted sites (for example, AltaVista, Excite, Google) grab some or all of the text on a page and store it in a database. When you search one of these sites, it will list every page with your keyword in it. The problem with these search engines is that often you will get a lot of garbage in your results (that is, pages that are not really about your topic at all).

USE ALL THE TOOLS AVAILABLE

If you can't find the information you need using one search tool, try another.

Try alternate terms. Sometimes after searching for your keyword for a while you realize from the information on the pages you are finding that there are other terms that would give you better information. For example, Jodi was once looking up information about Scopa (an obscure Italian card game with a special deck) and was not having much luck until she found the term "Neapolitan card games" on a Web site. Once she looked up this second term, she found the information she needed pretty quickly.

Know what you can and can't find on the Internet. People are often disappointed because they can't find in-depth information on Web pages. Sometimes, and for some topics, there is no substitute for a book or encyclopedia that can delve deeper and provide more information.

Although searching the Internet can sometimes be frustrating, it's like any skill: you'll get better with practice. The strategies above will help you get started (and hopefully keep you from wanting to toss your computer out of the closest window).

QUICK SEARCH TIPS

Use the following tips to help limit your searches. These simple commands should keep you from wading through too much information you don't need (note that these commands may not work with all search engines).

COMMAND	EXAMPLE
Use plus (+) and minus (−) signs to include or omit certain terms.	**+ union − Soviet**
Use quotation marks (" ") to search an entire phrase.	**"Hugo award winners"**
Enter the most important keyword first.	**loans college aid grants**
Use lowercase when entering your terms if you want to search *both* lower- and uppercase versions. Using capital letters will usually only search the uppercase term.	**china** This would look up both china *and* China. If you wanted information on China (the country), it would be best to enter the capital letter in your search so you don't have to search through sites about dishes.
The asterisk (*) is a "wild card" character. This can help you search for different forms of a word.	**Child*** This would give you child, children, childless, childhood, childish, childlike, and so on.
Refine your search if you get too much info. Use **AND, NOT, OR** to combine search terms (be sure to put these terms in all capital letters).	**McCartney AND Lennon OR Beatles NOT Wings**
Try typing in the keyword in your browser's address bar. Sometimes you just luck out and it is easy to find. Be careful though; *www.whitehouse.gov* gets you to the White House, but *www.whitehouse.com* gets you to something very different....	**www.thethingIamlookingfor.com**

Recently, there was a computer email going around entitled "HAHAHA." This email contains the opening paragraph to the story of Snow White and the Seven Dwarfs (told in a fairly sexy way that you probably didn't hear as a child) then refers you to the attachment to get the rest of the story. But should you open the HAHAHA attachment to read the conclusion, you'd get infected with a virus that would send the email to everyone in your address list (and do some other fairly nasty things). Basically, you cannot get a virus just from opening an email (at this point, but that may change) but you can get a virus from opening an attachment to an email, so be careful. Our general advice is to play it safe and never open an attachment that looks suspicious. And never ever open one with an ".exe" suffix (this means it's an executable file—basically, a piece of software). Executable files from unknown sources are very often nasty viruses. We also strongly suggest that you invest in a good antivirus program that will check your email before it downloads to your computer.

Trust and the Internet

You can search just about any topic and find many different sites about it. But be forewarned; the Internet allows anyone to post information without any fact-checking or screening. So how do you know whether you can trust the information you find? Use the following criteria to help you.

Can you tell who the author is? One of the most important things you need to consider is the source. Is this Web page written by a nationally recognized individual (or group) or is it Joe Schmoe's page? Does the author list credentials? If so, does the author's background make him or her qualified to write about this topic? Is the author cited by other Web sites on the same topic? Is the Web site sponsored by a national organization? If so, is it a for-profit or a nonprofit group? Is it a group you have heard of before or is it the National Society for the Promotion of Mustaches (or some other far-out sounding group)?

> Learning is what most adults will do for a living in the 21st century.
>
> —Bob Perelman

What is the purpose of the web site? Is it informational, personal, commercial? Is it trying to inform you about the topic, advocate a particular point of view, or sell you something? Why does the purpose matter? Well, if you are looking at a commercial site, you need to consider its goal (i.e., to convince you to buy something) when evaluating the information it presents.

Is the information biased toward a particular point of view? Let's say you visit the National Society for the Promotion of Mustaches' Web site. What do you think their view of mustacheless men would be? Most sites you visit will contain some form of bias. Your job is to figure out what that bias is and to factor that into your overall evaluation of the information you find there.

How does this information compare with other sources? If the material on one Web site seems to be way out in left field compared to the information you find on other pages, you probably want to discount that information. Basically you want to check enough sources to be confident that several credible authors agree.

How accurate is the information? Several of the preceding tips should help you evaluate the truthfulness of the information you find (especially looking for bias and confirming the information with more than one source).

☹ SAD BUT TRUE

Allison, one of our students, sent us an email that she had received from her mother warning about an ingredient in shampoo that causes cancer. The message instructed readers to check their shampoo bottles for Sodium Laurel Sulfate (an ingredient found in most shampoos). Allison was quite nervous about the possibility that her shampoo was increasing her risk of cancer and was sending the warning to everyone she knew (as instructed by the email she received). We took one look at the message and knew it was a hoax. By typing in the key phrase "shampoo causes cancer" on Google, we were able to quickly confirm that it was completely false (there was even a page from the American Cancer Society dismissing this email as a hoax). The moral: Check out anything that seems alarming before you send it along and perpetuate the hoax.

Who is the target audience? Is the site geared to consumers, academics, professionals (such as doctors or lawyers), kids? Are you the target audience? Sometimes Web pages offer very specific information that would only make sense to someone in the field. For example, if you searched for information about getting rid of migraine headaches, you might find yourself on a page geared to medical doctors, not the general public. So you probably would not understand much of what was on the page.

How current is the information? When was the last time the information was updated? Every page should indicate the last time the site was updated, and in most cases the more current the page is the better.

Basically, you want to use your best judgment. Think about the information in light of the guidelines above and remember: If something seems too good to be true or seems fishy in some other way, it probably is.

Avoiding Plagiarism and Other Taboos

We sometimes come across student plagiarism. Gasp! In fact, we come across it more and more often now that so many students have access to the Internet. We believe that part of the problem is that students do not really understand what plagiarism is or what counts as plagiarism. So let's review some of the basics of plagiarism.

Basically, plagiarism is when you take someone else's words or ideas and represent them as your own. As academics, your professors value intellectual property (because that is the foundation upon which academe is based) and truly frown upon any level of plagiarism. At some colleges, even small instances of plagiarism can get you into a world of trouble (they can even get you kicked out of school). You will not be plagiarizing if you provide references for where you got the material (but note that paraphrasing without citing the source is still plagiarism). This doesn't mean that you should not use outside sources to get information; professors expect you to do this. Actually, they love it when you find additional sources, as long as you give credit where credit is due.

To avoid plagiarism, be sure to use proper acknowledgment whenever you use part of someone else's work in your own work. This would include:

- a theory, thought, or idea

- a direct quote from either a written *or* a spoken source

- a paraphrase of an idea from either a written *or* a spoken source

- any pieces of information that are not common knowledge (including graphs, pictures, statistics, or facts)

Be careful with this last one. The fact that John F. Kennedy took office in 1961 is common knowledge. The fact that it was 22 degrees Fahrenheit on his inaugural day is not (we got that fact from page 917 of Bailey and Kennedy's *The American Pageant,* ninth edition, which was published in 1991 by D.C. Heath and Company).

We have unfortunately seen some sources of blatant cheating using plagiarism. Such cheating includes (but is not limited to):

- Buying a paper online. Several Web sites feature papers that you can purchase. Although these sites make claims that the papers are for research purposes only, it is commonly known that students have turned in these papers as their own. However, most professors do not give such general paper topics as those covered in these bought papers, so they are usually fairly easy to detect.

URBAN LEGEND

A student who belonged to a fraternity that kept a file of members' papers sorted through the pile and chose one that was about 20 years old to recopy and submit. When he got the paper back from the professor, he received an A along with a comment, "When I wrote this paper I got a C, but I always thought that it deserved a higher grade."

- Paying an "editing" service. If you are paying someone to revise and "clean up" your paper, many professors would consider that to be plagiarism, because some one else is doing the writing. However, using an editing service is not to be confused with seeking help at the college writing center. Writing center staff do not take your paper and fix it. Instead, they point out errors you are making in order to help you make corrections yourself.

- Turning in another student's work as your own. Self-explanatory, right?

- Copying pages, paragraphs, sentences, or even phrases from a text without quoting or citing the author.

All we can say about all this is that it is the same as stealing—you are taking another's ideas without permission or credit. So obviously you must take the time to do your own work.

SAD BUT TRUE 😟

Jason and Eric were both enrolled in Philosophy 101. At the end of the semester, Jason was caught turning in a shortened version of his roommate Eric's take-home final exam. Eric had one instructor and Jason had another, so Jason thought he was safe. While Eric was taking another final exam, Jason found his test on the computer and paraphrased it, making it about two pages shorter. What Jason did not realize was that professors talk to each other about their exams and about student responses. The exam consisted of essay questions that required students take a stance on a particular issue. No two students could have had exactly the same approach. When the instructors were discussing the interesting papers they received from students, they detected the problem. Jason was sent through the university's academic dishonesty panel. He failed the course and was ultimately put on academic probation. Of course, we know you would never make a mistake of this nature, but tell your friends that plagiarism doesn't pay.

Computers in Your Classes

Although your college professor may look as old as the hills, he's probably pretty knowledgeable about computers. Like all educators and researchers, college profs have had to stay somewhat current, and many are integrating technology (specifically computers and the Internet) into their classroom teaching in a wide variety of ways. You may encounter one or more of the following:

- **Computerized course management systems (such as Web CT)**. These systems allow professors to put syllabi, quizzes, homework assignments, and other course materials online. Students can often check their grades or meet in virtual study groups on these sites.

- **Course notes**. Some professors put lecture notes or other content online. These supports can help you evaluate your own notes or learn more about a topic you found especially interesting.

- **CD-ROM supplements**. Sometimes you will need to purchase a CD-ROM or other software supplement when you buy your textbook. They are becoming more popular in several content areas, but especially in the sciences, where the CDs present slides, videos, or demonstrations that could not be represented in a traditional textbook.

- **Exam modules or tutorials**. Many professors (and most publisher Web pages) offer Web-based exam modules. These sites provide practice questions so you can get a sense of what the exam will be like. They can also be used to help you monitor your learning of the material. If you take a computer module after you have finished studying for an exam and you do well, you know you've learned the material. If, on the other hand, you miss a lot of the items, you know what you will need to rehearse and review some more before taking the test.

- **Email assignments**. You can expect that some of your assignments will need to be turned in online. It may be just a one-page email journal, a lab report, or a full-scale paper that you will need to send via an email attachment, so be prepared. Your professors will expect you to know how to turn these assignments in.

LISTEN UP

Having a computer problem is no excuse for not getting your assignments completed on time. We think that "My printer didn't work" or "I lost my entire file by accidentally pressing the wrong key" are the modern-day versions of "My dog ate my homework." Most professors simply won't buy it.

- **Computerized exams.** This format is becoming more widely used on college campuses. You may take all of your exams in this format or, more commonly, only the final exam. In fact, many freshman English courses now require all students to write and edit their papers and their exams on the computer.

URBAN LEGEND

This one is almost believable. According to the story, a computer tech support person once received the following phone call:

CALLER: *Hello, I'm calling because my computer cup holder is broken.*

TECH GUY: *Did you say cup holder?*

CALLER: *Yes; it is on the front of my computer. I put my drink in there and it just broke off.*

TECH GUY: *Was the cup holder on your computer when you bought it or did you add it on later?*

CALLER: *No it was there. It is called an "8X" holder.*

At this point the tech guy begins to laugh as he realizes that the caller was using the CD-ROM drive as a cup holder.

Find out as much as you can about the role of computers and technology in your classes. Listen to what your instructor says about the subject and read over your syllabus. The more you know about what's expected in this arena, the better prepared you will be to do what's needed.

Reading on Computer

Reading from a computer screen is physically and mentally more demanding than reading from paper. Some current research has indicated that people tend to read more slowly and with less accuracy when reading from the screen. However, there are some advantages to reading information on your computer: you have access to a wide range of information through the Internet; computerized texts can make use of hypertext or other features that allow you to quickly compare different materials; and online texts can also include video or audio clips.

Most professors have not yet made the switch to having all text materials online. Even if you are taking a distance-learning course, you will probably have to buy and read a traditional textbook. However, should you be asked to read a lot of material on your computer, there are some things you should keep in mind. Some research has suggested that there is a decline in reading comprehension that can reach 40 percent when a person reads online. One factor that affects comprehension is the monitor's display: its flicker, glare, image quality, color, and font size. Some of this can be fixed by making sure you have a good monitor and that your monitor is at the optimal settings for picture quality and color.

But if you find you are having trouble reading on the computer, our best advice is to print out what you need to read (if you can). If printing out just won't work for you, another way to overcome any dips in speed or comprehension is to practice. Read as much information on the computer as you can. Maybe read the morning paper online, or read online movie reviews instead of watching them on TV. Basically, you want to gear up for computer reading if you know you will need to be doing a lot of it.

> Putting a computer in front of a child and expecting it to teach him is like putting a book under his pillow, only more expensive.
>
> —Anonymous

Taking Exams on Computer

Taking computerized exams is stressful for many students, but it is becoming an increasingly widespread practice. In fact, if you plan to go on to graduate school, the Graduate Record Exam or GRE (which is like the SAT for grad school) is *only* given on computer. Many professors are switching to computerized testing in their classes as well (particularly in mathematics and the sciences). There are several things you can do to help you do well when you take an exam on computer.

Don't abandon your normal test-taking strategies. If you always circle key words on an exam question to be sure you are addressing them correctly, keep a piece of scratch paper with you to jot down key words. If you leave questions blank to answer them later, find out if you will be able to go back on the computer test or if you will have to respond and then move on.

Become familiar with the technology. All too often, the computer is only used in a course for taking the exams, and students are wary about using the technology. Definitely do practice tests if the professor offers them. And if you know your exams will be given on a computer, make an effort to become comfortable using computers over the course of the semester.

THE INSIDE SCOOP

Research has indicated that students who can type fast tend to do better on computerized exams. So it is a good idea both to learn how to use your computer and how to type, if necessary, before exam time.

Find out as much as you can about the exams. We know professors who give basic multiple-choice exams on computer, but we also know several who fully utilize the technology when making computerized exams. For example, one chemistry professor on our campus integrates three-dimensional models and videos of chemical reactions into his computerized exams. To answer the questions, students need to stop the video at a certain point in the chemical reaction.

Taking exams on computers does not have to be scary. If you learn as much as you can about both the technology and the exam before you take the test, who knows? You may even find you prefer computerized tests.

Quick and Dirty

○ Using the Internet to find information can be a real time-saver in college. Use good strategies for surfing and for evaluating the information you find.

○ Don't plagiarize. Knowing what does and does not count as plagiarism often helps students avoid this pitfall.

○ Computers will be used in a variety of ways in your courses, so becoming familiar with how to use a computer is a real necessity.

CHAPTER 20

IT'S MORE THAN MULTIPLE-GUESS: PREPPING FOR AND TAKING OBJECTIVE EXAMS

As long as there are tests, there will
be prayer in public schools.
                                   —Bumper sticker

L et's face it. Preparing for exams is probably the least enjoyable part of being a college student. It takes a considerable amount of time and it's stressful. We guess the only thing less fun than prepping for tests is actually taking them. So why do professors continue to torture you by making you take exam after exam? Year after year? Don't they remember what it was like when they were undergraduates? Probably. But why should they let you off the hook? They had to take tough tests and so do you.

Actually, professors give you tests because it's important for them (and for you) to know what (and if) you're learning. Although it sounds like it would be great to have a college career where you never had to take a test, write a paper, or give a speech, the fact is that you probably wouldn't learn very much under those conditions. No matter what you do, knowing you'll be evaluated is an important part of learning, even beyond the classroom. It's what drives you to learn. Once you get out in the world of work, you will be evaluated for promotions and raises—not necessarily through tests, but through some kind of measurement of your performance. The message here is: Get used to it. Evaluation will continue throughout your lifetime.

URBAN LEGEND

This one has been around since the 1970s and is actually based on a real-life study that was conducted at Princeton University. The legend goes like this: seminary students are enrolled in a course that focuses on Christianity and the life of Jesus. When they arrive at the classroom to take their final exam, there is a note on the board telling them to go to another building way over on the other side of campus. As the students rush to the new location, each is accosted by a homeless person in tattered clothes who asks for help. None of the students stop to help him because they are panicked about being late for the exam. When they reach the classroom, the teacher is waiting for them. He tells them that the beggar was an actor, put there to see how they would react. Because they did not show that they acquired any compassion while studying the life of Jesus, they have all flunked the exam.

Examinations come in all shapes and sizes. In this chapter we will give you a feel for the most common type of exams—objective exams. We realize that you have probably taken all of the types of tests that we'll discuss somewhere along the way in your schooling. What you may not have done, however, is to adjust your studying according to the kind of test you will take. That's something you will most certainly have to do in college.

The most common types of objective exams are:

- multiple-choice

- true or false

- matching

These test types are referred to as "objective" because there is only one correct answer (or there's only supposed to be one correct answer), and this answer can be clearly articulated. For a well-written multiple-choice question, for example, there should be one answer that is obviously correct—that is, if you studied.

You have probably been taking objective tests in school, particularly multiple-choice tests, ever since you can remember. Maybe this is the way studying has gone for you in the past: the night before (or maybe even an hour before) the exam, you read over the chapters at lightning speed and looked over your notes. In fact, many students tell us that they think that this is the *only* way to do it, because they remember more of what they study at the last minute.

Studying for objective exams in college can take a bit getting of used to, especially if your experiences in high school encouraged memorization. You may have the idea that objective exams have only straightforward questions that demand straightforward answers—you know: just the facts, ma'am. So preparing for them should be a matter of memorizing the material. But college professors often ask questions that require you to pull together lots of information in order to answer them. This makes preparing for objective exams a little more involved.

THE INSIDE SCOOP

Some students believe that cramming for multiple-choice exams is more effective than studying earlier because you will forget the information if you study it too early. But we know that the way people learn is through repeated exposure to information. So you are more likely to learn if you have reviewed the information over several days rather than cramming over one or two days.

Studying for Objective Exams

If you have kept up in the course—you've done the reading, annotated your text, reviewed your lecture notes, and constructed appropriate rehearsal strategies (whew!)—getting ready for objective exams shouldn't cause much trauma. Preparing will be generally a matter of additional rehearsing and reviewing. However, two key factors will determine how you will do on objective tests: understanding the task and distributing your study time over several days before the test.

Think back to chapter 13, where we talked about tasks. Remember, it's important not only to know what kind of test you will have, but also the level of questions you will be asked. If you don't know the level of questions, you'll have a difficult time approaching studying in the most effective way. We know many students who memorized piles of facts only to discover that few of the test questions simply ask for the facts.

No more prizes for predicting rain. Prizes only for building arks.

—Anonymous

There are two basic kinds of questions asked on objective tests: memory-level questions and higher-level questions.

MEMORY-LEVEL QUESTIONS

Memory-level questions can usually be thought of as questions that focus on facts. That is, you don't have to put pieces of information together to come up with the answer. You can rely on basic rote learning or what is commonly called memorization. You may have encountered lots of tests like this in high school. Here are some examples of memory-level questions:

1. Short-term memory holds

    a. unlimited information

    b. just a little information

    c. 7 ± 2 pieces of information

    d. 9 ± 7 pieces of information

    (*Answer is c.*)

2. True or false: Chunking expands STM capacity by grouping pieces of information into units.

    (*Answer is "true."*)

Note that in both of these examples, if you memorized facts about memory, you would be able to answer these questions easily.

HIGHER-LEVEL QUESTIONS

However, most of the questions you will encounter will be more difficult, higher-level items. Higher-level questions go beyond facts and ask you for applications, examples, syntheses, analyses, and conclusions. Such questions are sometimes called "thinking" questions. Unless you luck out, objective tests in college will most likely include more thinking than memorization questions. Here are some examples of higher-level questions:

1. All of the following would be considered examples of maintenance rehearsal *except:*

   a. repeating a phone number several times so that you can
      call it again

   b. learning a date for your history quiz by relating it to something
      in your own life

   c. saying an address three times to yourself as you are on your
      way out the door to a party

   d. memorizing key terms in your biology book by looking them
      over several times

   (Answer is b.)

2. True or false: Short-term memory differs from long-term memory
   in both duration and capacity.

   (Answer is "true.")

STUDY ACCORDING TO THE TASK

Once you figure out the task—the kinds of questions your professor expects you to answer—you can focus your studying efforts to match the task. If the task is memorization, study by asking yourself primarily "what" questions. Answer the questions precisely and thoroughly as you are rehearsing and reviewing. Questions such as "What is the purpose of short-term memory?" or "Define 'encoding'" will provide you with the information you need to recognize the correct answer if a test item is multiple-choice or to know whether an item is true or false. The key in memorization tasks is to be able to categorize the information so that you don't get it mixed up. In the case of our examples, you want to be able to distinguish the characteristics of short-term memory from those of long-term memory.

For objective tests that ask higher-level questions, you'll have to take a different approach. You still want to ask yourself questions, but now you'll need to go a step further and ask yourself "how" and "why" questions, think of examples, and draw conclusions. If you ask yourself these kinds of questions, you'll be able to handle whatever your prof throws out on the exam.

STUDY WITH OTHERS

Students tell us that studying with others is a good way to prepare for objective exams. You can ask each other questions and get honest evaluations about how good an answer you have given. If you approach your questions and answers seriously, studying with others can also be a confidence-builder. If you study with someone else, writing questions on index cards can help you target your studying. Or if you have already made other written items such as concept cards or charts, you can formulate your questions directly from those. You can also use the questions you have posed in the margins of your lecture notes to test yourself.

☹ SAD BUT TRUE

Mason and a several of his friends were all in the same anthropology course. Because the tests largely consisted of objective-type questions, Mason thought it would be a good idea to form a study group so that they could all help one another out. No one really liked the course very much, but Mason thought they might all survive it and maybe even pull out half-decent grades if they got together on a regular basis. The group decided to meet every Thursday evening and also the evening before each exam. Their intentions were good: everyone was supposed to keep up, take notes as best they could, and be prepared to talk through the information. They planned on quizzing each other before the tests. Unfortunately, things didn't go so well. After the first week, the so-called study sessions turned into discussions of the places in town where they could hear the best bands, talking about relationship problems, and general gripe sessions about this and other courses. Then someone always got hungry, and it was off for pizza or wings. Most of the group fell behind. Mason's idea of forming a study group was good; his big mistake was involving friends who couldn't stay on task.

It's important to remember that being part of a study group requires that each member contribute something. The purpose of a study group is to exchange ideas and discuss information. But many students feel that working in study groups is a waste of time. We believe that opinion is common because most times, students meet in groups with their friends and goof off more than they study. To avoid this pitfall, have a plan of what you will do in your study group, and don't plan to meet until after each member has studied some on his or her own. For example, the night before an exam, members of the study group could ask each other questions to determine their readiness for the test—this assumes each member has already studied the material. So go to your study group prepared. Have questions ready about information that isn't clear to you. Be ready to ask (and be able to answer) challenging questions that match the task outlined by the professor.

STUDY OVER A PERIOD OF DAYS

Another key to being successful on objective tests is to distribute your studying and learning over a period of days. Although cramming can get you through occasionally, using cramming as your study method of choice can be stressful, unproductive, and in some cases downright foolish. Students who begin prepping a reasonable amount of time before the test usually are more relaxed and confident, and they do better. But what is a reasonable amount of time? It's different for everyone, and depends on the amount of information covered on the test, how much you already know about the topic, how much you have kept up, and the type of test you will have. In general, however, think about these questions:

- **What are the big concepts covered in this test?** You should be able to jot down the big picture.

- **How familiar are you with the concepts?** You should be able to gauge the amount of test prep time you will need by the amount of information you already know. The trick is to be honest with yourself. How much information do you *really* know, and how much do you only sort of know? Don't be in denial.

- **What does your schedule look like for the few days before the exam?** You'll need additional time built into your study schedule for exam preparation. You don't want your test preparation for one class to cut down on your regular study time for another class. If you let it, preparing for a big exam can make you fall behind in your other courses.

- **How will you group concepts for study?** Many students make the mistake of preparing for tests in a very unfocused way. They "look through" their text or they "read over" their notes during each study session. Quite frankly, this is a very inefficient way to study. It's much more effective to organize your studying by concepts, and to study so that you know one concept very well before moving on to another. For example, if one of the major concepts that you'll be tested on in biology is meiosis, study all the information on that topic from both text and lecture in one study session. Then, in your next study session, review what you have learned about meiosis—talk yourself through the information and ask yourself questions—and move on to mitosis. Studying this way helps you keep the information straight and also helps you really know and understand each concept.

In general, begin your study process a few days in advance (we suggest at least three days for most courses). And don't confuse studying with reading. Before you begin your exam prep, you should have all of your reading assignments finished. In addition, you'll probably need to add some time to your normal studying schedule to get ready to study for the exam. Before you start studying, organize all of your notes and other study materials and then divide the material into concepts to be studied. Be sure to have a goal for each of your study sessions. Begin each new study session with a review of what you learned in the previous session.

The pacing of your study sessions before a test also depends on when the professor stops lecturing on material that will be covered on the exam. Some professors lecture on test material up to the class period before the exam. If that's the case, you'll have to be sure you spend some time studying the information presented late so that you are prepared to answer questions. It helps, however, if you have done all of your reading and have studied most of the test material so that all you have to do is fill in the gaps with the lecture information.

LISTEN UP

Time ≠ learning (or, not necessarily). Students are fooled into thinking they know the information simply because they have put in some time (or even a lot of time). To really learn you need to really think, and you need to monitor what you know as you go along.

THE INSIDE SCOOP

Being successful on tests requires you to be honest with yourself and to clearly articulate what you know and don't know. This is called monitoring your learning, remember? Students who are good monitors tend to do better on exams than those who are not. So remember, as you are studying for tests, talk through what you know and then reflect. If you don't understand something, stop right then and get clarification. Know what you know.

Tips for Taking Objective Exams

All right. You have studied in a way that matches the task and you have distributed your studying over a period of days. You're confident that you know the information (at least most of it). You are seriously ready to kick some exam butt. However, there are some additional tips that may help you maximize your performance even more—tips for getting more questions right once you are actually taking the test.

Have you ever found yourself in this situation? You actually did study smart for a test. You knew the information and you had confidence in your ability to earn a good grade. But then you got into the testing situation and you forgot easy material, were distracted by minor noises, thought too deeply about questions, and got confused over ideas you were certain you knew very well. These things have probably happened to every student at some time or another, particularly in classes that are anxiety producing. But some of these events can be prevented if you know that they can be stumbling blocks. The savvy student acknowledges they can happen and does her best to cope with them. In order to maximize your performance try the following:

- Get to the testing situation early. Take your seat, get out your pen or pencil, close your eyes, and take several deep breaths.

- Don't talk with others about the course material right before the exam. We've all been there. You think you're prepared and then your classmate says, "What about transforming the units to mass? What was that all about?" You hadn't even considered this in your studying and you begin to panic. But it may be that the information is trivial, or that your classmate may have learned it incorrectly.

LISTEN UP

If a classmate tries to talk to you before an exam and you want to tell him to go away (but you don't want to appear rude), try telling him that you are taking a few minutes to relax before the exam but that you'd be happy to talk once the test has ended. Just try taking a few deep breaths and blocking out the distractions in the room. This simple relaxation technique can help you concentrate better on the test.

- Engage in positive self-talk. Tell yourself that you know the information and that you expect to make a good grade on the test. (Note: This is not a replacement for actual studying; it only helps if you really *do* know the material.)

- Read the directions carefully, especially on the first test. The directions will give you information about how to think about the questions. For example, you may be instructed to select the *best* answer. In this case, more than one of the answer choices may be correct, but only one is the best answer.

😟 SAD BUT TRUE

Lavon felt truly unprepared when he went in to take his psychology exam, but he figured, "What the heck. It's only multiple-choice, so at least I have a chance of guessing and with any luck, I'll pull at least a C." His day didn't start off well. He overslept (bad omen to begin with) and arrived in the classroom ten minutes late...and without a #2 pencil. The prof gave him "the look" when Lavon came to the front of the classroom to get a copy of the test, and was clearly annoyed about having to lend him a pencil. Because 15 minutes of class had already passed and he had 100 questions to get through, Lavon didn't bother to read the directions, which to his mind seemed rather extensive for a multiple-choice test. He just dove in and started bubbling in answers on his sheet. When the five-minute warning came, he did some speed-reading and ended up at least having an answer for each question. He turned in his exam (and returned the pencil to the prof) and headed back to his dorm. On his way back, he caught up with Alexis, another student who had just taken the psychology test. She was fit to be tied, ranting about how the scoring of the test was so unfair. "What are you talking about?" asked Lavon. "Didn't you read the directions?" she said. "Professor Miller put a penalty on for guessing. If you weren't sure of the item and left it blank, you only had a half-point taken off, but if you guessed and got it wrong, you had a full point taken off. I just think it's so unfair. I've never taken a test where there was a penalty for guessing." Lavon was speechless. Not only did he not study enough, he got to class late and he didn't bother reading the directions. He learned several valuable lessons that day, perhaps the most important of which was *always read the directions.*

- Do the easy questions first. What's easy will vary from one person to the next. If you're not sure of the answer to the first question, go on to the second. Continue until you have answered all of the questions you know. Then go back and tackle those that you're unsure of.

- Consider all of the alternatives. Read each choice, even if you are sure the best answer is choice "a." Sometimes a minor change in wording makes one answer better than another. Or sometimes choice "d" reads "both a and c," which you'd miss if you only read choice "a."

- Narrow your choices. Turn each of the answer choices into a true or false question if a multiple choice item confuses you. Sometimes this helps clarify which choice is correct. If you are unsure of an item, you can also use both what you know and other items that deal with similar information to eliminate implausible answer choices.

- Watch for qualifiers. On true or false tests, items that contain words such as "always" or "never" are usually false (things rarely happen always or never). Questions that contain words such as "seldom" or "frequently" are usually true.

- Tackle the items that you are least sure of last. Don't waste too much time on one item, only to have to "Christmas tree" the remaining items because you have run out of time. If it stumps you, skip it and return to it. Then eliminate answer choices that you know are incorrect, make a choice between what is left, and move on.

- Never leave an objective item blank, unless you are penalized for guessing. Even if you are clueless as to the right answer, you have a 50 percent chance of getting true or false questions correct and a 20 to 25 percent chance of getting multiple-choice question correct (for five- and four-choice answers, respectively). Chances diminish on matching items, but it usually doesn't hurt to guess.

Be test-wise. Putting these tips into action can gain you valuable points on all of your objective tests.

Eenie, Meenie, Minie, Moe...If You Have to Guess

Of course we know this will never happen to you, but here are a few quick tips to help that friend of yours who must guess make the best possible choices.

- On multiple-choice exams, look for patterns in answer choices for the items you are sure of. Most professors have a favorite answer choice spot, and if you don't have a clue about the answer, their favorite is the best guess you can make.

- If you can't figure out your prof's favorite and have no other idea (you haven't been able to eliminate any of the choices) "b" or "c" is usually the best choice. Most professors don't like to use "a" very often—they would rather bury the answer than make it the first of the choices.

- It's better to select a longer answer choice than a shorter one when you're guessing, especially if one of the four or five choices is significantly longer than the others.

- For true or false questions, do all the questions you know first and then go back and mark either *all* true or *all* false for the remaining items. This approach only works when you've really studied and know most of the answers. If you have 20 true or false questions and you only know the answers to 5 of them, marking the other 15 as all true or false may not buy many points—even with a 50/50 chance.

- Once you guess, move on. Go with your gut feeling and resist the temptation to go back and change your answers to the point where you have rubbed large holes in your paper. In fact, the only time you should change an answer on an objective test is when you have either thought of additional information that makes you change your mind or picked up additional information in another item.

> Procrastination is suicide on the installment plan.
> —Anonymous

An A+ for You: Evaluating Your Test Performance

For most students, the test is old news when it's returned and gone over in class. Our experience has been that when students do well, they yell something to this effect to someone across the room: "Hey, man what did you get? I got an A!" If, however, they did poorly, they cram the test in the back of their book and never look at it again. You know, that denial thing going on again—if I hide this it will just magically not exist. But you can learn a lot from your exams. Remember, all of college is a learning experience, even things you hate like tests. If you want to improve your performance (if you didn't do so well) or maintain high performance (if you did great) you should take a little time to examine the types of objective items you got right and wrong. There is usually a pattern to your errors. If you evaluate how you did, you'll also be able to figure out how to tweak your studying for the next exam.

If you did poorly on an exam, particularly if you thought you did well, it's important to figure out just what the problem is. If your prof doesn't go over the test in class or if he simply posts grades and all you see is a score, you need to make an appointment to go over your test. Don't feel as though it's an imposition. Having office hours and meeting with students is part of every professor's job. Once you're there, make specific note of the kinds of items you got wrong. Look for patterns. For example, did you miss lots of items that came from the textbook or from the lectures? Did you miss items that were examples? Did you miss more true or false items than matching items? Did you miss higher-level questions but answer all of the factual questions correctly? Once you have a better handle on the kinds of items you're missing, you can adjust your preparation for the next exam accordingly.

Evaluating your exam performance is important to do after every test, but it is particularly important to do after the first one. This is especially true if you didn't do so hot. The sooner you evaluate what you did right and wrong, the sooner you can get back on track and still pull a good grade in the course.

Quick and Dirty

○ Studying for objective exams usually requires more than just memorizing facts. In college, most professors will ask higher-level questions that require you to think critically about the materials.

○ Be test-wise. There are lots of little tips that can help you increase your score on objective tests.

○ When you have to guess, try to do it in an organized way. And remember, never leave an item blank on an objective test unless you're penalized for guessing.

○ Always, always, always evaluate your performance so you don't make the same mistakes over and over.

CHAPTER 21

BLUEBOOK BLUES: PREPPING FOR AND TAKING ESSAY EXAMS

Writing is easy. All you do is stare
at a blank sheet of paper until drops
of blood form on your forehead.

–Gene Fowler

The first question that is usually asked after a professor announces that she will be giving essay exams is "How long should each answer be?" Usually this question is asked in all sincerity, but because professors are sometimes frustrated that length is their students' main concern, many answer it in a deadpan manner, "As long as it needs to be to answer the question," and move on, hopefully to questions that focus more on intellectual or content issues.

There's no doubt about it: most students would much rather have a root canal than take essay tests. If they have to take tests, they would rather take objective tests, because they figure that on objective tests at least you can guess. It's almost impossible to guess on essay questions, because you either know the information or you don't. Essay exams seem to stress students out because:

1. They try to study for essay exams in the same way they study for multiple-choice exams.

245

2. They don't think of themselves as good writers who can organize their thoughts in a brief period of time.

3. They can memorize the facts but can't weave the information together, so they are not good at seeing the big picture.

4. They find it difficult to predict what the essays will be about and worry that they will study the wrong information.

If you are dreading taking essay exams in college, then this is the chapter for you. Using the strategies in this chapter should help you prepare for and succeed on your essay exams.

THE INSIDE SCOOP

When writing out your answers to essay exams or short-answer exams, remember this tip: when in doubt, leave it out. If you're not sure if the information you are thinking about including in your essay is correct, don't include it in your essay. If you include wrong information, your professor has no choice but to take points off your score, but if you leave out a relatively unimportant piece of information and the rest of your answer is correct, you will probably lose fewer points.

Studying for Essay Exams

Professors use essay questions to see if you can filter through the volumes of course information to find out what is important. Then they expect you to explain in your own words why it is important. Because you have to recall the information without any cues and because you have to put it into your own words, studying for essays is different than studying for multiple-choice exams. There are a few basic steps involved in preparing for essay exams.

Predict test questions. As you study, make up questions that could actually be asked on the test. That means that every time you read, annotate, or review lecture notes and other material you should be thinking about what kinds of essay questions could be asked using that information. It is actually a good idea to write down some predicted test questions as you go. Think about what the professor has stressed in class; often profs give away the essay questions by emphasizing the topics in lectures. Then once you have learned the information, you can evaluate your understanding of the concepts by answering the questions you predicted.

As you are reading, don't memorize material. For an essay exam, you really don't need to know the same level of picky detail that you need to know on objective exams. Instead, you will need to see how all of the information relates to the big picture. Rather than focusing on just the facts, look for relationships between ideas and use details as a way of supporting your points. This means noting themes, patterns, causes and effects, comparisons and contrasts, and other relationships as you see them. These are the things that essay exam questions are made of. Think about the examples in the text and how they relate to or explain the main ideas.

Elaborate on information as you learn it. This means you should expand on the information you are learning. One simple way to elaborate on information is to use examples from your own experience when you can (this can be tough to do in some courses, like history or entomology, but try it where it seems appropriate). You should also make an effort to connect what you are learning to what you already know about the topic, which helps make the information personal, and therefore, more memorable. Making maps, charts, or diagrams to help you reorganize the information can help you see interrelationships and connections between ideas.

Answer a predicted question beforehand. We realize that this is a lot to ask, but if you know that you struggle with writing or that you often have trouble organizing your essays, this is an essential step. All you need to do is answer one or two of the questions you've predicted. If you suffer from writing anxiety, practicing at home is a great remedy—really.

Studying for essay exams begins when you first open your book to read, not the night before the exam. Once you use our approach, you'll probably find that you feel a lot better prepared.

It's All in the Way It's Worded

You are sitting in the classroom looking at your test paper, when suddenly you realize you are not sure what the professor means when she asks you to "illustrate the tenets of the feminist movement." How does "illustrate" differ from "define"? Many students lose points because they do not pay attention or respond to the language used in the question. To help you interpret these questions, we offer a handy guide to typical essay question words. As noted in the last chapter, exam questions words generally divide into two types—memory-level and higher-level. The words professors use to ask essay questions can be divided along these lines as well.

MEMORY-LEVEL QUESTION WORDS

These questions ask you to recall information from your text or lecture notes. Suppose you were learning the information in the memory passage from chapter 16. An example of a memory-level essay question on that material would be "Summarize the three types of memory storage."

Some common memory-level question words include:

- **Define.** This is the most basic type of question. When you are asked to "define X" or you are asked, "What is X?" you need to give the meaning of the term or concept. (Note: If you discussed several different definitions in class, be prepared to give more than one definition in your response.) No matter what type of essay question you are given, it is always a good idea to define your terms.

> **URBAN LEGEND**
>
> A philosophy professor gave an essay exam that asked students to define "courage." The highest grade was given to the student who turned in his paper minutes after the exam was handed out after writing "This is."

- **Illustrate.** Generally this type of question is asking you to describe the concept using specific examples. You need to make sure that in your response you explicitly state how the examples connect with the concept and how the ideas you are illustrating relate to one another.

- **Summarize.** Briefly explain the concept you've learned.

- **Trace.** This question word asks you discuss events or developments over time.

HIGHER-LEVEL QUESTION WORDS

These question words ask you to explain or apply information you have learned; you'll typically find higher-level questions on college-level essay exams. These are generally more difficult than memory-level questions because you will need to interpret the information to be able to answer the question. An example of a higher-level essay question on memory would be "Compare and contrast the characteristics and functions of short-term and long-term memory."

Some common higher-level question words include:

- **Compare and contrast.** This phrase asks you to describe what two or more things have in common (compare) and how they differ (contrast). Remember, if the question asks you to compare and contrast you must do both (compare *and* contrast) in order to fully answer the essay.

- **Relate.** In this case you need to show relationships between ideas.

- **Cause and effect.** This type of question asks you to show how one event (or more) made something else happen and then to discuss the consequences of that event.

- **Prove (justify, support).** To answer this type of question you need to provide evidence and/or examples to support your stand.

- **Evaluate.** This type of question asks you to assess information about the topic and then discuss its pros and cons.

- **Analyze.** To respond to this type of question, you need to examine a topic closely and discuss its importance or what it means.

- **Synthesize.** This type of question asks you to pull together two or more pieces of information. This is not the same as a compare and contrast question because you need to provide a reason for putting these two or more ideas together (not just discuss their similarities and differences).

- **Argue.** This type of question asks you to take a side and defend your point against the other side.

One of the keys to doing well on essays is to take the time to read and reflect on what the questions are asking you to do. Remember to think carefully about the question before you begin to write.

Elements of a Good Essay

Although every professor has her own criteria for grading essays (and you should find out what these are before your first exam), there are some common elements to a well-constructed essay.

A GOOD ESSAY IS ORGANIZED

THE INSIDE SCOOP

Did you ever start to write an essay only to forget some of the points you wanted to make? Did a professor ever tell you that your essay would have been better if you'd only made a stronger argument? Making a jot list can help you with both of these issues. First, when you make your jot list, the act of writing down all of the information helps you remember what you know about the topic. Then, once it is written down, you can reorganize the order of the points in a way that makes sense, which creates a stronger argument.

Plan before you write. After you read the question, jot down all of the key points you want to cover in your essay. Then think through the best, most logical order for the points you will discuss.

A GOOD ESSAY IS FOCUSED

Be sure to answer each and every part of the essay fully, but don't try to BS the professor. In college, the person asking you the essay question is probably an expert on the question's topic. So there's a good chance he knows way more than you (or even your textbook) about the matter. Your professor will know if you are trying to pad your answer with a bunch of nonsense. Instead, stay focused on the question and write what you know, but don't worry too much about how long your answer is (unless, of course, your professor tells you that you should). Of course, you may want to be concerned if you've only written two sentences and your classmates have each filled a bluebook....

A GOOD ESSAY IS WELL SUPPORTED AND PERSUASIVE

Whenever you make a point in an essay, be sure that it is well supported or documented. Use information from your texts, lectures, and any other sources referred to in class. If your essay reads like you have just pulled the idea out of thin air, your professor will not buy it and you will lose points on the exam. So use examples, specific details, names, and facts to substantiate your argument.

A GOOD ESSAY IS GRAMMATICAL

When you are finished writing your essay, read it over looking for grammar and spelling errors. Although your professor may not take off points specifically for grammar issues (do find out your professor's policy on grammar and spelling errors before your first exam), your essay will certainly read better if it has few of these errors; this, in turn, will lead to a higher grade.

> **LISTEN UP**
>
> Be careful about using words such as "always" or "never" unless you are absolutely sure that the word is justified (and not an exaggeration). It is better to use generalizations when you can't remember an exact fact. For example, it is better to write "in the late 1960s" if you can't remember whether an event happened in 1968 or 1969. Usually the more general term will be sufficient.

Put It in Writing

The professor has handed out the exam and you are ready to go. But, wait. There are a few things you need to do before you start to write.

BEFORE YOU START WRITING

The first step in writing a good essay is to plan your time. Whenever you take an essay exam, spend the first few minutes budgeting the allotted time. Be sure to leave ample time for planning as well as for writing the essay and reviewing it when it's done. You also want to take the point value for each question into account when making your plan. Suppose you have three essay questions to respond to in a 50-minute class—which is a lot to do in such a short amount of time, but not at all uncommon. The first essay is worth 50 points and the other two are worth 25 points each. How would you budget your time? We'd suggest the following:

8 minutes	Planning and organizing
16 minutes	Essay 1 (worth 50 percent)
10 minutes	Essay 2 (worth 25 percent)
10 minutes	Essay 3 (worth 25 percent)
6 minutes	Review and proofread

This is a pretty tight time frame, and you'd need to stick to your plan to make it through all three questions. Notice that this plan leaves a good deal of time for getting your essays together at the beginning of the exam; students who take the time to do this step find they write out their responses to the essay questions faster and more easily than those who do not.

😔 SAD BUT TRUE

Lynn was unable to finish her political science essay exam because she did not read the direction stating, "Choose and respond to any two questions." Instead, Lynn attempted to answer all six, ran out of time, and was unable to give the level of detail needed in any of her responses. Basically, she just had time to write a few main points for each question, but not to use examples or details to support her arguments. In addition, Lynn's essays were loaded with grammar and spelling errors because she did not have time to review them. Lynn's professor only read the first two answers and took off a lot of points for responses that were too vague and too general.

If you are given a choice, the next step is to decide which question or questions you will answer. Then annotate the questions. Note key words in the margin and make a note of all of the tasks asked in the essay. Notice the key words annotated in this sample history essay question.

Chapter Twenty-One

Evaluate the factors leading to Johnson's decision to enter the Vietnamese
Conflict. Discuss the importance of both domestic and foreign affairs in
shaping Johnson's decision.

Evaluate factors in LBJ's
decision—need to make
judgment based on events

Discuss imp. of—
1. domestic affairs
2. foreign affairs

Next, make a jot list of the information you want to cover. A jot list for the question above might look like this:

1. Domestic affairs
   Great Society
   Civil rights movement
   Hawks and doves
   JFK legacy

2. Foreign affairs
   "Domino effect"
   Cuba
   China
   Ho Chi Minh
   Cabinet advisors' advice

A conclusion is the
place where you got
tired of thinking.

—Arthur Bloch

Notice how there are not a lot of words on the jot list, just enough to help you remember what you wanted to talk about. Your next step would be to organize the topics in order of importance.

ESSAY AS ONE, TWO, THREE

You probably learned to write five-paragraph essays in high school to suit all your essay writing needs. But in college you'll need to be more flexible in your writing (some essay questions may take upwards of twenty paragraphs to answer). So think about your essays as being composed of three main parts—the introduction, the body, and the conclusion—rather than five paragraphs.

1. **The introduction.** After you have annotated the question and made (and organized) your jot list, begin your essay with a good introduction. Your introduction can restate the question or pose a new one: "How did domestic and foreign affairs influence Johnson's decision to enter the Vietnamese Conflict?" The rest of your introductory paragraph should introduce all of the key points you will make in your essay so that the reader has a good idea of what you are about to discuss.

2. **The body of the essay.** The body of your paper is where you will develop your argument. Begin each paragraph with a topic sentence that expands upon one of the key points made in your introduction. Write in full sentences and complete paragraphs; use formal language (not slang or colloquialisms). Use transitions to get from point to point (or paragraph to paragraph). Words and phrases like *because, therefore, in contrast, as a result, first, second, third,* and *finally* will help the reader follow your train of thought. Each paragraph in the body of your essay should contain only one major point and your support for it.

Q THE INSIDE SCOOP

Students who write good, solid introductions receive scores that are almost one full grade letter higher than students who write just an average intro (even when the bodies of the papers were identical, researchers found that professors gave higher scores to the papers with the great intros). So your high school teacher was right when she told you to "write a snazzy introduction to grab the reader's attention."

3. **The conclusion.** The last paragraph of your essay should summarize the points you made and connect them to your central argument. It should also emphasize the importance of your argument.

LISTEN UP

What should you do if you run out of time while still writing your essay? Outline the points you would have made and point your instructor to your jot list of topics. You will probably at least get partial credit.

(We both love this one!) Two students went to Florida for spring break. They had a history essay exam on the first day back from break, but they were having such a good time, they decided to stay on one more day. Both students were doing well in the history class and had made As on the previous exam and felt that the professor would cut them a break. When they returned to school they went to their professor's office and told him that they were sorry for missing the exam, but that they had gotten a flat tire on the way home from spring break and couldn't get help for a long time, so they were late in getting back. The professor thought about this for a while and the students were very relieved when he said that he would give them a make-up exam the next day. Both students arrived promptly the next morning and the professor placed them in separate rooms, gave them the exam booklet, and wished them luck. Both students were completely caught off guard when they opened the exam booklet and read, "This item is worth 100 points—which tire?"

AFTER WRITING

Take a few minutes to review your responses. Be sure that you answered all parts of the question and that your response makes sense. Reading your responses can help you find and correct grammar and spelling errors. And, more importantly, sometimes when you review your answers you think of points to add that will strengthen your response. You may even find entire paragraphs that are off topic and that you will end up crossing out to make your essay more coherent. Don't worry about making correction marks on your paper or using arrows to guide your professor to information you've added at the end. Trust us, you will be glad you set aside some time to do this.

Taking essay exams does not need to be an overwhelming task, especially if you keep the structure of a good essay in mind as you write. We suggest that you revisit this chapter every time you need to take an essay test to remind yourself of the steps involved in good essay writing.

> How can I tell what I think till I see what I say?
>
> —E. M. Forster

Quick and Dirty

○ Prepare for the exam from day one. Every time you read or study, think about possible test questions, note relationships between ideas (such as causes and effects), and look for the big picture.

○ Decode your essay question. Take a look at the question words used by the professor to determine what she is asking you to do. Then think about the level of thinking required by the question—this will be either memory-level or higher-level thinking.

○ Organize your ideas by making a jot list and planning your time.

○ Think before you write, write well, then think about what you've written.

CHAPTER 22

IS THAT YOUR FINAL ANSWER?

Of course, it is very important to be sober when you take an exam. Many worthwhile careers in the street-cleaning, fruit-picking and subway-guitar-playing industries have been founded on a lack of understanding of this simple fact.

—Terry Pratchett

Exams. Tests. Quizzes. Whatever you call them, they have struck fear in the hearts of just about every college student we know. Although exams in college are a part of everyday life, most students probably would not view them as the fun part—challenging, maybe, but not their favorite part of the college experience. Most college students would acknowledge, however, that not only do you have to learn information, but you must also be able to document that you have learned something. That's what tests are all about.

Some students decide to wait until after the first test to really figure out what they need to do to prepare. But if you have only three exams and a final (and sometimes you'll face far fewer exams than that), you are putting yourself at a disadvantage if you wait. Instead, practice some of the general test prep and test-taking strategies we suggest to help you do well in almost any testing situation.

Smart Exam Prep

Although the last two chapters told you how preparing for essay exams differs from preparing for objective exams (i.e., multiple-choice, true or false, and so on), there are some general "good advice" tips that cut across all kinds of tests. You may have heard similar tips before, especially when you were getting ready to take high-pressure tests like the SAT or ACT, but it never hurts to hear them again as they relate to classroom tests.

Get a good night's sleep. It's plain and simple. You can't think straight or perform at your best when you are exhausted. You'll end up feeling muddled and won't be able to concentrate on your exam. So try to get a full night's sleep (or at least six hours) before your exams.

Make sure you have everything you need. Get all of your materials together the night before so that you don't have to rush around right before your exam. There is nothing worse than getting to your exam and realizing that you left your calculator (or pencil, or bluebook, or student ID) at home.

😦 **SAD BUT TRUE**

Will, a junior engineering major, would forget his head if it wasn't attached to his body. We're not sure if Will ever went to an exam with everything he needed. For exams in his civil engineering class he was allowed to bring a calculator and a page of notes with him. He also needed his student ID to show for each test. Will used to call his roommates in a panic several times before every test saying things like, "Could you just look through my desk? There's a paper somewhere on it that has a bunch of formulas written in very small print. Could you please find it and drive it over to me in the next 15 minutes?" The joke with Will's friends was that he was so forgetful that once he even forgot his shoes (honestly!). What Will needed to do was to pack up everything the night before his tests.

Distribute your study time. Rather than cramming all your studying into one or two sessions, plan to study over several days. In general, the more times you interact with the material, the better you'll learn it.

Monitor your learning. Know what you know and don't know. You can check your knowledge of the material on which you will be tested by asking yourself questions about the information as you review. This is really the most important part of studying. As we have heard from our students, there is no better feeling than walking into an exam knowing that you are ready for it.

Using these general strategies should help you no matter what the testing situation, but read on for strategies for dealing with special situations, such as the need to cram for exams and studying for midterms and finals.

A Word about Cramming

Its 7:00 P.M. on Thursday, you have been sick as a dog since Monday night, and you have a big exam Friday morning. You have been far too ill to study, but now it is down to the wire. At least you're able to drag your butt out of bed. But what will you do? In a word, cram. Cramming, as we have mentioned, is not the world's greatest way to prepare for exams. For some, cramming becomes a habit and a way of life (and we sincerely hope that those students have learned some alternative study methods in *College Rules!*). But even for the most conscientious student, sometimes cramming simply cannot be avoided. So for those (hopefully) extremely rare occasions when you need to cram, here is some good advice on how to maximize your time and focus your effort.

LISTEN UP

Some students think that caffeine or other substances will help them cram for exams (some even take Adderal, a medicine for ADD), but these chemicals can actually make it harder to remember the information while you are taking the exams. Have a few cups of coffee if it helps you stay awake, but don't overdo it—taking an exam with a hangover from drugs (or even too much caffeine) can make you do much worse than you would have otherwise.

Preview the material. Look at your syllabus, your text, and your notes to see what topics will be covered on the exam.

Be selective. Use the quick and dirty approach to reading. Read headings, subheadings, and boldfaced words to learn the main concepts in each chapter. Don't attempt to learn everything, because you just won't have enough time.

Target your lecture notes. Your professor generally emphasizes the most important points. Focus your attention on those key concepts and try to read about those topics in the textbook as well if you have time.

Spend time only on the material you don't know. If you had more time, we'd suggest that you review the material you know and then try to connect it to the material you don't. But when you are cramming, just focus on the new stuff and learn it as best as you can.

Repetition, repetition, repetition. The only way to learn a lot of material fast is to just repeat it over and over again until you have it memorized. Now, this is not a great way to learn information, as we have stated throughout *College Rules!*, but cramming is an occasion for emergency survival techniques.

Test yourself on the information. Better yet, midway through studying, have a friend or roommate ask you questions about the material. This can help you monitor your learning and determine where to focus your attention for the remainder of your studying. Even crammers need to monitor.

Get some sleep. Pulling an all-nighter to study will not help you if you are falling asleep while taking the test. You probably will not be able to get a full night's rest, but even a few hours' sleep can really make a difference in your ability to perform on the exam.

Stay calm during the exam. Because information studied in cramming sessions is not learned deeply, you are more likely to forget it under pressure. Take a few deep breaths, don't panic, and promise yourself that you won't put yourself in this situation again.

After you take the exam, take a few minutes to think about how you got into a situation where you needed to cram. Was it really a one-time emergency or were there things you could have done differently to avoid the pressures of cramming? Think about the changes you'd need to make to steer clear of cramming for future exams.

Acing Exams

You've read and annotated the chapters and reviewed your notes, and now the professor is handing out the test. You didn't need to cram this time and are feeling pretty good about the material, but a little nervous about taking the test. What should you do now? Well, there are a few tips and tricks we've learned that will help you do the best you can.

Relax. Take a few minutes to relax before the exam is distributed. When you get to your seat, close your eyes or put your head on the desk and practice some deep breathing. If you are feeling anxious about the exam, breathing deeply is a great way to calm yourself down.

Read the directions. We know far too many students who have lost points because they did not know what was expected of them. You may even want to circle the key words in the directions just to be sure you will remember them as you work through the test.

FOR ADULTS ONLY X

Many of our nontraditional students have told us that they get very nervous before exams. It may be because they haven't taken exams in a while or because they are worried about being compared to 18-year-olds and coming up short. Whatever the case, adult college students need to use good test-taking strategies so that they do not psyche themselves out. Remember, you've studied, you are prepared, and you will do well (repeat this to yourself as necessary during the test).

Preview the test. Look at the number of items and the exam format to be sure that the test consists of the items you had expected. Also, consider the point distribution for the questions. If the questions in section one are worth five points each and those in section two only two points apiece, plan to spend more time on section one.

Answer what you know first. You don't have to start with question one. When you are taking your test, answer the questions you know first and skip over those you do not know. Come back to the skipped questions before the end of the exam.

Resist the urge to change answers. Don't change your answer unless you find information in a later question or remember something specific that tells you that your first hunch was incorrect.

Don't be in a hurry to leave. We know that when you are done taking a test you just want to get out of there, but you can often find careless errors or skipped items when you take the time to review your answers.

Keep your mind on your own business. In other words, don't be distracted by what other students are doing. Sometimes students tell us that they lose confidence when they see other students leaving before they are even close to being finished. But our advice is to not worry about others; maybe those students are leaving because they don't know any of the answers.

LISTEN UP

What should you do if you think the professor has made a mistake in grading your exam, or if you think a question was really confusing? Most professors hate to talk to students about individual exam questions. This is most likely because they feel hounded for points. We think this is a shame, however, because students can learn a lot from reviewing exams (and professors can learn something about making better test questions). If you feel that your professor should reexamine part of your exam, speak up. But you may want to email your professor rather than confronting him in class. Support your point with page numbers from the text or information from your notes or describe your thinking on a particular question. Ask your professor to meet with you to discuss the issue further. He just might throw out the question altogether.

Some students have told us that there is a psychology to taking exams and that it is easy to make yourself overly stressed by reading too much into a question or worrying about what other students are doing. Try to remain calm as you enter the classroom, and congratulate yourself for a job well done (because hopefully you have aced the test) when you leave.

Surviving Midterms and Finals

It is that time of year again. All classes stop, yet a strange buzz of activity is present all over campus. Sales of caffeinated beverages soar as students desperately try to remember all of the material they've learned during the semester. And it is no small feat. If you are taking four courses and for each course you have had about 40 lectures

> It is hard to fail, but it is worse never to have tried to succeed.
> —Theodore Roosevelt

and read 25 chapters, that means that by the time finals hit you will need to study 160 sets of lecture notes and 100 textbook chapters. Wow.

Our best advice is to plan for finals throughout your semester by using the reviewing strategies we have discussed. But despite your best efforts throughout the semester, finals do present a unique situation. Here are some time-tested survival strategies for getting through these tough weeks.

Consider finals week to be finals *weeks*. In other words, start early. Rather than waiting until the night before the beginning of finals week to begin studying, start a few weeks in advance by beginning to organize the information and to review course content. Or better yet, plan to stay organized all along.

Set up study groups. A study group can be a real lifesaver when you're studying for big exams. After you have studied on your own, plan to meet with some classmates to quiz each other over the material. If it is a really tough subject and you are having trouble, you may want to have your group meet with a tutor.

GET WIRED

If you think you will be too busy to meet with your study group in person, set up a virtual study group. You can either plan to all be online at the same time or you can set up a Listserv where group members can pose and answer questions.

Find your pace for studying. We don't think that many students can study for ten hours a day and be particularly effective. Instead, figure out your studying threshold and take breaks before you burn out. In general, don't try to study for more than an hour or so without taking a short (ten-minute) break.

Know what kind of exam you will have. Will your midterm or final cover all of the material up to that point (is it cumulative)? Or will it only cover the material that has been presented since the last exam? You will prepare differently depending on how much material you need to review.

Study in reverse. Unless your professor tells you otherwise, focus your studying on the more current topics rather than the material that you were already tested on.

Know when and where your final will be. In most colleges finals are on their own schedule, so they will be at a different time and often in a different location than where you have met for class all term. You don't want to create further stress by realizing at the last minute that you don't know the building or room where you are supposed to take the test.

😦 **SAD BUT TRUE**

Sandy kept having nightmares that she would miss her 8:00 A.M. chemistry final exam. She set two alarm clocks and even had her mother call her to make sure she got up on time. Sandy got to the building with 15 minutes to spare, only to find an empty classroom. Panicking, Sandy remembered the overhead the professor had put up on the last day of class regarding the exam. She had written down the time and date, but had not written down the room assignment for the final, assuming that it would be in the same classroom. Now she had no idea where her exam was being held. When she finally found her class, she had missed 30 crucial minutes of exam time.

Plan your time strategically. Analyze your needs for each class when you plan out your study time. Now is the time to be realistic. If you are making a solid C in economics and would need an astronomical score on the final exam to pull a B, yet you're hanging between a B and an A in computer science, it may be better to spend more time on comp sci. In other words, put your efforts into pulling for the A and let the other class stay at a C. You need to make these judgment calls before you make your studying plan. This is just one of the many aspects of college that have to do with choices.

Plan several study sessions for each class. Your studying plan should include at least some time for each class. Remember, it is always better to spread out your studying for a class over several days rather than cram it into one session.

Break up your studying. No one can concentrate for five hours on physics problems. Work on one subject for a while then switch to another. It is best to switch to something that requires a different task, if possible. For example, switch from reading your history notes to working math problems.

Know what's at stake. Find out how much the midterm or final will count toward your final grade. In some classes, the final is worth the same as any exam; in others it can be worth as much as 50 percent of your total grade. Knowing this information can help you decide how to spend your studying time.

Don't burn out. Reward yourself, because studying for finals is hard work. At the end of each day, do something nice for yourself. Exercise to relieve tension, see a movie, hang out with friends, or eat a big bowl of ice cream. Basically, do something to take your mind off of studying for a while. Taking a little time off every day can help you avoid finals burnout, wherein you become so exhausted you can't really focus on studying at all.

Relax and have some perspective. When it all comes down to it, you really won't remember the grade you made on your sociology final in years to come. Although a final seems like this monumental thing,

URBAN LEGEND

A student was under a lot of pressure before final exams. He was worried that he wouldn't have enough time to study for the upcoming exams. He began to take amphetamines to be able to stay awake to study day and night. A week later he took the exam and left confident that he had done well. The next day he received a call from the professor asking him to explain why he handed in an exam consisting of nothing but sheets of paper covered with his own name.

in the long run it is just another test. So don't let yourself get into a panic. When you feel finals anxiety coming on, relax and take a deep breath (or a few deep breaths). If you put in the time, and put good study habits into practice, you will get through it just fine.

An ancient buddha said, "Mountains are mountains; waters are waters." These words do not mean mountains are mountains; they mean mountains are mountains.

–Dogen Zenji

If you have been keeping up with the advice offered throughout *College Rules!* preparing for finals may be easier for you than for some of your classmates. We wish you luck on your exams and in the rest of your college career.

Quick and Dirty

○ There are some general guidelines for smart exam preparation: get some sleep, get everything you need to take with you together the night before the exam, and distribute your studying rather than cramming.

○ Try not to cram, but if you have to, focus on your notes, review text material selectively, spend time only on the information you don't know, and test yourself on the information you are studying.

○ While taking your exams, try to relax and focus on the task at hand. Answer the items you know first to build your confidence and don't worry about what your classmates are doing. Don't change your answers unless you are sure that you have made an error. Otherwise, stick with your first hunch.

○ Preparing for midterms and finals requires some extra planning. Study in reverse by focusing on the material you covered last. Meet with a study group, because misery loves company.

ABOUT THE AUTHORS

SHERRIE NIST

JODI PATRICK HOLSCHUH

SHERRIE NIST received her Ph.D. from the University of Florida in 1982. Since that time, she has spent her career researching and writing about college student learning. Over the years, she developed a special interest in how students make the academic transition from learning in high school to learning in college. But it was her love of teaching that inspired *College Rules!* Years of university teaching has led her to a firm belief that students can make a smooth transition from high school to college, and should be able to if they are given the tools.

As a professor at the University of Georgia for the last 19 years, Sherrie has published numerous research articles and book chapters that focus on studying and learning. She has made over 125 presentations at professional meetings and continues to be an active researcher and sought-after consultant. In addition, she has written four textbooks focusing on reading, studying, and learning at the college level. These texts are used on college campuses nationwide.

Sherrie also has a keen sense of practicality. Because she has interacted with thousands of students over the course of her career, she knows firsthand the demands and stresses that are placed on them. She's heard all the excuses, learned all the lines, and listened to hundreds of students talk about their frustrations, mistakes, successes, and failures. These unique experiences, combined with her knowledge of research, enabled her to write a compelling, upbeat, and realistic guide for academic success in college.

Sherrie lives with her husband, Steve Olejnik (also a university professor), and her empty-nester dog, Mollie, in Athens, Georgia, home of the University of Georgia. She has one daughter, Kama, who lives in Los Angeles. When not working, she loves to cook (someday she would love to go to cooking school) and travel (her career feeds her travel habit).

JODI PATRICK HOLSCHUH is an Assistant Professor in the Division of Academic Assistance at the University of Georgia. For the past ten years, Jodi has been involved in helping students make the transition from high school to college learning. An award-winning teacher, Jodi currently teaches courses that are geared toward teaching students effective and efficient study habits. In addition, she has served as an educational consultant in Texas and Georgia public schools, teaching teachers ways to prepare their students for college learning.

Jodi has made many conference presentations and has written several articles and book chapters on the topic of helping students learn strategies for college success. She has also been involved in several projects with Sherrie Nist including the *Transitions to Learning in College* video program and *Active Learning: Strategies for College Success* (2000) a textbook published by Allyn and Bacon.

Jodi lives with her husband, Douglas, and her daughter, Maia (who at one year of age already seems to love books), in Athens, Georgia. When she is not writing, teaching, or researching, Jodi loves rediscovering the world as her daughter learns new things. She also loves to read good books and travel to new places.

INDEX